ROBERT FIFE & JOHN WARREN

A CAPITAL SCANDAL

KEY PORTER BOOKS

Canadian Cataloguing in Publication Data

Fife, Robert
A capital scandal

Includes index.
ISBN 1-55013-351-9
1. Canada.   Parliament.   2. Canada – Politics and government.
I. Warren, John.   II. Title.

JL136.F5 1991   328.71   C91-094507-1

Key Porter Books Limited
70 The Esplanade
Toronto, Ontario
Canada M5E 1R2

Typesetting: MacTrix DTP

Printed and bound in Canada

91 92 93 94 95 6 5 4 3 2 1

Contents

For Margaret Fife and Betty Warren

Acknowledgements

THIS BOOK IS THE PRODUCT OF MONTHS OF INTENSIVE WORK AND YEARS of collective observations and growing concern about how the nation's business is conducted. We expect to be criticized for taking too harsh a view of the system that governs us. Many who are part of it will undoubtedly feel that way. They have ample resources and personnel to make a case for themselves. Our object is a simple one: to draw attention to the failings and abuses and to suggest ways to correct them.

Many people have contributed to this book, from both inside and outside the parliamentary system. Many feel that system can only benefit from a tough appraisal. In particular we would like to thank the following people: Debra Broad, Gus Cloutier, Chuck Cook, Jim Cooke, Bob Desramaux, Mike Duffy, Bob Easby, Jim Fulton, Jean-Robert Gauthier, Michel Gratton, Angela Graves, Jim Hawkes, Derik Hodgson, Bob Horner, Frank Howard, Claire Hoy, Philip Laundy, Pat MacAdam, Mike McCormack, Ron MacDonald, Gerard McNeil, Bob Marleau, Pierre Menard, Peter Milliken, Judy Morrison, Pat Nowlan, Ed Riedel, Nelson Riis, Bill Rodgers, Doug Small and Jim Watson.

The *Hill Times* and its news staff, especially Jim Creskey, Katie Malloy and Paul Anderson, were a valuable source of ideas. They promise to continue the fight to make Parliament the open, honest institution Canadians deserve.

Two others deserve special mention. We deeply appreciate the wisdom and thoughtful analysis of *Toronto Sun* columnist Doug Fisher and the valuable observations provided by our friend Stewart MacLeod of Thomson News. Fisher deserves much of the credit for any virtues readers may find in this work, but certainly not any blame for its faults. We are also indebted to the wise counsel over the years of two departed parliamentary authorities: Eugene Forsey and Michael Kirby. Author and friend Stevie Cameron volunteered helpful insights and important contacts.

There are some people whom we cannot name in this list of acknowledgements. They are intricately involved in the place you are about to visit, and we are grateful for their wisdom and advice and, especially, for documents that helped us peek under Parliament's shroud of secrecy. This book would not have been possible without their kind assistance. Beyond these, there were more than a dozen parliamentary officials who shared their experiences and knowledge. To protect their job security we cannot list them in our acknowledgements, but they know who they are and, we hope, appreciate our thanks.

A special note of appreciation must go to staff of the Parliamentary Library. They allowed us to search for documents we needed to back up our story. Often they found information we could not. We particularly want to thank Louise Latour, Jocelyne Lafontaine, Sylvie Lauzon and Yves Lafortune.

Our chief hand-holders throughout were Key Porter editor-in-chief Phyllis Bruce and her assistant, Michele Melady. Toronto Sun Publishing Corp. chairman Doug Creighton, president Paul Godfrey and executive editor Les Pyette granted a three-month leave of absence and offered support. Support was also forthcoming from *Sun* friends Bob McConachie, Heather Bird and John Paton. We also appreciate the help of computer wizards Shelley Dooher and Ellis Solomon, who managed to make the Macintosh hum.

Gerard Vielleux, Patrick Watson, Terry Hargreaves, Pierre Racicot and other CBC executives who freed John Warren from his restrictive role as host of the House of Commons TV broadcast also deserve mention as do the Commons officers who contributed to that decision.

Finally there are Hazel Darragh, Greg, Steven, Ken and Adrienne Warren, Naomi Goldenberg and Natalie Goldenberg-Fife. Their support and encouragement sustained us.

1
THE HIGHER CALLING

"You scum! You give scum a bad name."
"Don't be so goddamn stupid, Roger."

COMMONS DEBATE BETWEEN LIBERAL ROGER SIMMONS AND TORY CABINET
MINISTER JOHN McDERMID, FEBRUARY 1990

A LL ALONG NOVA SCOTIA'S ROCKY SOUTH SHORE A CRISP SALT wind was grabbing leaves from the giant maples. At sea, fishermen strained against their nets in the rough Atlantic waves; inland, farmers on rusty tractors raked the earth into dark patterns in anticipation of winter. This day in 1990 seemed lean and hard, just as fall days had felt as far back as memory could stretch. For most residents of Lunenburg, Bridgewater, Carleton, Liverpool, Lockeport, Shelburne and all points between there were few luxuries. Hard-won dollars often fell short of costs.

This particular day brought mail from the nation's capital. It was a pamphlet titled "Keeping in Touch" from plump Peter McCreath, the riding's Member of Parliament. Certainly it was not as welcome as a cheque, but at least it brought information. As promised by the title of his newsletter, McCreath was telling the folks back home what he was doing in the job to which they had elected him two years earlier. This regular "householder" was one of the ways the forty-seven-year-old ex–school teacher served South Shore's 77,000 residents, 18,547 of whom had voted for him.

"Fall has come and with it the re-opening of Parliament," proclaimed their devoted representative. "For your MP that means the weekly shuttle back and forth to Ottawa is on once again." McCreath told readers how his work week began each Monday morning with an early flight from Halifax to Ottawa. There he labored long and loud in the public interest until his return to Hubbards, N.S., late Thursday. "This is the tough and lonely part of the job, often unseen by the the public," he revealed. "If you are happily married with a family, as I am, you like to be home at night. As an MP, that's just not possible, and an empty little apartment just isn't the same."

The outspoken and partisan Conservative might have explained to voters what Brian Mulroney's government was doing about interest rates or jobs for the depressed region endlessly plagued by unemployment. But McCreath, who earns five times the average income of other breadwinners in the riding and lists membership in the Chester Yacht Club in his *Parliamentary Guide* biography, chose instead to complain about the hardships of his job. Besides sharing with his constituents the difficulties of his lonely existence, McCreath assured them that he had learned a "great deal about politics, Parliament and the life of an MP" in his two years of public service. It was not an idle claim.

At the very time that his pamphlet was being dropped into mailboxes throughout the riding of South Shore, McCreath was indeed expanding his horizons. The effusive Nova Scotian was in Taiwan on an eight-day junket, compliments of that country's Chamber of Commerce. One thing he obviously had learned is that the tiny island is among the biggest suppliers of freebies for Canadian MPs. Even though Taiwan has no diplomatic relations with Canada and few trade or immigration links with Nova Scotia, the Asian country's hospitality has been enjoyed by both government and opposition members for years.

A few weeks after this Pacific jaunt, the hard-working McCreath was destined to slip into first-class seats on flights to Brussels, to Germany and later to Rome. These trips aboard the gravy plane doubtless helped him to bear the dreary monotony of his empty little Ottawa apartment. When McCreath's whereabouts were revealed in the Halifax *Chronicle-Herald*, his constituents had good reason to join the growing ranks of cynical Canadians.

Close scrutiny shows that most of Canada's MPs have a stain or two on the cloak of integrity and self-sacrifice that they like to wear in public. New Democrat Dan Heap, the billy goat look-alike from Toronto's inner core, has been one of the most conspicuous public consciences in the Commons. So has his blustery Edmonton colleague Ross Harvey. Yet both live in government-subsidized, low-rent townhouses designed for welfare mothers, poor refugees and others in need. A memo from the speaker was recently aimed at members who achieved even bigger savings by bedding down in their offices, a practice that some colleagues deemed inappropriate.

On February 26, 1991, when Michael Wilson rose in the Commons to deliver his seventh budget, he gave the country's 230,000 public servants special attention. Their wage increases would be capped at 3 per cent for the next three years. Any hike at all would result in two thousand lost jobs for each percentage point increase. Senior ranks of bureaucrats would be reduced by 10 per cent and their wages capped, although Wilson had neglected to mention that, two days before, cabinet had quietly slipped through retroactive pay increases of 4.2 per cent for fifty of the highest-paid civil servants, including Bank of Canada governor John Crow.

As a gesture of shared commitment to the cause of restraint, Brian Mulroney and his fellow ministers would have their pay frozen for one year. Other parliamentarians would have salary increases held to the same level as that of public servants. What Wilson failed to say was that the salary freeze would cause our lawmakers few hardships. Just months before, during Canada's worst recession in a decade, MPs had awarded themselves an additional tax-free allowance of $6,000. Senators had padded their pockets with a new allowance, too, which was later rejected by the Commons. Because they're tax-free, such allowances are worth roughly twice the same amount in pay.

Just two days after Wilson delivered his tough "tighten your belt" message to federal workers, the president of the Treasury Board followed up with details of the government's $159-billion spending plans for 1991-92. Buried in the fifty pounds of "Blue Books" tabled by Gilles Loiselle was startling news about Parliament. Its budget would jump by $20 million to $291 million, a hike of almost 7.4 per cent. Included in that figure was a boost of nearly $700,000 in the amount parliamentarians would spend on travel abroad and to entertain visiting colleagues. The biggest increase was in the Senate's budget, up 14.1 per cent over the year before at $45,741,000. Most of that was the cost of the eight special "GST senators" added to the chamber by Brian Mulroney to push through his new tax.

All that is enough to put our politicians smack in the middle of a severe credibility crisis. But there's much more – kickbacks, conflicts of interest, police investigations, convictions on criminal charges and allegations of influence peddling.

Canadians seldom see the name of prime-ministerial crony Michel Cogger in connection with the red chamber. The little senator is identified more closely with police investigations and courtrooms. Two former Quebec MPs have been convicted and two sitting MPs charged with bilking taxpayers, and Mounties continue to probe the activities of several others.

The crisis of confidence extends to politicians of all parties, although those on the government side are clearly closer to the trough, and thus more suspect. It was the same in the Liberals' day. As the fat politician explained in the cartoon "Shoe": "The people want help. We know that help comes to those who help themselves. So we're helping ourselves." For our parliamentarians that can mean not just goodies while in office but lucrative rewards afterwards. Among the sweetest plums in the patronage basket are well-paid appointments to the Senate, federal boards and commissions and the courts. No fewer than six former Liberal MPs are currently "double-dipping" on Federal Court benches, padding judges' pay of more than $140,000 with the handsome pensions they began collecting the day they left the Commons. Other former MPs, mostly Liberals and Tories, adorn County and District Court benches at $135,000 apiece, plus Commons pension.

What the public sees in all this is the refusal of its elected representatives to subordinate their own best interests to those of the public. Certainly many of those who represent us seem incapable of leading by example. The tales never seem to end – tales of renovations to the sumptuous "public housing" of our top politicians at 24 Sussex Drive and other exclusive mansions, of cars, drivers and limitless expense accounts, of unnecessary trips on near-empty VIP planes and of gratuitous office grandeur.

John Turner steps down as Liberal leader, disappears from the

Commons but does not resign his seat. Thus he continues to draw full salary. The suggestion that he retains his place in the House because the Liberals might otherwise lose it in a by-election may be true. If so it simply means that he believes the fortunes of the Liberal party are more important than the right of Vancouver-Quadra to be represented by an active member. Ed Broadbent takes top dollar in a Mulroney-invented job as president of the International Centre for Human Rights and Democratic Development (whatever that is) after denouncing Tory patronage.

Politicians fail to see that the excessive favors they bestow on themselves result in contempt from those who pay the bills. Some do understand the public's sour reaction but simply can't resist the temptation to dip into the cookie jar whose nuggets constantly beckon. The result is obvious public censure. All that criticism, however, does not drive many to resign. Most members would never consider abandoning the perks of office a second before they have to. In fact, they devote more strenuous efforts to ensuring their re-election than to law making. "The first duty of a politician is to get elected" goes the adage. It is one no MP either forgets or tires of talking about with colleagues.

Not all politicians are greedy or corrupt. Most are honest, well-intentioned and maybe even hard-working ombudsmen for constituents – even for those who voted against them. Constituency work, such as helping with passport hitches, immigration problems and unemployment-insurance snarls, is a big part of the job. Most MPs' four or five staffers are excellent at it. This is the stuff that can win their bosses re-election.

But an MP's job is more than constituency work. The title Member of Parliament means he or she is supposed to have a substantial role in making laws and guarding the public purse. The fact is that ordinary MPs don't carry much weight. That may account for the public's high level of dissatisfaction with the political system. Debates are ritualized, third-rate performances played out in an empty Commons theatre. Only Question Period has any spark; but it is meant to ignite headlines and TV coverage, not to assess policy or produce legislation.

Nor do most of the thirty-nine ministers in the most bloated cabinet in our history have any real clout. Power is reserved for a small cadre around the prime minister that controls both public policy and the public purse. Occasions when Parliament diverts a majority government from its course are as rare as diamonds in a manure pile. Equally unusual are members who dare to stand up for their constituents in speeches or votes if that means disagreeing with their party's line.

For Canadians, that reality has contributed to a massive loss of confidence in politicians and the political system. All that jawing in Parliament is simply irrelevant. A few insiders wield all the power, make all the decisions. The rest of the parliamentary playhouse is little more than costly window dressing. The fundamental problem is that our political system has lost legitimacy.

Polls show that the public believes politicians to be self-serving buffoons or cunning manipulators, rather than dedicated public servants. "The system is corrupt," declares John Bulloch, president of the Canadian Federation of Independent Business. He argues that MPs are not in a position to influence important decisions. After twenty years of observing the Ottawa power game, Bulloch has no doubt that only a few cabinet ministers and senior bureaucrats have real clout. Ultimately, "everything is controlled by the prime minister."

According to Tory pollster Allan Gregg, Canadians trusted their politicians far more a decade ago. Back then, says the president of Decima Research Ltd., a full 70 per cent of the public described MPs as hard working. Parliamentarians also got a positive score as principled (63 per cent) and competent (57 per cent). In his book *The Big Picture: What Canadians Think about Almost Everything*, Gregg reports that "a majority of Canadians find them unprincipled; 81% think they are more concerned with making money than with helping people; 65% call them incompetent; and only 32% of the population say they hold generally favourable views about them."

Parliament has become an ivory tower where grown-ups play follow-the-leader and leaving the path is a dangerous game. The show is staged to provide dramatic "bites" for the nightly news.

Television focuses on the inflammatory rhetoric and convinces the viewer that Parliament is a place for the simple-minded. There's lots of shouting, growling and righteous indignation, but the place has lost both its grip on the nation's purse strings and any ability to nudge the government from its fixed course.

Loss of faith in the parliamentary system could not come at a worse time. A country with more promise and potential than almost any on the globe today appears ready to self-destruct. There is mutual distrust between Quebec and the rest of the country. The nation is ready to split apart or, at the very least, become highly decentralized. The people we elect cut jobs and services, but our debt remains an uncontrolled $400-billion monster, growing by the minute. At birth every Canadian owes $15,000. Each of us believes that those in some other part of the country are getting favored treatment. And a national survey published by *Maclean's* magazine to launch the new year concluded that Canadians think Parliament is not responsive to their needs.

Why does our central democratic institution no longer work? Its members have more staff, skills, time, equipment, money, education, travel opportunities and communication capacity than ever before. Everything is there except power. MPs do not control the public purse, hold ministers to account or have anything much to say about formation of government policy. The prime minister and a tight circle around him have gradually won it all. The provinces, bureaucrats, the courts and lobbyists seem to have more clout than do elected representatives. Power is concentrated in the Prime Minister's Office, and in the Privy Council Office, which controls the bureaucratic machinery. Thousands of critical decisions issue from that central core each year, joining others passing through cabinet as Orders in Council. Parliament's role in the process has been reduced to one of ex–post-facto review.

Most of the laws we live by are actually regulations. They are the detailed working parts that cabinet, not Parliament, puts in place. Regulations set safety standards for bicycle helmets, new ways of grading beef carcasses and restrictions on pulp-mill effluent to protect fish. They prohibit duck hunting at Point Pelee National

Park, keep shoddy cordless phones out of the country, determine how pill bottles will be labelled and upgrade the standard of brakes on trucks. The cabinet does all that, appoints judges, sets the pay of top bureaucrats and – well – runs our lives.

The men and women in cabinet who can make those things happen with a single stroke of the pen get their advice from an exclusive clique surrounding the prime minister. As *Toronto Star* columnist Carol Goar pointed out in March 1991, the power elite is drawn to a remarkably large extent from a single group – bilingual Montrealers. Even more striking is the close parallel among power-brokers in opposition leader Jean Chrétien's tight circle of top aides. In Mulroney's case, they include chief of staff Norman Spector, top bureaucrat Paul Tellier, communications director Dan Gagnier and press secretary Gilbert Lavoie, along with former staff chiefs Stanley Hartt and Bernard Roy. Knowing that all that power emanates from a single centre in Quebec leaves most Canadians feeling out of the circuit.

And then there is the civil service. The mushrooming of the bureaucracy since the Second World War has also eroded the influence of MPs, stealing their ability to understand and steer an infinitely complex government vehicle. The futility of attempts by mere parliamentarians to control the giant machine is compounded by many civil servants' deliberate steps to keep its working parts secret.

Much ado surrounded the creation of new Commons committees during Mulroney's first mandate. They were to keep the bureaucracy in check. With the right to hire experts, command anyone they chose to appear before them and subpoena documents, these committees could curb bigwig bureaucrats. In that first term many MPs took the responsibility seriously. But it turned out to be primarily a device to keep the huge cast of otherwise bored Tory back-benchers busy and out of trouble. Conscientiously drafted reports hardly slowed down on the way through cabinet to the dustbin. MPs quickly realized the futility of their efforts. Many turned their talents to harmless pursuits such as tax-funded travel and the purchase of new office toys.

In the last two decades much of Ottawa's most important power has been handed to commissions that are almost immune to the influence of those we elect. The Canadian Human Rights Commission, the National Transportation Agency, the Information, Privacy and Official Languages commissions are just a few of the levers that MPs can't get their hands on, but that wield power once assigned to Parliament.

The Charter of Rights and Freedoms has given the courts astounding new authority to run our lives. The Supreme Court, in particular, now has authority that once resided with elected representatives. Law making was the prerogative of Parliament; the courts interpreted the laws Parliament passed. Former chief justice Jules Deschênes of the Superior Court of Quebec explains the old order this way: "Canadian courts did not set themselves up as judges of the wisdom of legislation; they respected the power of Parliament in this area and they recognized that defeat at the ballot-box constituted the only remedy for parliamentary abuse."

No longer. We now have a charter under which the Supreme Court decides, for instance, between the rights of the unborn and a woman for control over the woman's body. The court struck down a 1976 abortion law – a fine compromise, which is what politics is all about. Parliament has been unable to agree on a replacement. Mr. Justice John Sopinka confirmed the transfer of power that elected members are sometimes reluctant to admit: "When you're deciding a charter case, the court is in a sense legislating. I think it took a little while to sink in that when the court is dealing with charter cases, they're not dealing with the law as we used to deal with it. Now, when the court is asked to strike down a statute, it is often dealing with the types of decisions that were made previously by elected representatives. . . ."

Robed judges used to sit in regal isolation while Parliament wrestled with pressure groups. But omnipresent lobbyists are now as likely to appear at the art deco Supreme Court building as on Parliament Hill a few hundred yards away. Extradition cases have brought Amnesty International to make its point in court. The Canadian Civil Liberties Association shows up on hate propaganda. And the Chantal Daigle abortion case brought them flocking from the Canadian Abortion Rights Action League, Campaign

Life Coalition, Canadian Physicians for Life, REAL Women of Canada and the Women's Legal Education and Action Fund.

Business and interest groups now channel the demands of their supporters directly into the corridors of power in a way MPs no longer can. They choose lobbyists for their connections, cunning and insight into the power structure. Books, guides and even a monthly newsletter now steer those who want government action to the operatives who can get it for them. Quickly and quietly. A company would rather hire high-powered lobbyist Frank Moores, the former Newfoundland premier and a buddy of Brian Mulroney and Mulroney's deputy Don Mazankowski, than seek help from the local Tory MP.

Big interest groups, such as the Business Council on National Issues or the National Action Committee on the Status of Women, prefer one-on-one encounters with cabinet ministers or top bureaucrats. None of them wastes much time cultivating ordinary MPs. All have discovered that appearances before Commons committees rarely influence political decision making. Young people shun political parties in favour of interest groups such as Pollution Probe, while the disadvantaged, such as Native people and other minorities, are forced to participate in similar groups to seek redress.

Rare exceptions occur when so-called free votes are held in the Commons on issues of conscience, such as capital punishment or abortion. MPs and senators were lobbied by both sides on abortion (capital punishment was killed before it reached the Senate). However, such parliamentary votes are never truly free. Mulroney insisted that his cabinet ministers and thirty parliamentary secretaries vote for the abortion bill, and other strong-arm tactics were used to defeat capital punishment. In the upper chamber, a dramatic tie vote meant defeat of the abortion bill. Mulroney was unable to browbeat Tory senators with threats of reprisals into voting for the bill or to persuade them with promises of goodies. Senators already have the ultimate prize – a seat in Patronage Heaven until age seventy-five – and the PM can't withdraw it.

Federal-provincial conferences, task forces and royal commissions have further drained influence from Parliament, leaving it oddly erect but impotent. Whether it be Keith Spicer's stumbling, costly circus on national unity or Maureen McTeer's commission on reproductive technology, the special appointees have usurped the traditional mandate of MPs to listen to Canadians and develop the policies they want. The bill for four royal commissions operating in 1991 will be between $50 million and $100 million. In the end we'll see fat and glossy reports on passenger transportation, electoral reform and party financing – all studies that could have been handled by parliamentarians. These consultative forums have virtually no links to those whom we have elected to represent us and are immune to influence from them. Other research bodies, like the Economic Council of Canada and the Canadian Institute on Peace and Security, advise cabinet directly.

Another non-parliamentary process is the one that ended in the collapse of Meech Lake – the federal-provincial conference. They're held by first ministers, finance ministers or any other crown princes who can find a reason to strut the national stage with TV cameras and media mobs hanging on every posturing word. Provincial gladiators use the conferences to tilt against oppressive Ottawa policies, from the National Energy Program to rural post office closings, to the abandonment of local rail services. Sensing the frustration that Canadians feel towards ineffective federal legislators, provincial premiers claim to be the people's voice. Lost in the battle between the haves and have-nots – West and East, Quebec and the rest – is the House of Commons, ostensibly our national democratic forum. The Senate, where regional interests are supposed to be aired and balanced, has been ineffective for 124 years. The unelected upper chamber woke up during the GST fiasco only to convince many Canadians they were better off when it slept.

The Trudeau adage that MPs become "nobodies" when they move fifty feet from Parliament Hill has been reversed. They can still command some attention at parades, weddings, funerals, rallies and garage sales back home. But in Ottawa no one takes them seriously anymore. While Canadians pay handsomely to send representatives to Ottawa, most have no influence over what they do there. More often than not, MPs ignore the majority view of constituents if that view runs against the party line. Experts say that party discipline is more sternly enforced in Canada than in any other country with a similar parliamentary system. Certainly the practice in the "mother of parliaments" at Westminster is far less rigid. Members in Britain can spout views contrary to those of their party leaders, and dissenting votes are frequent when the government's survival is not at stake. Thirty-one MPs, for instance, voted against Margaret Thatcher's hated poll tax without being penalized or expelled from caucus.

Not here. Every issue in Canada is treated as though defeat and a general election depend on it. Views that diverge from the party line bring harsh punishment down on any MP who foolishly believes he or she was chosen to exercise independent judgement. The system provides the party leader and his trusty whip with thousands of ways to keep members in line. Caucus appointments, committee assignments, office space, seating in the House, a role in Question Period, speaking dates and TV spots, overseas freebies or long duty days in the green chamber can be offered or withheld. Nobody understands carrots and sticks better than a Canadian MP.

From cabinet posts to plum commissions upon retirement, the prime minister dispenses favors from the biggest treasure chest in the country. The promise of a prize or the threat to withhold one is enough to keep most members in tune, regardless of what their personal views or constituency opinion might suggest.

In Mulroney's first term about two dozen Tory MPs, mainly from the West, were under pressure from their electors to oppose amendments to the Official Languages Bill. There were dire warnings from the grass roots that they'd pay at the polls if they backed their own government. Mulroney's palace guard responded with painful arm twisting. They said that open division would wreck the party's delicate French-English coalition and scuttle the Tories' chances of returning to power. A few stubborn hold-outs were offered attractive foreign assignments that coincided with votes on the language bill, to allow them to be "unavoidably absent" when the crunch came. Most fell reluctantly into line, grumbling their objections to one another but avoiding a public fracture. Several abstained from the critical votes and paid in lost perks. The willingness of others to compromise their own convictions and the wishes of their constituents for the sake of party solidarity cost them votes in the 1988 election. It was a factor in at least one loss, that of Jennifer Cossitt in Leeds-Grenville, a United Empire Loyalist stronghold in eastern Ontario.

Once in a while one of them gets mad as hell and won't take it anymore. Their shattered careers are held out as examples to others who might be tempted to abandon ship. Big Jack Horner, once the most popular politician in Alberta, was lured from the Tory herd by the evil Grits with a cabinet post. In the next election there weren't enough Horner votes in Crowfoot to save his deposit. Wealthy Winnipegger Jim Richardson debarked the other way, from Liberal defence minister to the opposition benches, to oblivion. The language policies he challenged thrive today.

Today the opposition back-bench is strewn with defectors. There's former Calgary Tory Alex Kindy, sitting as an independent, and former Edmonton Tory David Kilgour, now a Liberal. Both were pushed out the door for refusing to sing from the Tory book. There are almost a dozen Bloc Québécois members arrayed around Lucien Bouchard, the former environment minister and ambassador to Paris. Only one was elected under that label. The others entered the House as Liberals or Conservatives, then abandoned ship after the sinking of Meech Lake. All stand as a sad testament to the failure of Parliament.

Kindy and Kilgour faced the wrath of Mulroney and his loyal caucus for various misdemeanors culminating in their votes against the GST. Kindy, a Hungarian immigrant and medical doctor fluent in French and English, had been a thorn in the party's side almost since his election in 1984. He bridled at caucus solidarity. "We have no say and yet we are the ones who have to go back to our ridings and defend actions we don't agree with," he complained. "We are not puppets around here," he added, likening the strangle-hold of the leader to that of regimes in Moscow and Beijing.

The first warnings that he would pay a political price came from party whip Jim Hawkes. He accused Kindy of seeking to "grab the media nipple" and removed him from the Commons Justice Committee. Kindy was nearly dumped from caucus itself in June 1989 when he sent a pamphlet to his Calgary Northeast constituents criticizing the GST and warning that the tax would drive Alberta voters into the arms of Preston Manning's Reform Party. Many in the Alberta caucus demanded that Kindy cross the floor to sit as an opposition member, but caucus chairman Bobbie Sparrow intervened. "We send out householders four times a year. We're pretty free to say what we want," she reminded them. Athabasca MP Jack Shields argued that Kindy cast his colleagues in a bad light by expressing the views of his constitutents. "He's actually inferring that the remainder of Alberta caucus is not. I resent that most thoroughly."

Kilgour, another smoothly bilingual Alberta MP, served in the Commons for twelve years as a restless Conservative. In April 1990, after his and Kindy's anti-GST votes, they were expelled from caucus by the prime minister. "For voting with your constituents, you're booted out of your caucus," said Kilgour, amazed at the speed of his expulsion. The name-plate on his House of Commons desk was moved to a back-row seat on the opposition side overnight. When he later joined the Liberals, Kilgour was removed from his Centre Block office to a more remote one.

Mulroney heaped scorn on Kilgour, who had accused the Conservative government of favoring Ontario over the West and dishing out too many patronage appointments. The prime minister contended that Kilgour never understood parliamentary tradition, which calls for full and frank discussion in caucus but a united front in public. "He never said a bloody word in Alberta's defence, ever," fumed Mulroney. "He never once spoke, he never once rose in my presence, he never once wrote me." The prime minister may not have heard Kilgour. A lot of Albertans and other Canadians did.

Most dramatic of all the floor-crossers is twenty-six-year veteran Pat Nowlan. The giant, hard-drinking, cigar-chomping Nova Scotian has Tory bloodlines as pure as any in the country. His father, George, was once finance minister in Diefenbaker's cabinet. But in fifty-nine years Pat has never quite learned the virtue of taking the loot and keeping quiet. In 1990 he found out just how fast an outspoken MP can be shuffled to the sidelines and out the door. Nowlan's differences with Mulroney dated back some time. The leader's withholding of a cabinet post obviously rankled. But Nowlan sincerely believed that the party was wrong on crucial issues such as Meech Lake and the Goods and Services Tax. In June he announced his withdrawal from caucus meetings in protest. He simmered through the summer.

The party's solidarity machinery was hard at work when Nowlan returned for the fall session. He was stripped of his hard-won jobs as chairman of the Commons Transport Committee and head of the Canada-U.S. Parliamentary Group. He was also unable to get assurances from the Prime Minister's Office that Mulroney would sign his nomination papers for the next election, a requirement for anyone running as a Tory. So Nowlan formally resigned from caucus in a sadly forthright letter that explained much of what is wrong with the political system.

"The yoke of caucus and blind loyalty to the leader have been very difficult for me to follow," he said of the system that forces MPs to sacrifice their convictions to party discipline. "We have forgotten from whence we came and the people feel betrayed. That's why the polls have hit new lows and the mood is angry."

Members of Parliament have become irrelevant, he stormed. If MPs were truly allowed to represent their constituents instead of numbers on a caucus scoreboard the government wouldn't have to run around the country constantly soliciting and measuring the public's views. "It's trust and credibility more than specific policies that got us to rock bottom," said Nowlan of the party's lowest-ever poll result on the second anniversary of the 1988 election victory.

That day Pat Nowlan was moved to the opposition bleachers from the front-bench seat he'd won with more than two decades of loyal Tory service. The Conservative whip even rose to object to Nowlan's chosen designation as "Independent Conservative," insisting that the label must be simply "Independent." Speaker John Fraser deliberated for days before ruling in favor of the old war-horse from the Annapolis Valley.

Harsh party discipline applies not just to the government party. Vancouver New Democrat Ian Waddell was stripped of his cherished job as culture critic when he voted against Meech Lake. Liberal

Donald Johnston lost his post as external affairs critic when he opposed the accord. The same thing happened to another Montrealer, Liberal David Berger. Liberal MP Paul Martin, Jr., was chastised in caucus early in 1991 for publicly urging his party to sketch out a constitutional vision. And John Turner lost his spacious office in the Centre Block when he spoke in favor of Canada's military role in the Persian Gulf War.

Sheer trickery is also used to eliminate dissent. Veteran Liberal Marcel Prud'homme is a meticulous expert on Commons rules and tops in attendance. Nevertheless, he got caught short by an all-party conspiracy in October 1990. The Commons was debating a resolution that dealt with Canada's position during the build-up to the Persian Gulf War. There were a couple of amendments that would have curbed Canadian participation, motions that the pro-Palestinian Prud'homme in particular was eager to vote on. But officials of all three parties scuttled the amendments and substituted another motion "by unanimous consent" while Prud'homme was briefly absent. Even Speaker Fraser conceded that "an abuse of Parliament by consent is just as much an abuse."

Pat Nowlan's complaint that the "vitality of debate, discussion and, yes, even dissent is no longer here" is one shared by many parliamentary observers. As political scientist Paul Thomas has noted, MPs are conditioned to see party voting as an essential feature of the parliamentary system. They believe that the media and public expect party unity, even though the seventh annual Decima/*Maclean's* poll shows that 89 per cent of respondents want politicians to make decisions based on their individual consciences or on petitions from constituents.

It is not as though our politicians don't know that mind-numbing party rigidity stifles open debate and creates a problem of public perception. The comfort of having everyone on side is too much for leaders to resist, however. They brainwash, bully and bribe their followers into obedience. Changes to the standing orders of the House of Commons in the spring of 1991 give the government even more control over Parliament. Revisions to the parliamentary calendar have reduced the number of sittings by 40 days per year from the previous total of 175 (which was rarely met). Legislation will be pushed through with even less debate. The public will have less time to learn about proposed bills and exert pressure for changes or delays. There will be 40 fewer Question Periods to hold ministers to account.

Another reason Parliament can't function is the extreme lengths to which members take the adversarial system. Judith Maxwell, head of the Economic Council of Canada, blames part of our economic problems on pointless parliamentary bickering. "One of the fundamental weaknesses of the Canadian economy is that we may be too adversarial," she says. When one side vows to "launch a form of parliamentary resistance not seen in this country ever before" and another bellows back that it will "triumph over the hijackers," you have a poor start towards meaningful dialogue. Unquestionably, it's the government's job to govern and the opposition's to oppose. But outsiders can't understand why every difference must provoke a fight to the death – or at least the melodramatic pretence of one. Nor do Canadians understand why the government regards the smallest modification to a minor bill as an unthinkable surrender.

Canadians are now looking beyond their traditional parties for political relief from a system they feel does not serve them. They are turning to a more self-centred regionalism and more populist solutions. Deep disenchantment with Parliament as the country reels under economic and unity crises plays into the hands of both Preston Manning and the Quebec separatists. Lucien Bouchard's loosely knit group of nationalists has become a registered party with hopes of winning fifty of Quebec's seventy-five seats in the next election. Manning's Reform Party is riding a wave of anti-establishment rage at huge rallies in every province west of Quebec. "Canadians are very angry at what seems to be a lack of leadership in the country," says Winnipeg pollster Angus Reid. "Everyone is looking for a political messiah. Maybe Preston Manning can become that." Experts say Reformers could win up to fifty seats in the West, and more now that they are expanding to the East. The Mulroney government reacted to the threat in its 1991 budget with the assault on public servants and the move of the National Energy Board from the capital to Calgary's oilpatch.

Manning is an unlikely-looking revolutionary. But so was his father, Ernest, who entered the Alberta legislature in William Aberhart's first Social Credit government of 1935. Ernest became premier in 1943 and served longer in that capacity than anyone in our history – instilling lessons in old-time religion and politics in his son. Preston, a slender, studious teetotaller, is selling a simple message to Canadians who are fed up with political deception, high taxes and perceived favoritism towards Quebec.

"Support for the Reform Party is not a figment of some Reform Party individual's imagination," says the University of Manitoba's Paul Thomas, who has written extensively on Parliament and political parties. Manning's political credo – fiscal responsibility and prairie populism – is simple (some say simplistic) and appealing. He promises a system that will make elected officials more accountable to those they serve. "Populism is the idea that there is common sense among the common people and if you can get at it you can apply it in public policy."

Few observers doubt that Canada is ripe for a protest vote. The failings of the parliamentary system and profound dissatisfaction with those now in it make the Reform Party and the Bloc Québécois attractive alternatives. Their success may only contribute further to political fragmentation. On the other hand, they might bring more people into the process and re-legitimize Parliament. In any event, what Canada needs is a working system of checks and balances in Parliament and a hefty dose of political integrity. Unless some authority is returned to Parliament, our so-called democratic system will become a farce. It is very close to that now.

2
A LONG TIME AGO

*"It is his duty to sacrifice his repose, his pleasure, his satisfaction,
[to his constituents] and above all, ever, and in all cases,
to prefer their interest to his own."*

EDMUND BURKE, ON THE DUTY OF POLITICIANS.
SPEECH TO THE ELECTORS OF BRISTOL, NOVEMBER 3, 1774

T HE ROUGH LUMBER TOWN DRESSED AS NEVER BEFORE. Shops were closed to allow every one of its 18,000 residents to take part. It was the biggest event Ottawa, formerly Bytown, had ever seen. The buildings were festooned with Union Jacks and banners as gentlemen in formal attire escorted expensively gowned ladies to Parliament Hill on that bright, brisk November day in 1867. Sir John A. Macdonald, with his blazing eyes, curly black locks and whisky-veined nose, cut an imposing figure. Silk-robed judges and clergy stood nearby as Governor General Viscount Monck arrived to open officially Canada's first Parliament.

Monck had strolled from Rideau Hall, which he called his "miserable little house," to the imposing stone structure perched on a cliff overlooking the Ottawa River and the Gatineau Hills beyond. It was the unlikely spot Queen Victoria had chosen ten years earlier as capital of the Province of Canada. Now, its first Gothic buildings, ornate turrets and iron grillwork were complete, and the business of running the new Dominion of Canada was about to begin.

Pomp and pageantry were concentrated in the scarlet splendor of the Senate, as they are to this day. But the key figures of Confederation were down the hall in the House of Commons. Canada's first 181 MPs were ready to go to work for the people who had elected them.

The workplace was crowded. The chamber was built for the 130 members of the colonial assembly of the United Province of Canada. To handle the overflow, fifty extra green leather chairs were squeezed behind seven rows of oak desks on either side of Speaker James Cockburn.

When the business of this experimental new country got underway, the public galleries in the white-pine–panelled chamber were packed, far beyond any standard of safety and comfort, with curious, excited and often drunken onlookers. Crowding and clutter were part of the parliamentary atmosphere from day one. The stone buildings housed not just MPs, senators and the few employees who served them, but all the departments and civil servants needed to run the new Dominion. Parliament Hill housed the country's entire government operations.

The atmosphere was hot and stuffy as gas lamps and wood fires consumed huge quantities of oxygen in their battle against Ottawa's bitter winter. The heavy wool suits and scarce bathing facilities of the time did little to improve the atmosphere as MPs trudged from nearby boarding-houses for the long days and nights of each session in the late winter. With cloakroom space at a premium just outside the chamber, there was a huge clutter of boots, scarves, coats and hats.

Immediately below the house was Ottawa's newest saloon, a jam-packed retreat for Hill boozers and those just passing by. It was open to the public and, by virtue of parliamentary privilege, immune to the rules and restrictive closing laws the province enforced on nearby watering holes. In those days the Commons had its own restaurant where MPs enjoyed wine or beer with their meals. At the other end of the Centre Block was the Senate eatery and saloon. Its staple was said to be port, while the Commons drinkers favored rum, which one newspaper observed "was very comforting to the wounded heart."

The attractions of these parliamentary facilities were obvious to members who were stuck miles from home for two or three months a year without offices, staff, families or handy diversions during late-night sittings. Their charms became equally obvious to thirsty locals, who could take a short detour off Wellington Street for a grog after the nearby pubs had closed for the night. Parliament's immunity to provincial liquor laws remains to this day, although the bar does not.

A well-worn staircase ran from the Commons bar to the chamber next to the speaker's chair, allowing members to stumble right into the action, while guests had to climb one flight farther for a view of the show from the public galleries. Occasionally some MPs griped about the "unmannerly behavior of the townsfolk," just as they complained about journalists who used the saloon as a "spy head-quarters" to catch politicians with their guard down. Because the Commons usually sat until midnight or later, the unparliamentary activities in the basement bar often led to what another newspaper termed "rude and disorderly conduct above."

When Wilfrid Laurier arrived in 1874, it was not uncommon to find more than half the MPs "more or less under the influence of liquor when the House adjourned at midnight." Speaker Cockburn bent to the wishes of more temperate members that year by closing the saloon. But MPs and the private operator of the restaurant did not quit easily. The thirsty Commoners headed down the hall to the Senate bar. Sir John A., ever sympathetic to such a cause, told the House it was unfair to the Commons' saloon-keeper and led to overcrowding in the Senate bar. "This House has no control over the Senate restaurant, and the consequence of preventing the sale of wine in the Commons restaurant was that everybody went to the Senate, and made the fortune of the man in one end of the building, instead of the other."

Newspapers were bluntly critical of the saloon and the boozy behavior it fostered in the chamber above. In 1881, the Toronto *Globe* stormed: "If it were not for the fatal facility with which members obtain intoxicating liquor within a few steps of this chamber, the brawls and scenes which have disgraced not only this but previous Parliaments would never have been witnessed." In 1878, the *Canadian Illustrated News* railed: "if the debates go on as they have begun, we may expect to see a cheap edition of the *Hansard* brought out . . . for the special benefit of cabmen and omnibus drivers . . . whose vocabulary of abuse and retort would be greatly enlarged by a careful study of that publication."

The fondness of members of the old boys' club for "intoxicating liquors" made life hell for speakers whose job was to maintain order and a semblance of decorum during raucous debates. One account of an all-night sitting in the spring of 1878 shows just how tough it was to maintain control. "While points of order were being argued, members hammered at their desks, blew on tin trumpets, imitated the crowing of cocks, sent up toy-ballons, threw sand-cracks or torpedoes and occasionally hurled blue-books across the House," E.B. Biggar wrote in his 1891 book *Anecdotal Life of Sir John Macdonald*. "Once in a while amid the din some member with a good voice would start up the 'Marseillaise,' 'God Save the Queen,' 'A la claire fontaine,' 'The Raftsman's Chorus,' or some plantation melody and then the whole House would join in song, with an effect that was quite moving."

Not all the horseplay could be traced to the basement saloon. Members did what they could to distract and annoy their opponents, sometimes with more imagination than they demonstrate today. One member, Joseph Cauchon, would duck behind the back row of seats to render loud and discordant music on a jew's harp when he felt a speaker was becoming too long-winded.

Even the public got into the act. Guests were often invited to join MPs on the floor during proceedings until the friend of a Conservative MP from Toronto got a little too caught up in the action one night in 1880. The distinguished guest could not contain his feelings, shouting that a Liberal MP was a "cheat and a swindler" until he was forcibly removed by the sergeant-at-arms. He returned to repeat his charge, to be escorted out a second time, and since then "strangers" have not been permitted inside the chamber curtains.

Alcohol-fired debate remained a part of the parliamentary life long after the basement bars shut down. To this day a refrigerator and liquor cabinet are basic furnishings in many Hill offices. More than once the speaker's pre-holiday "reception" has been blamed for bizarre conduct and glitches in proceedings. More than once the speaker was unable to adjourn the sitting, turning that task over to a less-inebriated deputy.

But boozy night sittings ended with a rule change in 1982 that set the daily quitting time at 6:30 p.m. or earlier. (In April 1991 the house revised its hours again, with 6:30 the normal quitting time, except on Wednesday when the house now sits until 8:00 p.m.) That, along with changing social and drinking habits, killed the last wide-open "blind pig" on Parliament Hill. It had been run for generations from a tiny room behind the Press Gallery work area. Gallery clerks there supplemented meagre pay by operating a beer machine and a bar where shots at half the "street price" drew not just reporters but MPs, senators, cleaners, guards, *Hansard* staff, postal clerks, party flacks and guests to join in the magic of alcohol and gossip.

The early administration of Parliament was haphazard and undeniably corrupt. All employees were patronage appointees, right down to the $1.50-a-day pages. Parliamentary staff and officials were hired by the party in power and instructed not to help opposition members. The prime minister and speaker spent much of their busy days dealing with requests for Commons jobs, which they filled with cronies, relatives and loyal supporters. The practice was so outrageous that an investigation was undertaken in 1884. It concluded that too many job winners were "selected without regard to qualifications or habits." Journalists working for newspapers that supported the government got work as sessional clerks to supplement their meagre salaries. Members had no offices or staff, but the speaker hired a few "extra writers" to help with correspondence during the annual sessions, which usually began in early February and wrapped up business by the first week in May.

An illustration of just how closely politics and publishing were intertwined is the case of the Commons speaker from 1874 to 1878. Timothy Warren Anglin continued to publish the New Brunswick *Freeman* during his term in the chair, often using it to berate opposition members. He took part in a debate on postal rates that affected his newspaper and appeared before a committee dealing with printing contracts. While speaker, he also argued strenuously against prohibition in a Commons debate on the subject.

Hansard reporters, recruited from among pals and friendly newspapermen, sometimes polished up the prose before locking it forever in the historical record. That, along with a potential annual saving of $18,562.50, prompted the member for Inverness, a Mr. MacDonnell, to call for *Hansard* to be scrapped. On March 7, 1881, he told the House that even greater savings would be achieved because members would deliver fewer and shorter speeches once the "irresistible inducement" of seeing their words in print was removed. Those words were often improved versions penned by talented wordsmiths so that some members "afterwards show their speeches around to their fellows, expressing the most profound surprise at their own eloquence."

Despite the rewriting of the record, Sir John A. noted that future historians would learn more about what moved Parliament in 1881 from back-benchers than from leaders. "It is the expression of opinion by the mass of members that shows really what the feelings of the people are as expressed by their representatives."

Those first representatives received just $600 a year for their efforts. Pay was called a "sessional indemnity," a term that is used to this day, although modern MPs claim that their task is full-time and year-round, justifying the handsome package of pay, benefits and pensions they receive. The reward for service was first increased to $1,000 in 1873 and to $1,500 in 1901. Most members had other jobs to supplement their skimpy Commons pay.

Back-benchers worked at their desks or at shared tables in one of the smoke-filled common-rooms. Their only "free" supplies were a tightly limited allowance of stationery, a penknife, glue, scissors and red tape, and a travelling trunk. Trunks and stationery in the Senate were of better quality than in the Commons, which prompted one MP to burst out: "If there is to be any difference at all to be made, we ought to get better stationery than the senators do." Former MP Doug Fisher recalls that there was still a limit of 2,000 sheets per MP when he arrived in Ottawa in 1957. An increase in the paper ration was among the benefits he fought for over the next few years.

Free-wheeling and sometimes drunken debates among the men who got together in the House of Commons for a couple of months each spring did not necessarily mean that public business was ignored. Opposition members found lots to criticize and did so loudly, just as they do today. They stormed against cabinet ministers who made policy announcements around the country for political advantage, instead of in the House. They objected to government by cabinet order then, just as they protest VIA Rail cuts or postal changes today. They railed against political patronage by Sir John A., who had at least as many friends lined up for rewards a century ago as Brian Mulroney does today. And, just as now, the government fought off Commons committees that wanted to stick their noses into cabinet business. Moreover, there was no auditor general to scrutinize spending until a dozen years after Confederation. Money was regularly transferred illegally from one department to another, or worse. Even after the overseer's office was established in 1878, it was given far too small a staff to do its job as watch-dog of the public purse. As they do today, opposition members in the 1800s had a lot more suspicions about wrongdoing than provable charges.

Unlike their counterparts today, those early MPs were "somebodies," both in Parliament and back home. They were prominent community leaders, not party yes-men riding to Ottawa on a multi-million-dollar wave of television advertising. While national leaders and national issues always played a part in campaigns, it was a far smaller one than in today's instant image communication. Individuals got elected on local issues, and made a noise about them when they reached Ottawa.

While the prime minister and cabinet had a pre-eminent role then (as now), the Commons got far more attention than it does today. Its members, and its debates, were listened to inside the House and read about outside. The late parliamentary scholar professor Norman Ward of Saskatchewan wrote of those formative years: "The member of Parliament was a strategic figure and a man of note."

To begin with, Commons rules in the nineteenth century permitted broad participation by MPs. They could speak on a subject for as long as they could stay on their feet. Party whips who tried to tell them when they could take part would have been ridiculed out of business. So would caucus "researchers," had there been such people back then to stuff a prepared text into a member's hand.

Members said what they believed, not what the party directed. That made them a very real check on the government or on any party leader whose ideas they disagreed with. A lot of those early MPs sat officially or unofficially as independents or what Sir John A. called "loose fish" and "shaky fellows." Allegiances would shift, depending on the issue under study and the impact it had on an individual's riding. MPs who had other jobs or outside wealth depended less on currying favor for future patronage jobs, which were not as numerous or as lucrative as today's.

Governments were frequently defeated without being forced to resign or call elections. In his first four sessions as prime minister, Sir John A. lost votes five times on minor bills. Some of the MPs who voted against him later sat in Macdonald's cabinet. They may have been back-benchers, but they were up front with opinions and private members' bills. Considerable time was spent debating bills put forth by ordinary members, and many such bills were adopted. "The House of Commons had a decisive role in the making and un-making of ministers and ministries," says academic Roman March in his book *The Myth of Parliament*. "Debates were listened to because the Commons was a place where the most vital decisions were taken."

MPs had the power in those days to oust a prime minister, even one resolutely determined to hang onto office. Sir John A. was forced to resign in the Pacific Scandal of 1873. Old Tomorrow, sick and drinking heavily, had accepted $300,000 from the Canadian Pacific Railway Company to bankroll the Conservative party's 1872 re-election. Before the campaign ended he sent a deadly telegram to CPR owner Sir Hugh Allan: "I must have another ten thousand. Will be the last time of calling. Do not fail me. Answer today." The Conservatives won a narrow victory, but Macdonald was forced from office when the fatal message and the campaign funds it produced were revealed in the Commons.

Despite booze and shady dealings, Macdonald was a dramatic and eloquent speaker whose performances in the House were a special treat for those who crowded the galleries each day. D'Arcy McGee was a scholarly spellbinder and Sir Wilfrid Laurier's rhetoric was in part responsible for making his the longest career – forty-five years – in our Commons history. Passion and grace were essential to leadership and to victory in Commons votes. They were required in the daily competition for the hearts and minds of the independent men who decided issues of the day. Grattan O'Leary, legendary journalist and Tory senator, wrote of that period: "the fight for natural freedom, for democracy, for the deliverance of intellect from the old fantastic bondages, was won largely by the power and the appeal of eloquence."

The rule against reading speeches was strictly enforced in the early days and, in fact, until after the Second World War. In his memoirs, O'Leary said: "Men like Laurier, Borden, Meighen, Bennett and King put on virtuoso performances with only a few notes to assist. A member who rose in his place and read a speech through from beginning to end would have been quarantined." Now, as any Commons viewer can observe daily, members stumble through the bloodless texts that hired researchers pump from their word processors. Admonitions to speak, not read, are routinely ignored. So are the rules against repetition and irrelevance. Back then, "it was a different House," O'Leary tells us. "It was a time when . . . people spoke as they felt; there was more openness."

The so-called golden age of parliamentary power was gradually tarnished. The advent of strict party discipline chipped away at the independence of individual MPs. New rules were imposed on proceedings as the people's business became more complex and cabinet power grew. With parties to draw divergent players together from across the country, the tolerance for rebels diminished. Uniformity imposed from above was needed to override regional complaints and French-English animosity.

Protest parties emerged in the early twentieth century. The Progressives, the United Farmers of Alberta, the Liberal-Progressives and the Labor Party sprang up, then shuffled into a variety of combinations. In 1921 there were 65 Progressives elected to the 234-seat Commons, 15 more than the Conservative total. In 1935 two new parties bloomed on the prairies, Social Credit and the Co-operative Commonwealth Federation (forerunner of the NDP's uneasy alliance of farmers, labor and socialist academics). Each was born out of economic and regional frustration and fuelled by the misery of depression. The resulting name games produced, among others, the oxymoronic "Progressive-Conservative" label our government wears today.

As independent-minded members were corralled into new groupings in the Commons, power shifted from back-benchers to party leaders. Gradual changes came with such little things as Laurier's 1906 imposition of a limit on the number of times MPs could move adjournment motions.

The most dramatic single rule change came in 1913 when Sir Robert Borden first introduced "closure" to push through the Naval Aid Bill under which Canada would pay $35 million to build ships for use by the Royal Navy. The new Commons guillotine cut off debate on that measure after a two-week, day-and-night filibuster led by Laurier. Journalist Arthur R. Ford described the clash as "perhaps the most boisterous, the noisiest and the most disgraceful session of any Canadian Parliament." He reported that Sir Wilfrid was "white with anger" when the closure motion was passed.

Closure was invoked fewer than a dozen times in the next two decades, and not at all between 1932 and 1956. Then in 1956 the St. Laurent government used closure four times to cut off opposition to its Pipeline Bill. Anger over this "steam-roller" tactic was whipped up by John Diefenbaker into a huge protest against "Liberal arrogance" and led to the defeat of St. Laurent in the 1957 election. Today the frequent use of closure by the Mulroney Conservatives is hardly noticed by press or public.

Until 1927 there was no time limit on speeches. A forty-minute cap was imposed that year, and later rule changes continued to reduce it. Opportunities for members to take part in major debates on the budget and Throne Speech were also reduced. Government back-benchers were often forbidden to "use up valuable time" speaking on legislation, and only a rare renegade disobeyed. Private members' bills, the main source of legislative activity in the nineteenth century, had been virtually eliminated from serious consideration by the 1980s. On rare occasions when a private member's bill proved acceptable to the government, it would usually be allowed to die on the order paper, only to be revived as a government initiative in a later session. The effect of all these practices was to move almost all important decisions from the public Commons forum to the secret sanctums of cabinet and caucus. Even those in the government caucus had little idea what was adrift in cabinet circles.

By the time Paul Martin, Sr., arrived on Parliament Hill in 1935 as a freshman Liberal MP, the "trained seal" role of government back-benchers was well established. Clap, bark and vote on cue in the hopes that the leader would eventually toss you a fish. He recalls his consternation at cabinet's iron-fisted control of the Commons, where debates were pointless and government back-benchers had no input. "Government bills were not presented to caucus ahead of time, there were no caucus committees to investigate policies, and few back-benchers made special efforts to have government matters brought before caucus – which was basically a gripe session. We were therefore called upon in Parliament to approve measures without having had an opportunity to amend or influence them," he laments in his memoirs of a time before he became a powerful minister himself.

The opposition had it even worse. No amount of ranting and raving in the chamber, no suggestion – however constructive – had any impact on policy. Governments considered any amendment to legislation as an admission of wrong. They would rather pass a flawed bill and correct it with future legislation than approve an opposition change. Ministers won their leader's approval for competence and efficiency by getting the bills through quickly without change, not by encouraging debate on them.

What little work Commons committees accomplished was usually routine. Some of them went years between meetings. For the opposition there were two basic mechanisms for bringing the government to account: Question Period and the Committee of the Whole. The latter provided clause-by-clause study of some bills and of budgets and spending estimates. Debate there took on a free-wheeling question-and-answer format rather than simply adding feckless speeches to the *Hansard* record. Ministers, with top bureaucrats beside them, had to account in the House for every penny of departmental spending. Not only was there an accounting, the process clearly revealed which cabinet members were on top of departmental business and which were not. That process too was later eroded.

As MPs lost power and stature, their role became less attractive to men of top calibre – at least according to O'Leary, who was one of Parliament's closest observers for more than half a century. As a young reporter he did miss a (very) few things – such as the start of the 1916 fire that destroyed the original Centre Block. He was in a card game at the nearby Château Laurier Hotel when it began. He started his career at the *Ottawa Journal* as cub reporter in 1911, retired from the *Journal* as president in 1966, and sat as a senator from 1962 to his death in 1976. In sixty-five years of Parliament-watching he credited at least two-dozen MPs as first-rate. Both he and this century's best-known parliamentary observer, the late Eugene Forsey, named Arthur Meighen as the premier performer in the green chamber. But there were many others with sharp tongues and keen eyes in the early 1900s. No government would "lightly take chances with half-baked legislation or with doubtful public accounts," O'Leary wrote in 1939. "In Parliament today, these men have no counterparts. Indeed over a period of nearly two decades the Public Accounts Committee has been called but rarely; in some sessions not at all. Instead of addressing themselves now to the public accounts and the Auditor General's report, members . . . use Parliament as a sounding board for political propaganda."

If Parliament did not always function as it should have, at least it was not costing taxpayers a fortune. By 1935 it had 245 MPs. Pay of $4,000 a year and a few perks meant that most candidates were more interested in public service than personal rewards. They got train travel, free postage and little else. One office and a sessional secretary were shared by two MPs.

"Dozens of MPs did not know how to dictate a letter easily and would tie up a secretary for hours while their office mate sat there fuming," Martin recalls in his autobiography, *A Very Public Life*. Journalist Austin Cross felt that most MPs earned their pay and usually ended up poorer at the end of their terms. "An MP can hardly stick his nose inside the House of Commons some days, so busy is he wrestling with all the mail he gets. . . . Then there are delegations that are likely to land on the member's hands, and they must all be fed at the member's expense!"

The Parliamentary Restaurant helped out there, providing excellent meals in sumptuous surroundings at give-away prices. With night sittings, it was a packed rendezvous for entertaining and political star-gazing. When Speaker John Bosley jacked the prices up by over 100 per cent to almost market level in 1985, business dropped dramatically. Grumbling MPs admit it was a factor in their low opinion of Bosley's performance in the critical Commons position from which he was forced the next year. With the end of night sittings, the buffet lunch is now the restaurant's main attraction.

The Second World War saw the scope of government extend to almost every sector of society. There was a surge in the transfer of provincial power to Ottawa that began in the Depression. During the war more than 25,000 cabinet orders, on every conceivable activity, were passed without parliamentary oversight or approval. Government agencies made greater changes in Canadian life than had all the legislation passed by Parliament since Confederation. The civil service expanded from 46,000 in 1939 to 116,000 by the end of the war. Crown corporations and new departments mushroomed. The "extraordinary powers" granted to the King government in wartime were extended first to the post-war reconstruction period, then into the Korean war years. C.D. Howe, the strongman of the King and St. Laurent cabinets, objected to a proposed curtailment of these powers after the Korean conflict. The trade and commerce minister barked: "That would mean coming back to Parliament every three years, and I've more to do than spend my time amusing Parliament." He apparently did not amuse the voters of his Port Arthur riding for much longer either. They replaced him with a relative unknown in 1957, CCFer Doug Fisher.

By 1953, Parliament had virtually lost its power to amend or even delay government spending and legislation. There was lots of talk signifying little in sessions that seemed endless. In the angry Pearson-Diefenbaker years of the late 1950s and early 1960s, MPs began to battle for restoration of their former might. Debates were as dramatic as those in the Macdonald-Laurier years. The chamber was filled, the galleries crowded. Canadians woke up and looked with renewed interest at their House on the Hill.

In 1956, the Liberal government's view of Parliament as a clumsy rubber stamp was shattered by the great pipeline debate. Howe's decision to invoke closure to meet his construction schedule for the

Trans-Canada Pipeline brought the House into a state of near-anarchy. With Diefenbaker's enthusiastic help, the public image of the Liberals changed; once considered a team of competent managers, they were now seen as arrogant Mafia dons. The opposition screamed "dictatorship," sang, whistled and waved fists in some of the most unruly performances since the 1913 fight over closure on the Naval Bill. "The Pipeline Debate was not a sudden expression of disregard of Parliament in respect of one bill," wrote John Diefenbaker in his memoirs. "This was the culmination of a process that had continued virtually unabated from the days of the war."

The final explosion came in June when Speaker René Beaudoin made a ruling to cut off debate. "You can't do this," shouted the normally mild-mannered CCF leader M.J. Coldwell. In an outburst that amazed him along with everyone else in the House, he rushed the Speaker's dais and shook his fist in Beaudoin's face. Diefenbaker described the event as "Parliament at its worst and Parliament in its greatest hour." The government won the parliamentary battle but lost the election war that followed.

The public concluded that its democratic institution had been hijacked. Howe's famous, "What's a million?" was widely misquoted as an example of Liberal arrogance. (What he actually said was: "So I hope the Honourable member will agree that to operate a department with 1,100 people for a year, $3 million is not exorbitant. Will he go that far with me?" Diefenbaker and the public liked the shorter version.) Another culprit in the perceived hijacking was Jack Pickersgill, who endeared himself to voters with this humble election claim: "It is not merely for the well-being of Canadians but for the good of mankind in general that the present Liberal government should remain in office." That whopper helped the Tory chief to a narrow win and enough momentum to follow quickly with a second election victory of record proportions, 208 of 265 seats.

Diefenbaker's landslide and his oft-proclaimed devotion to Parliament gave hope for its restoration. The Chief had campaigned on a pledge to put the nation's business under effective parliamentary scrutiny. With considerable fanfare, he put his back-benchers to work in committee. But the Commons makeover was more illusion than reality. Meddling endlessly, Dief kept a stranglehold on committees, controlling every bit of business through hand-picked chairmen and majority membership.

The opposition turned its weakness to advantage, showing that the Tories were stubbornly unwilling to listen to minority voices. Four years after the biggest win in Canadian history, Diefenbaker could salvage only a minority. He lost even that the next year as his cabinet, along with Parliament, crumbled around him.

The 1960s, which had begun with such promise of democratic renewal, the return of power to the House of the people, had produced just the opposite. The Commons became a vipers' pit of partisanship, with party discipline ruling over all else. The example of Diefenbaker's self-destructive caucus has been used ever since to control mutinous elements, or even those who try to express understandable differences on any subject.

The punishment meted out to Doug Harkness, who resigned as defence minister in 1963 over the nondeployment of U.S. atomic warheads in Canada, is an example of political nastiness. Diefenbaker neither spoke to him again nor allowed him any role of parliamentary importance. Entitled to a large office by virtue of his seniority, a re-elected Harkness returned to Parliament to find his files dumped on the floor. His new office was so tiny his secretary had to leave when the Calgary veteran wanted to talk in private.

But those years also saw great Commons debates that stirred the blood of the nation – debates on the flag, a national pension plan, unification of the armed forces, medicare and bilingualism. Each aroused fierce battle inside and outside the green chamber. The thirty-three-day flag debate raged through July and August of 1964, ending with closure and prompting further measures to limit opposition powers. The unlimited ability of MPs to hold up passage of the spending estimates was about the last major weapon the opposition had with which to rein in the government. The Pearson government gained power to override that, promising to send most government bills and all department estimates to Commons committees in return. But the committees were dominated by the party in power whose members voted exactly as they were told. The opposition was sold a toothless watch-dog.

Finally, there was the ultimate question of votes of confidence. Parliamentary tradition held that defeat on a budget measure meant loss of confidence in the government. An election or handover of power should follow. In 1967 the Liberals finessed a new wrinkle. With Pearson catching rays in Jamaica and his House leader asleep at the switch, the Tories under new leader Robert Stanfield won a surprise vote on a spending amendment. Pearson scurried back, convinced Stanfield through Bank of Canada governor Louis Rasminsky that an election would cripple the Canadian economy, and persuaded Stanfield to allow a second vote, which reaffirmed the confidence of the House in the Liberal government. Trudeau succeeded Pearson, and the Liberals swept back into power. Stanfield remained in opposition until the day he retired. He was unforgiven to the end by old-guard Tories who had missed their grab for power and patronage.

All that contributed to still more complaints from back-bench MPs about their lack of influence. "Our system does not allow any real purpose for back-benchers," protested New Democrat MP Arnold Peters in 1965. "All an MP is expected to do is get elected." That view provided little incentive to work in committees. Many MPs turned their attention completely away from the House, "vegetated" or looked after their ridings. "When I entered the House in the fall of 1967, the consideration of estimates seemed to me to be a farce," remarked Stanfield. "I found an emasculated House of Commons which was still capable of greatness on occasion but which was no longer in effective control of the public purse."

Liberal Phil Givens put it a bit less elegantly in 1969. "At the end of Question Period every day the House flushes out like a toilet bowl – members leave, cabinet ministers leave, the press gallery leaves and you get up and talk to 240 empty seats. . . . The people who might be in a position to help implement an idea are simply not there."

Although the Diefenbaker landslide did not restore Parliament, it launched the era of big-league spending. In 1958 MPs received $8,000 plus a $2,000 tax-free allowance and unlimited free rail travel. Parliament then cost about $7 million a year or about $30,000 an MP. When Doug Fisher arrived he shared 260 square feet of Centre Block office space, a phone and a secretary, just as Martin had two decades earlier. A year later Fisher began a drive for higher pay and better services for MPs. It was an uphill battle against a notoriously frugal prime minister and the frugality of some elders in his own party. (CCF statesman Stanley Knowles was defeated in the Diefenbaker sweep and did not return to set a personal example of austerity until 1962.)

Speaker Roland Michener was sympathetic to Fisher's pleas. He believed that each MP should have his or her own office and a full-time secretary. Fisher and a small group of Liberals and Conservatives also pushed for two "perks" – free air travel to and from their ridings and free long-distance phone calls. By 1963 MPs had boosted the rewards of office to $18,000, of which $6,000 was tax-free. Fisher, who is now a political columnist for the *Toronto Sun*, was sure that if MPs were offered sufficient pay and services they would not only do better work, but the position would attract a better calibre of candidate. He later lamented that he had opened a Pandora's box. "Alas, it hasn't worked out that way," he says with a sigh today. "And what's more, parliamentary spending is spiralling out of control."

Commons costs began to skyrocket in the 1970s, particularly during Trudeau's minority government of 1972-74 when Liberal planners bought a bit of job security by keeping opponents comfortable. In 1970 MPs received a "sessional allowance" (pay) of $18,000 plus a tax-free allowance of $8,000. A decade later they got $30,600 and a tax-free $13,500, plus a lot of new fringe benefits. By then they had two full-time secretaries in their parliamentary offices, which had spread out from the Centre Block to expanded quarters on and off the Hill. They are now housed in five buildings. A full-time staffer was added in constituency offices in 1977. The year after that MPs were given an office budget of $58,000. Pay hikes and perks grew as fast as MPs could invent reasons. They were given three-room, carpeted office suites. Research assistants were added. Today, each office has four telephones, a fax machine, a photocopier, two personal laptop computers, two office computers and printers, two color TV sets, a video tape recorder and a multichannel television system that provides everything from selected hometown newscasts (recorded via satellite and available on demand) to airport arrival and departure times, to two U.S. C-Span public affairs channels. Each member has another fully equipped office back in the constituency.

During the recession of 1981, Knowles was the only MP to protest a hike in salary and expense allowances to $47,100. In a heartfelt but futile speech, Knowles rebuked his colleagues for their excessive appetite for personal benefits. He reminded the House that there were "good men in Parliament when the pay was $4,000 and no extras." He acknowledged that times had changed but declared that the rewards were getting so high that Parliament was attracting "people looking for a good-paying job" and not public service. "Everyone who has spoken in this debate thus far has justified it [the pay increase]. I say, and I speak only for myself, that I do not want to be in a position of improving my situation when we have done so little for those out there." Many members quietly snarled that Knowles could get by on almost nothing because "he lives on tea and crackers." The bill passed.

Today it takes a 476-page manual to detail the "allowances and services" for MPs. Here are but a few of the blessings that come with a life of sacrifice and public service in Parliament. Free first-class air travel for an MP, spouse and family members; a private health club; cheap haircuts; $1 shoeshines, a tailor shop and dry-cleaning service; masseurs; elegant dining at bargain prices in the exclusive Parliamentary Restaurant or several cafeterias; a billiard room; free picture framing; a free buffet in the Commons lobby on Fridays and any evening the House sits; the services of a furniture and upholstery shop; little buses to whisk them around the Hill; printing and postal services for "householder" newsletters; messengers on demand; a daily news digest; a library and professional researchers; in-office individual language lessons and free parking at the door (worth more than $1,300 a year, according to the auditor general's office).

An MP receives a basic salary of $64,400, plus a tax-free allowance of $27,300 ($6,000 of that is to pay for accommodation).

Members from large, remote ridings get an extra allowance of $5,000 to $7,000. The tax-free allowance amounts to nearly double its face value at a time when federal and provincial income taxes take away half of a regular pay cheque. As taxes have risen through the years, the benefit of tax-free income has also jumped. MPs are now hard-pressed to explain why they need more than $27,000 for unitemized expenses on top of such benefits as free flights and free drinks in the exclusive first-class airport lounges while waiting to board.

There's an understandable disagreement between new MPs and older ones about which is better, a pay increase or a hike in the untaxed allowance. Fresh MPs prefer the tax-free cash, but those contemplating post-parliamentary life favor a boost in the pay on which their pensions will be based, 5 per cent for each year of service up to a total of 75 per cent after fifteen years in the House. Pay increases, however, must be dealt with (however quickly) by passing legislation in public. A hike in the expense allowance or other bene-fits can be slipped into their pockets much more quietly. No change in the law is needed for that.

The budget to cover an MP's staff salaries and office expenses has shot up from $58,000 in 1978 to $165,000 in 1991. There are also free rail passes, long-distance phone service, gold-plated pensions, free post-retirement life insurance and counselling services when they leave. There is subsidized day-care for those with small children.

Just how astoundingly the bills have mounted is shown in statis-tics since the Second World War. In 1949, the tab for the Commons was $2.9 million; for the Senate $900,000. With $100,000 for the Parliamentary Library, the total came to $3.9 million. In 1991 those figures are $229 million for the Commons, $46 million for the Senate, and $16 million for the library – a seventy-five–fold increase, to a total of more than $291 million. The cost per MP, not counting the library, is more than $770,000 a year. Even the explosion in overall government spending, with medicare, Canada Pension Plan, federal-provincial transfers and all the other post-war benefits, is less, about fifty times what it was in 1949. The consumer price index has multiplied less than six times in the same period.

MPs argue that their precarious future and career interruptions warrant extra compensation. But at a time of universal job layoffs and mid-career changes in the real world off the Hill, the term of MPs is about as secure as that of anyone else. And few outsiders obtain the prime patronage rewards and pension bonanza that cushion the transition to post-parliamentary life.

The example of self-service set by those chosen to safeguard the public purse carries over into ever-fatter rewards for bureaucrats, especially those at the top. They too enjoy huge offices, support staff, cars with drivers, first-class travel and a cornucopia of treats that includes free personal counselling on how to invest their money.

In the view of Doug Fisher, "The increasing opulence of our parliamentary institutions is the visible symptom of the declining political morality. It might even be one of the causes."

Aside from stuffing their pockets with four or five times as much income as the average Canadian, parliamentarians have other things to do. Not the least of them is keeping up with constantly changing Commons rules. Among the promises each prime minister makes along the path to office are vows that power will be restored to the people's representatives in the House. Invariably, delivery on those pledges falls short of the hopes of both back-benchers and the people who elect them. Governments make commitments to get things done. Nothing makes that tougher than an uncontrolled Parliament, a dangerous obstacle between a prime minister and his goals. Those "reforms" become twisted into devices to help the government, not Parliament. Members realize this, of course, but if sufficient treats are handed out they usually don't rock the boat enough to tip themselves overboard. They may complain about the unique demands of the job, and about its frustrations, but most hang on until they are retired by the voters.

The explosion of salaries in the 1970s came on the heels of reforms introduced by Pierre Trudeau in 1968-70. These were radical in their scope, designed to make the Commons work better and to give MPs more input through committees. Detailed debate on all estimates and virtually all legislation was diverted from the chamber to committees. All spending estimates were to be returned to the House within a set timetable. Opposition concerns were to be raised on "allotted" or "supply" days, when those arrayed against the government could put a motion forward for a full day's debate, sometimes ending with a pro-forma vote. (Since the government considered such recorded divisions as votes of confidence, it defeated every such opposition motion regardless of the content.)

In 1969 time allocation rules were introduced to allow the government to overcome almost any opposition obstacle and to push legislation through each stage in a couple of days. Not surprisingly, the government needed closure to end that fiery debate and pass the new rule. That was the occasion of Trudeau's now-famous pronouncement about parliamentary "nobodies": "The opposition seems to think that it has nothing else to do but talk. . . . The best place in which to talk, if they want a forum, is, of course, Parliament. When they get home, when they get out of Parliament, when they are fifty yards from Parliament Hill, they are no longer honourable members – they are just nobodies." Brian Mulroney followed with his own variation when he shuffled his cabinet in April 1991 to put his western-based ministers in front-line jobs to counter the rise of the Reform Party. "Albertans will have to decide whether they want this or some back-benchers," said Mulroney, sneering at the role of ordinary MPs.

Trudeau's reforms virtually neutered Parliament's remaining ability to scrutinize and control the outflow of public money. Government spending estimates were deemed to have been passed automatically on June 30 of each year, regardless of whether committees had examined them. All these changes prompted Auditor General J.J. Macdonnell to report in 1977 that Parliament "has lost, or is close to losing, effective control of the public purse." Two years later the Lampert Royal Commission on Financial Management and Accountability concluded: "The review of estimates is often meaningless."

By the early 1980s the opposition felt it had so little power to influence legislation that it resorted to one final, drastic tactic. It shut the place down. In March 1982, the Conservatives, led by Erik Nielsen, forced a vote, then walked out of the chamber and refused to return in response to the division bells. At issue was a massive, controversial energy package. By collecting half a dozen or more subjects in a single omnibus bill, the Liberal government would be able to push through several contentious items at once. "The government will use this as a dangerous precedent to steam-roll legislation through the House," declared Conservative leader Joe Clark.

The bells summoning members back rang for an unprecedented, nerve-racking fifteen days while constitutional experts huddled with Speaker Jeanne Sauvé and Nielsen stared down government House leader Yvon Pinard. The critical sticking point was a convention that delayed votes until party whips on both sides entered the chamber, signifying their readiness to proceed. Finally, the government agreed to split the bill into four separate parts in return for a resumption of business. At least as significant, however, was the resulting rule change that allows one side to vote even if the other refuses to show up.

The Conservatives mounted a loud campaign for real parliamentary reform that would restore to ordinary MPs the power that had fallen, bit by bit, into the hands of the prime minister, his tight inner circle of advisers, a few key bureaucrats and a handful of powerful cabinet ministers.

"Our system has been changing for a long time, gradually giving more power to governments and parties and gradually limiting the right of Parliament," Clark declared in 1982. "If that continues, we will waste the talent of the members who serve here."

Mulroney wrested the Conservative leadership from Clark soon after, then rode to power in 1984 vowing to restore Parliament to its rightful place and politicians to respectability.

3
KING OF THE HILL

*"The next prime minister who ignores
MPs is history."*

BRIAN MULRONEY, 1986

I
T WAS AS CLEAR AS THE CHIN ON HIS FACE. IN THE SPRING OF 1991
Mulroney's sour self-absorption magically changed to buoyant
enthusiasm. The brooding withdrawal that followed the wreck
of Meech Lake was gone. He again oozed the confidence and
control that had won the only two-in-a-row Tory elections this
century. He even charmed his way into the hard hearts of the media
for a few hours at the Press Gallery Dinner with jokes about his once-
fabled drinking and Mila's equally stupendous shopping binges.

Every pulse-taker in Ottawa detected the new Mulroney beat.
The top columnists commented on it, but seemed totally at a loss for
an explanation. Marjorie Nichols of the *Ottawa Citizen*, Michel
Gratton of the *Toronto Sun* newspapers and Jeffrey Simpson of the
Globe and Mail, three of the best plugged-in observers of his office,
were in the dark. The upbeat mood seemed to defy reality.

After all, his support was somewhere between 12 and 18 per
cent, depending on which poll you saw which day. His strongholds
in Quebec and Alberta were about to be wiped out by regional
parties. The Bloc Québécois, headed by his turncoat pal Lucien
Bouchard, was poised to pick off fifty or so of the sixty-three seats his
Conservatives had captured in that province in 1988. All twenty of
his Alberta members appeared doomed at the hands of the mushrooming Reform Party. So did up to half of his twelve British
Columbia seats and six or seven more of his eighteen in Manitoba
and Saskatchewan. Even seats in Ontario were threatened by the
explosion of "Presto" Manning's Reformers.

The NDP was already flying high with whiz-kid Bob Rae at the controls in Ontario. The Big Blue Machine was a heap of rusting, sadly remembered scrap. Today's no-name Ontario Tory leader was in a distant third place. Provincial Conservatives were seatless and leaderless in New Brunswick. In Nova Scotia, Mulroney's brazen Senate rescue of Premier John Buchanan left a stench that would soon be cleared out by the voters. The NDP was expecting to topple the Tories under Premier Grant Devine in Saskatchewan. Tory-by-another-name Bill Vander Zalm had just been chased from Fantasyland in Victoria. The socialist hordes were poised to take over there within months. Alberta Tories under Premier Don Getty had just voted to save themselves by severing ties with their national party.

The country was about to fly apart, and even Keith Spicer's $25 million flying circus could not save it. A solemn joint committee headed by Senator Gérald Beaudouin and Tory MP Jim Edwards was sadly listening once again to constitutional tinkerers across the land. After Oka, the natives were restless, demanding a place at the unity table and action on land claims, environmental threats and dozens of other grievances. Unemployment was at its highest level in years. The deficit hung like a leaden cloud over the government. The economy was mired in recession with no signs of breaking loose. Tens of thousands of Canadians were grocery shopping in the United States. Poll after poll showed that Mulroney himself was neither liked nor trusted. There seemed little reason for the good cheer that had so clearly overtaken him.

But Mulroney still held the reins of power. He had a sense, for the first time since the Meech Lake fiasco, of where and how to guide his team. Straight for the election two years away.

The Senate débâcle was behind him. The "GST senators" had done their messy job, leaving him in control of the upper chamber. From now on he could easily club Allan MacEachen and the hated Trudeau remnants into submission. The GST itself was pumping money into the federal treasury to be used when the campaign demanded it. After the colossal parliamentary battle to push it through, the actual start-up was almost painless. Saddam Hussein and George Bush had neatly diverted everyone's attention.

The treacherous Bouchard was getting increasingly tangled up in a Quebec turf war with Jacques Parizeau. While they quarrelled over the top separatist spot, Bourassa was ever-ready to help plot whatever would help keep him in power and to do the same for the prime minister. Mulroney had not only staunched the flow of deserters to the Bloc, he had even regained one. Gilbert Chartrand publicly whimpered that it had all been a ghastly mistake. He was really a federal Tory – and a Mulroney-worshipper to boot. He won a standing ovation from his former and future colleagues as he scampered back across the Commons floor.

Jean Chrétien was recuperating from his lung operation but showed no sign that he was about to regain the "first place in our hearts" popularity that peaked with his near-victory in the Liberal leadership race seven years earlier. The Grits still sagged under a huge debt and were waging internal fights for top party and parliamentary spots. A shake-up in their Commons team had made it even more difficult for them to gain any momentum. In contrast, Tory coffers were full and the party brains trust was clicking.

An experiment in budget drafting had worked out just as Mulroney had hoped. All MPs had been asked to contribute ideas to the process, measures that were important to them and their constituents. Enough of those were incorporated into Michael Wilson's final package that all Conservative MPs were back in step, able to tell anyone who asked that they were making their influence felt. Those who did not have anything to show for it this time were told to pitch in some fresh ideas for the Throne Speech. There, or in the next budget, they would find fresh booty to flash for constituents.

The main budget theme was always popular with Tories – save public money by kicking around the fat-cat public servants. Since the Conservatives had already lost all the Ottawa-area seats in the last election, they had little to lose when the hired help retaliated. The one regional seat that might be lost was Paul Dick's, a sacrifice his colleagues would be happy to make. The gains to be made certainly exceeded any political cost. The entire country would be delighted to see the bulging bureaucracy cut down to size in the capital city. The move would rip out a key Reform Party plank. Just to make that perfectly clear, Mulroney uprooted the National Energy Board and replanted it in Harvie Andre's Calgary riding, next to where the high priest of Reform, Preston Manning, would run against Conservative MP Barbara (Bobbie) Sparrow. That made sense in the oilpatch, which did not know or did not care that the board does more work on eastern pipelines and Ontario and Quebec hydro matters than it does on Alberta oil and gas. Its responsibility is at least as much to eastern consumers as to western producers, but this is irrelevant when seats are at stake. As for the 300 employees involved and their families, they were just early casualties in a pre-election war. After all, they were merely public servants.

A new assault on the CBC was also going well. They whined in Windsor, Calgary and Saskatoon when local stations were shut down, but the CBC's left-leaning friends were not the kind who voted Tory anyway. Mulroney's message was clearly delivered through columnists such as Nichols. The Crown broadcaster was fat, overfunded and unfair competition for unsubsidized broadcasters and publishers who had to compete for advertising dollars in a tough market. Every Conservative in the country was primed to tell any CBC defender that the Crown broadcaster received $1.4 billion a year, which should be enough to stop its bleating for more.

Even the new CBC chairman's sensitive ego played into Mulroney's hands. Patrick Watson moaned that the prime minister had misquoted him as claiming that the CBC was amply funded. With a golden invitation to retaliate, Mulroney named bombastic right-wing economist and CBC News foe John Crispo to Mother Corp's board. The Toronto professor had complained to the federal broadcasting watch-dog that the CBC did not give him enough air time to voice his pro–free-trade ideas. He apparently qualified to sit with Watson on the board because he believed that the CBC was "a lousy left-wing, Liberal-NDP pinko network."

That sent shudders through news and public-affairs personnel who were already wrestling with government-forced cutbacks. There was more. An unpublished report by the former head of the Canadian Radio-Television and Telecommunications Commission, John Meisel, mysteriously surfaced through Unimedia columnist Michel

Vastel. The report (later published) attacked political reporting by CBC TV English News. Meisel accused the journalist-boss of the CBC's Ottawa bureau, Elly Alboim, of unconscionable bias in the 1987 coverage of the Meech Lake Accord and said that, while the federal-provincial constitutional deal was taking shape, Alboim saw it as a fraud perpetrated on the people of Canada for the sole purpose of feeding the Mulroney ego. Meisel charged Alboim with scouring the country for critics to discredit the agreement. Vastel's initial column on the Meisel charges was followed up by Michel Gratton in the *Sun* newspapers, Marjorie Nichols in the *Ottawa Citizen* and officially commissioned Mulroney biographer Peter C. Newman in *Maclean's* magazine. A few columnists, such as the *Citizen*'s Robert Lee and the *Sun*'s Mike Duffy, supported Alboim. Nichols darkly described an anti-Meech campaign that included "even sending a daily CBC messenger to Pierre Trudeau's Montreal office to solicit negative public statements." Alboim had concluded that the "remarkable consensus was a fraud and thereupon embarked on a surreptitious campaign to destroy the deal," Nichols charged.

Oddly enough, three years later the same Elly Alboim was accused of deploying the CBC-TV News team headed by Peter Mansbridge, Don Newman and Wendy Mesley on a mission to save Meech Lake. Critics said that they and "Journal" host Barbara Frum promoted the view that failure of the deal meant national disaster. What was just as peculiar as the crazed scheming attributed to Alboim was how it came to light. No one explained just how a Quebec journalist who happened to be well connected in the PMO had unearthed an unpublished report by a retired Queen's University professor and former Tory appointee. Was Alboim's dastardly hand-iwork the real threat to the nation? Or was the fine hand of Mulroney agents involved? In any case, the publicly funded service that is the most influential news agency in Canada was scorched again.

The fuss clearly reminded CBC management and journalists where their money came from. They were being closely watched for unfair coverage of the prime minister and his works. Joe Clark, Harvie Andre and other key ministers chipped in about the same time with suggestions of anti-government bias on CBC News. The threat that an even tougher CBC financial crunch could follow was obvious. It was clear too that the Tories were laying a solid base for future claims that criticism of them was the result of partisan reporting.

The Mulroney government's clear, constant and destructive meddling with an institution that reports to the people through Parliament upset far more than the "leftie friends of the CBC." After all, it was the Conservatives in opposition who had protested against "interference" by Prime Minister Pierre Trudeau when he requested CBC network time once every year or two for an announcement of "national importance." The CBC was careful on such occasions to offer equal time to the other parties. Once in power, though, Mulroney's Conservatives were clearly unsatisfied with just the right to appoint the president and chairman. Or with the right to request time for prime-ministerial statements. They wanted to gut the place and intimidate those who were left. That Mulroney strategy would be firmly in place in good time for the election two years away.

Possibly the neatest bit of remodelling Mulroney's hired hands completed last spring was in the House of Commons itself. It took four months of inter-party negotiations, four days of debate and a closure motion to do it, but his team pushed through sixty-four changes to the rules. The net effect was to reduce Parliament's ability to subject the government to scrutiny.

Using such words as "efficiency" and "businesslike," the government cut 40 sitting days from the Commons calendar. Members would now be in the House for 135 days a year, back in their ridings or somewhere else for 230. The government maintained that the sitting hours each day were being extended so that no total House time was lost. But the Commons works more on a timetable of days than of hours. For example, there would be 40 fewer Question Periods in which opponents could grill ministers in the House and be seen doing it on the nightly news. Time for individual members to speak in the Throne Speech debate was cut by 25 per cent and in the budget debate by a third. Those are two rare opportunities members have to cover any topics they want, usually ones close to their constituents' hearts.

A powerful government-dominated committee would take on the

work of three previous ones in controlling other committees, private members' business and the management and services of the House. It was expected to meet mostly behind closed doors, its business and its minutes kept confidential.

Committees would be grouped in five subject "envelopes" within which the party whips could freely move members from one committee to another – for instance, from Labour to Aboriginal Affairs, to Health and Welfare, to Multiculturalism. Meeting times would also be scheduled by the overriding government authority, meaning it could keep a squad of reliable loyalists on hand to cover all committee demands, and let most of its members go about the business of getting re-elected. Television coverage of committees would be allowed only when the government representatives chose.

One interesting wrinkle suggested by the Liberals was inserted into the new standing orders. It would cut the power of small parties and independent members to stall business. Under the old "unanimous consent" provisions, a single member could prevent the House from quitting early, for instance, or changing the order of business. Elijah Harper had used this tactic in Manitoba, and the same rule was used by Independent MP Alex Kindy to stop the three parties from a deal to shut down the House during the Persian Gulf War. With the change, it now takes twenty-five members to hold things up. That not only makes it tougher for the NDP but anticipates the arrival of small parties in the next Parliament and curbs their impact.

During negotiations on the changes, NDP House leader Nelson Riis assured his Liberal and Conservative counterparts that his caucus would approve what the three leaders agreed to. But his party colleagues refused to go along with much of the package Riis brought back to them. Riis then publicly accused the government of trying to impose "Draconian" measures in a "fascist" way. Harvie Andre, the government House strongman, was enraged by the turnaround and the charges. He retaliated by cutting NDP speeches to half the time Conservatives and Liberals are allowed at the start of a debate. Under the old rule the lead-off speaker of the "third party" got the same forty minutes as the preceding two. The new rule reduced the New Democrats' allocation to twenty minutes.

Andre also accused Riis of bringing the Commons into disrepute by using excessive language. Later, New Democrat Bill Blaikie suggested that Parliament's reputation was damaged more by Harvie's own horrifying behavior of ten years before, when a shouting gang of fist-waving Tories had charged the chair to protest a rare Liberal closure vote. Harvie insisted that he had not threatened Speaker Lloyd Francis at the time. Instead, he had been in a snarling near-punch-up with another Liberal who had advanced menacingly towards his leader, Joe Clark. In putting the oft-told "charging the chair" story to rest, Harvie drew attention to the very kind of "schoolyard" spectacle that so disgusts Commons viewers.

Mulroney has used closure and a rule called "time allocation" to cut off debate dozens of times since 1984. This tactic is now so common that the press and public no longer cry foul when it is invoked. Rule changes make it still easier, ensuring that the government can push any measure through the House in five sitting days. The Senate, of course, is no longer a problem.

The age-old right of "grievance before supply" was also weakened drastically. That's the historic reason for having a Parliament – to let the people study and criticize government programs before their money is spent. Not only was the budget debate cut from six days to four, but the number of opposition days was chopped from twenty-four to twenty, with further reductions to follow if the Commons did not sit its full schedule (it rarely does). The chance for detailed committee examination of departmental spending was also reduced.

Finally, there was the three-weeks-on, one-week-off schedule. It clearly worked in the government's favor. In order not to be defeated in any Commons vote, the government must keep its defences up, its members in Ottawa when the House sits. The opposition has no such obligation and has thus allowed its members much more time with constituents when the Commons is in session – or, in the case of MPs like Liberal John Nunziata, more time for his law practice. Now everybody will get at least a week each month to "work the riding."

No doubt that has streamlined the process. But it also runs completely contrary to the purpose of Parliament, which is supposed to give the people's representatives time and opportunity to question the government's plans and spending. The rule changes cut that opportunity down, drastically reducing the ability of the opposition to hold a particularly odious measure up in the House while public protest is mobilized outside. Clearly the most "efficient" and "businesslike" Commons would be one that met for just a day to pass everything the government put before it. Mulroney and his Andre-the-Giant House leader stopped short of that. Nevertheless it was a dramatic about-face for the leader who had come to Parliament vowing to restore its original powers and give individual MPs a meaningful role in running the country.

Despite the national gloom, Mulroney had reason for high spirits with a couple of years left in his mandate. Few were reminding him of his own publicly stated conviction that no prime minister should remain for a third term. That was then, this is now. GST revenues were piling up for strategic dispersal before the next election. He had the Commons and the Senate tamed. The CBC was wounded and off balance, if not on side. But there was still more reason to smile as he clicked more campaign buttons into the "ready" position.

He allowed himself an expensive little joke with his April cabinet shuffle, placing travel-mad Marcel Masse where the planes are, in Defence. He put two trusty Alberta henchmen, Don Mazankowski and Harvie Andre, in control of the purse and the House of Commons. In danger of being toppled from their own seats by surging Reformers, they could be relied on to use money and Parliament to the best election effect. Alberta's other minister, Joe Clark, had been happy and effective at External Affairs for more than six years. To remind him who was in charge, the boss handed him a grenade labelled "Constitutional Affairs." Clark's new job was to keep it from going off. Mulroney could take credit if the country were saved. If the grenade exploded, Clark would go with it.

In some ways, things were almost as hopeful as that June day eight years before when Martin Brian Mulroney vanquished Charles Joseph Clark in the Ottawa Civic Centre to become king of the Conservatives. He had promised that when he ascended to the Canadian throne he would bring peace and prosperity, a magic consensus among East and West, English and French, business and labor. He would create jobs, wipe out deficits. Inflation would be tamed. Puffed-up bureaucrats would be brought under control and the dreadful excesses of Liberal patronage would be wiped out – or, he joked, replaced by some of his own.

His record speaks for itself. But it was his promise of parliamentary reform, of restoring power to the people's elected representatives, that seemed to offer real hope. Now the total reverse of that promise offers equal cause for gloom.

Mulroney had never been elected to public office when he became Conservative leader. Untested in Parliament, he nevertheless knew it was weak and discredited, that individual members had lost their sense of purpose, that public displeasure was growing towards contempt, that Trudeau treated the institution almost with scorn.

A lawyer, conciliator and self-made corporate fixer, Mulroney would forever tilt against the positions of the disdainful Montreal intellectual who had reigned for most of the two decades before him. He would fix what Trudeau could not: the Constitution, the economy, Parliament. He would also avoid the bumbling of predecessors Clark and Diefenbaker, who had led the Tories into power, then back to the political wilderness in shattered disarray. Unlike Trudeau, he would buy his own groceries at 24 Sussex and would even invite guests to share the $200,000 pool that had been built by unnamed friends of the Liberal prime minister.

This was not some fantasyland dreamed up in the Ritz Hotel bar, but a rebuilding plan carefully drawn up by hard-headed advisers with long experience, men such as deputy Erik Nielsen. Old school chum, sometime drinking buddy (like Mulroney, he has now quit) and backroom veteran Pat MacAdam was particularly close. MacAdam recalled the Diefenbaker débâcle when the largest majority in Canadian history fell apart as idle MPs indulged in cards, booze and late-night plots. MacAdam had been Mulroney's key operative in the *putsch* that unseated Clark. Mulroney made him "caucus liaison" agent, the first time any prime minister had named an unelected aide to handle relations with back-bench MPs. Mulroney sold the idea to his members as a way for them to get his instant attention, but it was an even better way for him to keep an eye on their activities.

In his 1984 election campaign, Mulroney vowed to make Parliament a place where individual MPs would be significant players, no longer the "nobodies" of Trudeau's time. Dominance by the executive would be weakened and the power of hired mandarins would be broken. Tories were convinced that bureaucrats were too cosy with Liberals and more interested in their own well-being than the public's. Ironically, Liberal leader John Turner campaigned on the same "new broom" theme, pointing out that he had cut his short-lived cabinet from thirty-seven to twenty-nine members, reduced the number of cabinet committees and curbed the power of bureaucrats. On September 4, 1984, the people chose Mulroney along with 210 Tory colleagues in a gigantic sweep.

To breathe new life into the democratic process and provide work for the biggest Commons caucus in history, Mulroney chose a tough, disgruntled veteran, Jim McGrath. Possibly smarting because he had been passed over as key Newfoundland minister in favor of rival John Crosbie, McGrath and his all-party team attacked the job with a vengeance, building upon the excellent foundation provided by the previous "Lefebvre committee." Naturally, Liberals and New Democrats saw nothing but good in a "power to the Parliament" exercise.

The McGrath report in June 1985 recommended sweeping changes. Commons committees would have power and budgets to design and initiate policy, to travel, hire consultants, subpoena witnesses, even examine some of the prime minister's 3,500 patronage appointments. It would be made easier for private members to push important ideas through the process into law. MPs should be free to vote as they saw fit except in a very few "confidence" situations where the result could turf a government from office. Those votes would be clearly identified in advance so that tricks could be avoided.

In a sly jab below the cabinet's ample belt, the McGrath committee called for ministers to vacate their choice Parliament Hill office suites, retaining only the same space as other MPs. Ministerial business belonged in the glass towers scattered elsewhere in the city, the report declared. "This place will never be the same again," McGrath bragged as he turned in his report.

Mulroney was already learning about the exercise of power in a democracy where opponents' voices sometimes drowned out those of the people in charge. He and his elite guard received the report with grim smiles. They implemented the recommendations in a way that left the reins of power firmly in their own hands. Some, like those about vacating prized offices and allowing free votes, were ignored.

One of Mulroney's greatest assets is the ability to disarm others with charm. He told the House that the reforms would make MPs "somebodies" with independent authority, "asserting their control over Parliament. And that is as it should be," even if it meant that the prime minister himself would occasionally suffer "egg on my face." At one point he told the Tory caucus that "the next prime minister who ignores MPs is history."

There were some early successes. The Finance Committee under the loud chairmanship of Don Blenkarn studied the failure of two western banks and achieved improvements. Sky-high interest rates on credit cards dropped after committee scrutiny. Refugee and unemployment-insurance legislation got started in other committees. There were endless studies of child-care, acid rain, illicit drug and alcohol abuse, security services, VIA Rail, and on and on. The committees kept members occupied, but most accomplished little more.

That was, of course, because Mulroney and his cabinet, along with a few key bureaucrats, realized that handing power to MPs meant loss of their own authority. Besides, it was messy. Crown princes in the Mulroney court did not take kindly to having a gang of frisky new "somebodies" question their wisdom and undermine their work. The Tory whip was advised to remember that power emanated from the top down, not the other way around. Independent-minded committee chairmen were replaced by docile ones who awaited the boss's orders. Committee participation was limited largely to those who "understood the system" and would not embarrass those who ruled it.

Bob Horner, the well-liked Tory from Mississauga West, stirred up a number of unpleasant issues for the authorities, despite the government's wishes. Returned in the 1988 election after four years' service on the Justice Committee, Horner decided he wanted to be its chairman. He was told by government whip Jim Hawkes that the spot was to be given to a brand-new lawyer MP from Quebec. Horner went to the top, to Deputy Prime Minister Don Mazankowski, who runs such things for Mulroney, and told Mazankowski that he would resign his seat if his own party prevented him from seeking the committee chairmanship. To avoid the fuss that would follow, the power-brokers backed off. Today the veterinarian and former Mountie enjoys stirring up the justice system, recommending a freeze on judges' ample pay, release of secret prison documents and new laws in areas ranging from prostitution to the extradition of murderers. He admits that "most of our reports go nowhere," because ministers and deputies shelve them. Still, he asserts, "I have to keep trying. That's what I was sent here for."

The old committees designed to keep the huge crowd of 1984 Tories occupied and their opponents run ragged would not work in Mulroney's second term. Members were tired of seeing reports fly through the cabinet room into the garbage. Witnesses travelled to Ottawa meetings that were never held because not enough MPs showed up to form a quorum. "You see three people [MPs] come and you sort of wonder, 'Does this mean that this is obviously not a high priority on their agenda?'" complained Mary Pat MacKinnon in February 1991. She had just made a presentation on child poverty to near-empty seats.

Obviously the vaunted committee system was getting a bad image outside the House as well as inside it. There were dozens of examples, including some that undermined the very promises that had brought Mulroney to power. It didn't help when freshman Tory Garth Turner, who was briefly chairman of the Consumer and Corporate Affairs Committee, insulted a witness who arrived with speaking notes in English only. Turner dismissed Nicholas Murray of the Consumers Association of Canada with the warning that he must "religiously adhere to this country's policy of bilingualism and respect it when you come before another committee."

Commons legal advisers later told Turner that it is proper to present material to committees in either of the official languages. Murray had been correct.

In 1984 Mulroney accused Liberals of "stonewalling" and promised an "end to the obsession with secrecy." He told a campaign audience in Kingston that "the present government believes you have only limited rights to know. . . . Conservatives believe you have every right to know." Three years later his government replied to Justice Committee appeals for more access to information by rejecting its 108-recommendation report. The government threw out an exhaustive all-party study of the Canadian Security and Intelligence Service and accepted only two of its 117 recommendations. It refused for months to hold meetings of committees it could not dominate and steered a committee meeting on the 1990 crisis at Oka away from visiting the reserve. Fernand Jourdenais was fired as chairman when he did not toe the line with his Labour, Employment and Immigration Committee. The final straw that dumped him in 1987 was his call for an inquiry after Mila Mulroney became involved in the immigration request of a French citizen who had taught Mila's children in a private school.

The Communications and Culture Committee had its own horror story. After a year of hundreds of meetings and as many witnesses, it produced a huge draft Broadcasting Act. The minister told it, in a few sentences, to go back and start again.

When he returned to office in 1988 with a reduced majority, Mulroney abandoned any pretence of making Parliament work through all-party consensus. According to MacAdam, he concluded that the House of Commons was "a very necessary evil. It was perceived as a theatre for the opposition . . . a launching pad for a quick hit." By the time Mulroney was well into his second mandate he was accused of showing the same fabled contempt for Parliament as Trudeau had. In just over two years from his 1988 re-election, Mulroney's palace guard has shut off debate with closure and time allocation two dozen times. They have used the guillotine on free trade, the Goods and Services Tax, unemployment-insurance changes, a bill on plant breeders' rights and the motion to revise Commons rules. In his sixteen years in office, an "arrogant" Trudeau used the power of closure to stifle opposition just three times.

Much has been made of Trudeau's unilateral imposition of the War Measures Act during the 1970 October Crisis. To this day his critics say that Parliament should have been recalled. The same should surely have held true before Canadian troops were sent to join in an imminent war. With unseemly haste, Mulroney dispatched three naval vessels to the Persian Gulf before the United Nations had even reacted to the situation there. In committing first troops, then ships, then sophisticated planes to the war, Mulroney acted first and consulted Parliament after. He held up the final debate on Canadian involvement until the day of a United Nations deadline that produced the bombing of Baghdad. And on such issues of moral concern, he insisted that MPs vote the party line, not their consciences.

Few things so enraged Trudeau's opponents as his aloof, presidential style. The growth of the Prime Minister's Office (PMO) and the Privy Council Office (PCO), his attitude towards Parliament, his extravagant travels, the donated swimming pool and, of course, Grit patronage were all big targets for his critics. So big that Mulroney could not miss as he fired away at them on the way to his 1984 election.

There was not a lot of extravagance in the offices of our early leaders. The first private secretaries were hired when Alexander Mackenzie became prime minister in 1873. Until the Second World War, prime ministers had only a few aides – usually from the civil service – to help with the flow of information. Before 1939 King's staff numbered a dozen, mostly secretaries. Other ministers ran things more or less from their hip pockets.

The war brought sudden expansion. Cabinet was organized into committees, and a small secretariat was set up in the Privy Council Office to serve the key war committee. The PCO grew after the war, as did the PMO. During the King and St. Laurent years, PMO staff gradually increased to thirty. The PMO remained small under Diefenbaker and Pearson; in 1968, Pearson left a PMO staff of forty with a budget of $330,000.

After 1968 the PCO became an adjunct to Trudeau's office, responsible for far more than its previous clerical duties. It grew from 142 under Pearson to 352 by 1975 when Trudeau appointed his friend Michael Pitfield to the top job of privy council clerk. All policy from departments flowed through his office. Trudeau even created a federal-provincial relations office there, which was answerable to Pitfield rather than the minister of justice.

The sweeping changes not only rationalized policy making, they added immensely to the prime minister's power. In one bold stroke he had created an alternative to cabinet ministers and their mandarins as the sole source of policy. He also created an unprecedented centre of power and policy making in his own office. PMO personnel doubled to eighty-five by 1970 and its budget was hiked to $900,000. By the time Trudeau left, his staff numbered ninety and the budget was $4.4 million. Trudeau insisted that the growth was a response to the increasing size and complexity of government.

The changes certainly shifted power and the media focus away from Parliament. All policy from the PCO flowed through the PMO. Trudeau's staff attended cabinet meetings, decided cabinet agendas and even sent back cabinet decisions to be reconsidered. From 1968 to 1972, principal secretary Marc Lalonde acted as though he was vice–prime minister. Power-broker Jim Coutts was another who wielded great influence. So important did the inner circle of advisers become that even cabinet ministers were relegated to the sidelines. The best example was in 1978 when Trudeau returned from talks with West German chancellor Helmut Schmidt to announce $2 billion in federal spending cuts. He did not even consult his finance minister, Jean Chrétien. The only people who knew about the huge budget reversal were Coutts and Pitfield.

The Trudeau years produced presidential-type power without congressional-type checks. All key decisions were made by the prime minister with the aid of unelected advisers, top bureaucrats and a few privileged cabinet ministers. The job of the parliamentary majority was to keep the prime minister in office, not to constrain his use of power. The prime minister had truly become more powerful than the U.S. president in terms of authority over his subjects.

Mulroney promised change. He pledged to reduce the influence of public servants and restore cabinet control over the vast bureaucratic machine built by Trudeau and Pitfield. "In a Tory government the minister will run his department," Mulroney said in a stern warning to the unelected elite. "Any deputy minister who doesn't understand that will have a career notable for its brevity."

He did simplify the cabinet system and increased the importance of senior ministers *vis-à-vis* the mandarins. But he also vastly increased his own powers. When Mulroney took over, the PMO grew by a third to a record 120 people. Its budget was nearly $7 million, or 54 per cent more than that of Trudeau's last year. The size of the PCO increased by six to 156, with a budget of $10.3 million. The Federal-Provincial Relations Office (FPRO) got a staff hike and a budget boost of 17 per cent to $4.7 million. The total budget for the administration servicing Mulroney in 1984 was $31 million.

Today his office has the air and functions of a White House, including the latest in electronic communications equipment. Like the White House, the PMO plays a pivotal role in the formation, co-ordination and implementation of foreign and domestic policy. It controls top government appointments, which are instantly cross-referenced by computer. Trusted back-roomer Marjorie LeBreton, whose Tory connections date back to the Diefenbaker days, oversees some 3,500 patronage positions in her confidential job jar. The total budget for the offices under Mulroney's direct command is nearly $86 million, up from $61 million in a single year. He has a staff of 592 at his manicured fingertips, including 90 aides in his own office.

Part of the reason for the huge increase under Mulroney is the addition of a separate Deputy Prime Minister's Office to handle day-to-day operations. Another big bill is rung up on royal commissions and task forces, some of which do work that might well be handled by MPs. The $25 million Citizens' Forum under gadfly Keith Spicer skittered around trying to find out what Canadians think of their country. MPs are paid to know that. Royal commissions on electoral reform, on transportation and on aboriginal issues (the last-named designed to give Mulroney a little breathing room in a dangerous area) are running up similar bills.

In his early years, Mulroney and his collection of old buddies turned top advisers followed their noses directly into every stink that befell the government and its ministers. Mulroney was showered with the fall-out from one disaster after another. John Fraser's tainted tuna, Sinclair Stevens' fancy financial footwork, Bob Coates' strip-club caper, André Bissonette's Oerlikon land flip and a cluster of crooked MPs, all landed on Mulroney's lap. Tory popularity crashed, and Mulroney was taught a lesson former U.S. president Jimmy Carter learned too late. "The people who got him there weren't the people he needed when he got there" is the way former U.S. speaker Tip O'Neill put it in his book *Man of the House*.

So Mulroney put his friends out on the street. Not far, mind you. Most are just a few blocks and an ever-welcome phone call away, scooping up enormous fees as lobbyists and consultants. Some, such as former chief of staff Fred Doucet, faithful insider Pat MacAdam and communications honcho Bill Fox, are at the top of Mulroney's private invitation list. Any organization seeking the prime minister or a senior cabinet minister for a speech could do much worse than contact them for service. The price may be high, but the product is guaranteed.

Mulroney brought in a senior External Affairs official, Derek Burney, to straighten out the mess his pals had left. As chief of staff, he was the conduit for every important piece of information that flowed to Mulroney. Burney was such a crucial player that he hovered over the table in Washington when the final free-trade deal was hammered out in 1988. He was later rewarded for his services with the top ambassadorial post, Washington.

The prime minister removed himself from daily trouble-shooting, handing that task to Don Mazankowski, who replaced Erik Nielsen as deputy prime minister. An office and large staff was assigned to "Maz" in the Langevin Block, across Wellington Street from Parliament, where the prime minister's top staffers work. "Maz" also kept an office suite just forty feet from the Commons door for instant action if necessary in the House.

Mulroney has changed other top aides in the past few years in response to the issue of the moment. Long-time friend Stanley

Hartt ran the command centre during the GST phase. He has recently been replaced as chief of staff by constitutional trouble-shooter Norman Spector.

What has not changed is Mulroney's aping of the U.S. presidential style, right down to the type of podium, backdrop flag, and TelePrompTer he uses for public appearances. When he first took over, Mulroney often usurped the role of Governor General Jeanne Sauvé in welcoming foreign heads of state. During the "Shamrock Summit" he made sure Sauvé was not around to greet President Ronald Reagan and his wife, Nancy. Sauvé was told by the PMO that the Reagans were on a "working visit." In the PMO, wrote former press secretary Michel Gratton, "we chuckled all the way while the woman scorned almost fell off her royal sofa in her Rideau Hall living room when she saw Brian and Mila stealing her starring part on TV." The Mulroneys had taken over the governor general's Quebec City residence, the Citadel, for the occasion.

Mulroney was up to his old tricks again in March 1991 when President Bush came calling on his first trip outside Washington after the Persian Gulf War. For reasons left unexplained, Governor General Ray Hnatyshyn scurried off on a Florida vacation. Gratton knew why the Hnatyshyns left. "The Boss still comes first. If Bush is coming to town with a 91 percent approval rating in the polls, our boy Brian sees no valid reason to share his greatness with a paper-pusher who simply signs Royal Proclamations once in a while."

The prime minister's love of the limelight is matched by the Mulroneys' love of luxury. Investigative journalist Stevie Cameron revealed some of the personal excesses at 24 Sussex Drive in her book *Ottawa Inside Out*. Her account revealed closets full of fancy footwear and expensive suits and gowns that took up as much space as a nearby food bank. Carpets in the prime-ministerial residence were changed four times while Canadians were hit with tax hikes and prime-ministerial pleas for restraint.

The Mulroneys' former chef cast off personal restraint in 1990. He gossiped about something that Canadians had long suspected. Mulroney, the electrician's son who brags about buying his own groceries, does not foot all the bills himself. François Martin spent four years as the Mulroneys' chef before he quit, complaining of over-work, underpay and unconscionable excesses by his employers. He says staff were sent on such personal errands as moving Mila's sister to Toronto, picking up antiques to take as gifts for Mila's mother in Montreal and catering the sister's wedding in Toronto. He talked of the "care package" of food, cleansers and other items packed off to the Pivnickis (Mila's parents) in Montreal.

Martin says that not a cent was paid for food or entertainment from Mulroney's $164,300 salary and benefit package. "I hated their abuse of power, the fact they were telling taxpayers to tighten their belts and they weren't doing the same."

On April 21, 1991, the *Calgary Herald* reported that the Mulroney entourage had booked twenty-eight rooms on the Palliser Hotel's most exclusive floor (including VIP suite) for a four-hour touchdown in the city. The report said that the rooms were reserved and paid for, for both Sunday and Monday, although Mulroney was in town for a single luncheon speech before flying to Victoria. Mila and their four children were with him. Only a handful of advance staff was actually staying the first night, and there was no information from press secretary Gilbert Lavoie that anyone stayed the second night. The office insists that it cannot divulge details for "security reasons." That report came on the heels of a six-day paid-by-taxpayers visit to Paris by Mila on which she helped a French charity raise $2,500 for the mentally disabled. Security is also the reason for having an official food taster for Mulroney when he travels outside Ottawa.

The prime minister also loves to globe-trot in regal style, usually with an entourage of about forty, including a valet. A retired Armed Forces officer has been hired to carry the clean shirts Mulroney dons several times a day. He has two four-man sound crews leap-frogging to each stop on foreign excursions to record his speeches and scrums with reporters. In 1989 he even flew two bullet-proof limousines to Costa Rica for an international gabfest that was attended by President Bush.

One of the best examples of Mulroney's cavalier attitude towards public spending was demonstrated at a cocktail party in Beverly Hills in October 1989. It was at the $2.5-million mansion of Joan Windser, Canada's consul general in Los Angeles. The lady Mulroney calls "Joanie" earned her job after years as a loyal friend and fund-raiser. Brian and Mila arrived by chauffeured limousine under a requested police escort, to be greeted by such expatriate glitterati as Suzanne Somers, Geneviève Bujold, Alan Hamel and assorted business/movie-star fat-cats. French wine and smoked salmon were served, and fired-up propane heaters guarded against potential chill, although the evening was balmy and beautiful.

A feature of the festivities was a brief Mulroney speech praising the United States and batting down Canadian foes of free trade. The real thigh-slapper came when he described his close relationship to the Montreal bagwoman. "Joanie asked me to come over because she's been describing this place to me for five years," chuckled Mulroney. "She said, 'Brian, come down so you can see some real public housing.' " It was a hoot for the crowd of millionaires. No one laughed louder than Mulroney.

His means of getting around the world is not as opulent as that of many of his counterparts. The twenty-five-year-old Boeing 707 he has used on trips to Europe, Asia, Africa, Central America, Japan and the Soviet Union pales in comparison not only to George Bush's Air Force One, but also to the aircraft used by the leaders of some distinctly poor nations. Mulroney once told reporters he hated arriving at international conferences to see some tin-pot African leader with a swanky jet that was probably paid for by Canadian aid. To get around the problem, Mulroney rented a 747 Canadian Airlines jet to fly him on his tour of Hong Kong and Japan in May 1991.

Some overseas trips have little public purpose. Canada's first couple flew to London in July 1989 – a year in which Mulroney visited eight countries – supposedly to confer with Margaret Thatcher. But a British official let slip to Canadian Press reporter Jim Shepperd that the meeting was simply to allow Mulroney to have his picture taken with Britain's Iron Lady for the newspapers and television newscasts back home.

"Your prime minister is the PR man," the official said. "He wants to get his picture with the prime minister [Thatcher] outside of

No. 10. Nothing else matters." Mulroney's staff denied the claim, even though Thatcher assistant press secretary Michael Bates said, "There's no substance to the talks." Bates also said that Mulroney had requested the meeting with Thatcher. Thatcher press secretary Bernard Ingham added: "Everyone who comes through here likes to get their photo taken. We organize photo calls for them."

The British leader herself seemed to erase any doubt about the purpose of the get-together when she asked photographers, "Have you enough?" and brought the session to a close. High Commissioner Donald MacDonald got Thatcher to wipe the egg from Mulroney's face when the photo-op foolishness reached Canadians back home. He asked Thatcher to issue a statement describing the tête-à-tête as "extremely full, detailed and friendly."

While globe-trotting Mulroney gets a lot of valuable gifts from foreign leaders. Some are in return for ones he handed out on behalf of taxpayers. An extravagant example was the $1.5 million Canadian painting that Mulroney gave to France during the bicentennial of the French Revolution. The impressionist work by Quebec artist Jean-Paul Riopelle, considered a Canadian national treasure, now hangs in the new Paris Opéra de Bastille. The painter refused to attend the ceremony at which a beaming Mulroney turned over the painting to the French. Mulroney's handlers said that Riopelle couldn't make it because he was a "recluse" with "a drinking problem."

Riopelle's daughter, Yseult, had a different version from Mulroney's spin doctors. "He'll come, but not for this," she said. "I don't like this either. It's not fun." It wasn't fun for Yseult because her father didn't want the painting taken from Pearson International Airport, where it had hung for twenty-five years. "He was surprised, because it was made for the airport," she said with a shrug. "It was the only order [commissioned work] from the government." Sadly, she said her father wished Mulroney had asked for another painting rather than the one he had "designed for the airport." But Riopelle's feelings didn't matter much to Mulroney. He was out to impress the French.

Few Canadians know that Mulroney has kept thousands of dollars' worth of gifts that have been presented to him by foreign leaders. Among them are an ancient cup of the Roman period given by Israel, a replica of the Gutenberg Bible from France and an antique pot and clock from billionaire the Aga Khan. Conflict of interest guidelines require him to list any gifts over $200. But he does not have to state their value or hand them to the public. In the United States, the president must pass such items to the state.

Antique appraisers say it's impossible to tell the value of such gifts without seeing the objects. But an art expert at the National Gallery said a good replica of the Gutenberg Bible could sell for as much as $4,000. Other gifts kept by Mulroney include silver vases from Emperor Hirohito of Japan, a decorative plate from China, two cultured pearls and a cabinet from Japan, two antique maps and a porcelain vase and cup from France, a jade horse from Toronto's Chinese community, a teapot from Russia and a marble sculpture from Italy.

Liberal MP Don Boudria says it is wrong for Mulroney to keep them, even though other prime ministers have accepted valuable gifts from foreign leaders. "It's not the other prime ministers who wrote the rule book. He's the one that said that others have been lax. He shouldn't pretend it's a personal gift when clearly it is not. If Brian Mulroney was a janitor of the Hawkesbury General Hospital, would he have gotten the gifts? Not likely, so it's not a personal gift. It's a gift to the prime minister of Canada and not to Brian Mulroney."

Mila Mulroney has assumed the role of Canada's "first lady." She is a warm, caring person with a sincere love of children. Her good work in raising money for cystic fibrosis is respected. But, like her husband, Mila loves power and the symbols that go with it. She jumped at the opportunity in April 1985 to attend a "first ladies summit" on drug abuse sponsored by Nancy Reagan in Washington. It gave her the legitimacy she has coveted. Her husband took a step in that direction by providing her with an office, and a staff of three in the PMO at a cost of well over $200,000. It was the first staff ever given to a prime minister's wife. "I like to be a forum," Mila told *Saturday Night*'s Robert Fulford in April 1987. "I like to be a place where people can come and tell me what they want the government to do."

What is so sad about all this extravagance is that prime ministers used to set the example for the nation. Mackenzie King checked over the receipts of his cabinet ministers. Louis St. Laurent was embarrassed when officials made the decision to buy, repair and refurnish a run-down mansion at 24 Sussex. He had lived in a downtown apartment from which he customarily walked to work. When he moved in, St. Laurent insisted that he would pay the state $5,000 annually in lieu of rent. That excellent example was followed by John Diefenbaker and Lester Pearson. All three paid for their own food and drink, charging the taxpayers only for official entertaining.

Nobody expects the prime minister of Canada to live like a pauper. The job makes tremendous demands on its holder, and he is certainly entitled to adequate assistance and comfort in return. But today there is a clear feeling on the part of taxpayers that, while asking them to bite the bullet, he is biting into more tasty treats.

4

THE CROWN PRINCES

*"Part of the problem with this whole thing is we have
a Loblaws operation – no-name products everywhere."*

DON BLENKARN, MP, APRIL 1991

THE 148 HORSES UNDER THE HOOD OF THE MIDNIGHT-BLUE
Chrysler Fifth Avenue leaped to life as the minister of
Indian and northern affairs rushed from his East Block
office towards it. Tom Siddon was in the urgent mode
that afflicts male MPs when they acquire cabinet rank. Scurrying to
keep up was the beautiful blonde aide that typically accompanies this
august status. They had scarcely scrambled inside when the chauf-
feured limo sped from the curb towards Siddon's next date with
national destiny. Ten seconds later they were there, at the front door
of the Centre Block, having just covered the length of a football field.
Fresh and alert after his journey, Siddon rushed inside for a 10:00
a.m. cabinet meeting.

His car and driver, along with those of three-dozen cabinet colleagues, would spend the next several hours picking up the family
groceries or responding to other equally important ministerial imper-
atives before heading back to the comforting shadow of the Peace
Tower. There, the high-priced limos would idle nose-to-tail for hours
more with phones, sound systems, air conditioners and heaters set at
the optimum comfort level, as their liveried drivers exchanged secrets
about Canada's crown princes. It is a sight that invariably impresses
visitors as they peer through the exhaust for a glimpse of greatness.

Including the prime minister, who appoints all the others, there are
thirty-eight elected members and one senator comfortably seated in the
largest cabinet in the democratic world. The British cabinet has twenty-
two ministers, including Prime Minister John Major. The United States,

with ten times Canada's population, gets by with fourteen.

While merit plays a role in selection to top government rank in much of the world, geography, sex, ethnic background, religion and electoral prospects are the Canadian keys. Each province and region has its quota. There must be an Anglo Montrealer, one from Prince Edward Island (unless, as today, the four islanders all sit as Liberals), representatives of Metro Toronto and the West, of women, and the Jewish community. Montreal pharmacist Gerry Weiner recalled, when talking about his duties as minister of multiculturalism and citizenship, that he had been a victim of anti-Semitism on occasion. He did not acknowledge that his religion also won him a place in cabinet just two years after his first election in 1984.

Those, of course, are not legal requirements but individual criteria used by the prime minister. He can go outside Parliament for talent if he has a personal favorite to reward. Mulroney did just that with his old university pal Lucien Bouchard. Just a year after taking office, Mulroney appointed his lawyer friend ambassador to Paris. He put him in cabinet as secretary of state in March 1988, and rewarded a Tory back-bencher with a federal post for vacating the safe Lac-Saint-Jean seat so that Bouchard could enter the House of Commons in a by-election three months later. The by-election saw millions of federal dollars rain down on the riding, invoking the spirit of former Quebec premier Maurice Duplessis. Unable to do enough for his faithful old buddy, Mulroney elevated Bouchard to the environment minister's post at the end of the year. He was rewarded for his good judgement and generosity by Bouchard's defection to set up the separatist Bloc Québécois.

Pierre Trudeau, perpetually short of western MPs, kept putting westerners who defected from other parties in his cabinet. They were a varied bunch. Hazen Argue was a former CCFer/New Democrat, Bud Olson a one-time Social Credit member and Jack Horner a former anti-Trudeau Conservative. Trudeau put his friend Pierre Juneau in the cabinet, but the culture czar proved so politically inept that he lost a safe Quebec Liberal seat and was forced to leave cabinet. Juneau had to settle for Trudeau consolation prizes as head of the CRTC and, later, the CBC.

Siddon became a crown prince for his good judgement in backing Brian Mulroney's coup against party leader Joe Clark. Others who demonstrated the wisdom to undermine their leader in favor of the man who preaches loyalty above all else were: Otto Jelinek, Robert Coates, Sinclair Stevens and Paul Dick. Elmer MacKay contributed his refined eloquence to that cause by observing that campaigning with Clark was "like trying to market bad dog food." MacKay gave up his Nova Scotia seat temporarily to allow Mulroney's entry to the House in a by-election. He then won it back in 1984 when Mulroney took a seat in Quebec. Such unselfishness won Elmer a cabinet post from which he has not been shaken loose either by questionable business/political connections or by a private chat he had while solicitor general with the late Richard Hatfield about the latter's problem with marijuana as premier of New Brunswick.

Coates and Stevens fell from cabinet and federal office when their bad judgement was revealed. Paul Dick remains minister of supply and services, not so much for his ability to keep track of federal pens and pencils as for his position as the sole Tory in an Ottawa-area sea of Liberal MPs. Besides, his wife, Judy, is a good friend of Mila Mulroney's.

Siddon moved into the Fisheries portfolio with all the adroitness of a wrecked rowboat after the "tainted tuna" scandal drove John Fraser from office. The man who later rose to fame and comfort as Commons speaker had proved singularly oblivious to the concerns of Canadian consumers when he approved the marketing of below-standard canned fish to protect jobs in Atlantic Canada. Fraser also earned a special place in the autobiography of Mulroney's deputy, Erik Nielsen, who revealed the rating Nielsen awarded to various potential ministers. Fraser won "unsatisfactory" marks in more categories than any other Tory member, plus the following observation: "His sole purpose for being is re-election and a cabinet post. His total inability to organize or direct makes him a prime candidate for bureaucratic cannibalization." Fraser's bureaucracy as top man in the House of Commons today is the best entrenched in Ottawa.

Nielsen's ratings placed current cabinet insiders Don Mazankowski, head of Finance and deputy prime minister, and Harvie

Andre, House leader, at the top of the talent pool in 1984. Pat Carney ("overwhelming self-esteem") and Flora MacDonald (a "persistent source of disharmony") rate down near Fraser on the unsatisfactory scale. Both are now gone.

Siddon's academic background and loyalty were highly rated by Nielsen, but "his stubbornly polarized views on some policy issues could prove to be volatile." That assessment appears to apply to his awkward handling of crises in both Fisheries and Indian Affairs. But it was in a 1985 appearance in the House of Commons that Siddon drew Mulroney's sharpest reaction. While Michael Wilson was retreating on de-indexing seniors' pensions, a grinning Siddon entered the chamber and slid into a seat directly behind the finance minister and in full view of cross-Canada TV viewers. He was fresh from his son's graduation. Reporters began to giggle in the press gallery above the chamber. Mulroney turned to see Siddon, sitting like a peacock in a full, flowing graduation gown, complete with the hood that marks his Ph.D. in engineering. With a glare Mulroney hissed, "Get that fucking thing off." Ever obedient, Siddon did.

Monique Vézina, whose qualifications for cabinet rank include being female, grey and representative of the rural Quebec riding of Rimouski, also made an early mark. As the brand-new minister for external relations in 1984 she briefly epitomized the difficult adjustments Mulroney's new ministers went through. Surveying the world from the window of her brand-new office in the Lester B. Pearson Building, she spied a Union Jack flying conspicuously nearby. "That has got to go," she reportedly ordered an aide, only to be told that the flag in question was atop the British High Commission residence.

Cabinet ministers quickly learn to enjoy power, prestige and the attentions of the sycophants who surround them. They have jobs and trips and rewards of various kinds to hand out to friends, relatives and party workers. One senior minister for each province is the patronage chief who approves all appointments in his home turf. It is a tremendous bonus when it comes time to recruit troops for campaigns.

Right in Ottawa, the size of a minister's personal staff, entirely apart from the tens of thousands of departmental workers under a minister's authority, can be staggering. When John Crosbie was minister for international trade, before the April 1991 shuffle, there were twenty-six names on the staff telephone list in his personal office. There were ten special assistants, four policy advisers, a chief of staff, an executive assistant, a press secretary, a person in charge of cabinet documents, another whose title was "Question Period" (presumably an aide to help the minister prepare answers if he were quizzed in the House) and three people listed under "Minister's Registry." A number of secretaries completed the office world of the minister from Newfoundland.

Crosbie and some others have enjoyed lifelong wealth and the privileged status that cabinet rank bestows. Some believe that Michael Holcombe Wilson was born wearing an Upper Canada College blazer. But others have fought every step of the way to the cabinet table.

Erik Nielsen, the son of an iron-disciplined Mountie, fell deeply into debt during his early period in Parliament. He spent a full year back home in the Yukon combining law and bush flying to supplement the pay he drew as an MP while nowhere near Ottawa. He later learned enough about the system of power and pay-offs to combine a big cabinet pension with a top patronage appointment for a hefty retirement income.

When he was first elected in 1962, Eugene Whelan lived in a rooming house that cost seven dollars for four nights (the other nights he spent back in his Windsor-area riding). It was run by "two old ladies who locked the door at eleven o'clock and put the chain on," Whelan recalls in his autobiography. After the 1963 election, Whelan, along with newly elected MP and Toronto Maple Leaf star Red Kelly and rookie Liberal Larry Pennell, moved into an apartment. "Larry and I had twin beds in the single bedroom and Red slept on the studio couch – it was a fold-down thing that didn't even have a mattress and just a sheet for a cover."

A few years before he crossed the floor to become Liberal trade minister, Jack Horner was a Tory back-bencher from Crowfoot, Alberta. He supplemented his income by selling made-to-measure western suits, displaying samples on racks in his West Block office, measuring customers and sending orders off for tailoring and speedy delivery.

Though it can take a long time to get to cabinet, ministers may be there for only a short stay. Newfoundland Grit Roger Simmons was named mines minister by Pierre Trudeau on August 12, 1983, but resigned for "personal reasons" ten days later, ending the shortest term in Canadian cabinet history. Charges of tax evasion on $28,000 worth of income during an earlier five-year period were then laid against him. Simmons was convicted and paid a fine of $3,500. He lost a bid for re-election to the Commons the following year, but one year after that won election to the Newfoundland legislature, serving as opposition leader there until the federal 1988 election brought him back to Ottawa. All federal cabinet ministers are sworn into the Privy Council, a largely ceremonial body that confers the right of members to use the term "Honorable" for life. No mere criminal conviction can remove the "Hon." from Roger Simmons' name.

There have been 581 federal cabinet ministers through our history, some of them in more than half a dozen ministries. The one who has held the most different portfolios – thirteen – is Senator Allan MacEachen who was sworn into the Privy Council in 1963. There are about 230 privy councillors living, a few of them former provincial premiers and other honored "special cases." More than 200 are former or active federal cabinet members.

Cabinet scandal and wrong-doing date right back to Canada's start. To date, 152 federal ministers have resigned since 1867. Number one was Sir Alexander Galt, a Father of Confederation, who quit as finance minister because of a bank scandal just one month into Canada's first parliamentary session. Sir Hector-Louis Langevin, another Father of Confederation, was forced to resign from Sir John A. Macdonald's cabinet twice, first during the Pacific Scandal and later during some unpleasantness over public-works patronage. None of that prevented his name from being honored on the building where the offices of the prime minister and Privy Council are now housed.

Reasons for the departure of crown princes and princesses are amazingly varied, but "ill health" and foolishly phoning judges have been popular. Judy LaMarsh said simply that she would not serve in the cabinet of Pierre Trudeau, whom she called "that bastard" during the 1968 convention that made him Liberal leader. In sixteen years after that Trudeau lost twenty-one other ministers by resignation for various reasons, not all scandalous. Mulroney lost thirteen in seven years. The first was Bob Coates, whose late-night visit to a West German strip club cost him the defence minister's job. The latest was housing minister Alan Redway, whose airport joke about a gun in a friend's luggage had the same result.

Obviously, it is not hard to get out of cabinet. For some, it is not very hard to get in either. Joe Guay made it six years after his first election to the Commons. The owner of Guay Shoes in St. Boniface, Manitoba, had an almost unique qualification. He was a Trudeau Liberal from the prairies. Guay's comment on his appointment gave hope to all MPs: "You don't have to be a brains trust" to get into cabinet. Nor into the Senate. Guay served there happily from 1978 to 1990, when he retired at age seventy-five.

MPs covet cabinet rank for lots of reasons. Pay and privileges rate high. Junior and senior positions pay $140,800, nearly $30,000 of it tax free. All ministers get another $2,000 "car allowance," a hold-over from the days, decades ago, before each was given a car and driver.

Many ministers might earn as much money in private life, but few could obtain the ego gratification that comes with cabinet rank. With even the tiniest government responsibility comes not just the limo but a minimum personal staff of twelve and an array of offices. Ministers have suites on Parliament Hill, elsewhere in Ottawa's high-rise luxury, in home ridings and often in other cities. The average cost of running each minister's offices in 1986 was just over $1 million a year, with the price-tag for personal staff at around $400,000. The government stopped releasing cost figures that year. Treasury Board official Lise St. Jacques Ayoub says, "It has gone up like everything else," in the five years since the numbers have been hidden from the taxpayers who foot the bills.

Ministers of state each have an executive assistant earning $68,300, a senior policy adviser, a legislative assistant, two to five special assistants, a scheduling assistant, a correspondence assistant, a constituency assistant and a personal secretary. It is usually one of the special assistants the public sees just over the shoulder of a minister who is being interviewed on television. That job is worth $58,300, the same amount paid to legislative assistants, who most often are the striking young blondes with briefcases who escort their male bosses as they strut into daily Question Period in the Commons. There is no limit to the number of special assistants a minister can hire. Seniors get more of all that, plus a chief of staff.

What does a chief of staff do for nearly $95,100 a year? A variety of things, including, in the case of William Winegard's Jim LeBlanc, making sure the press get his boss's title right. LeBlanc wrote to Canadian Press bureau chief Kirk Lapointe the day after the April cabinet shuffle to point out that Winegard was not a junior minister. "I was disturbed to note that Honorable William Winegard was incorrectly listed as 'Minister of State [Science and Technology],'" huffed LeBlanc. "Dr. Winegard's official title is 'Minister for Science.'"

The chief-of-staff job is one invented by the Mulroney government to put political agents in the system between ministers and top bureaucrats whom the Conservatives suspect of latent Liberalism and other evils. It turns out to be a handy place to keep high-priced former MPs plugged into the system after they have been rejected by the voters. Former MPs Joe Price and David Daubney are chiefs of staff, as was ex–Manitoba MP Leo Duguay before he became a lobbyist. Daubney was accused of being amazingly inept in the handling of the Mohamed Al-Mashat immigration file. Daubney said he was unaware of the importance of the former Iraqi ambassador to Washington whose fast-track immigration caused wide government embarrassment. Although identified as a bumbler, Daubney kept his patronage job with Joe Clark.

Ministers of state, annoyingly identified in the media as junior ministers, have cabinet rank and pay, but often few duties. A senior official in Indian and Northern Affairs said Hamilton-area MP Shirley Martin received copies of ministerial items while serving as Siddon's junior in that portfolio but, "I'm not aware of anything she did. I never had a memo or correspondence [from her] or anything like that." Martin became the junior transport minister in the spring shuffle of 1991.

Martin did not win cabinet rank because of any special knowledge of Native people or brilliance as a parliamentarian but because she was in danger of losing her seat in the 1988 election. Several embattled MPs make it that way just before the end of each Parliament. The hope is that the prestige of government office will get voters to send them back for another term. It worked for Martin, a former Bell Canada supervisor. She won by 400 votes over a much-maligned opponent, ex–Liberal minister John Munro. For Gerry St. Germain and some other late appointees, a cabinet post was not enough to gain the electors' favor. The former B.C. member was defeated and had to pursue his political career in other ways – as president of the federal Conservative party and as one of two commissioners appointed to recommend increases in pay and perks for MPs.

Ministerial rank provides both obvious and little-known benefits. For instance, executive suites are maintained for visiting ministers in Vancouver, Edmonton, Winnipeg, Toronto, Montreal and Halifax. Ministers get to them aboard the fleet of Challenger jets that Ottawa keeps for its exalted crown princes, although competition for bookings sometimes forces them, and their assistants, to rough it in first-class commercial seats. This means of travel proved to be an embarrassing inconvenience to one senior Maritime minister who was helped off an Air Canada flight in Vancouver in April 1991 after sipping too many liquid delights. Ministers need never produce receipts for entertainment or other expenses in Ottawa or on the road. Their "honor system" ensures that Canadians get value for each dollar spent despite complaints by the Public Accounts Committee and the auditor general that the honor system is not good enough.

Occasionally, a few details leak out about expenses, such as the $9,500 Marcel Masse spent for a desk and nine chairs while communications minister, or the nine trips he took at a cost of $100,000 in his first year, including a $14,000 junket to Paris. When Masse's furniture purchase was revealed, an irate university student put it in perspective by writing to the *Ottawa Citizen* to point out that the desk and chairs were equivalent to three years' tuition. Lucien Bouchard spent $35,000 redoing his Hull office when he became environment minister. When criticism followed a leak of the cost, he claimed to have saved money by turning to a build-it-yourself store for some shelves.

To win the comforts of cabinet office an MP must be the right person at the right time – this often means being the right sex or ethnic origin or coming from the right home town, rather than having the right knowledge, intelligence or work habits. Those who become ministers, of course, claim that merit alone was responsible for the appointment. Being from the wrong place can be a serious liability. With Joe Clark, Don Mazankowski and Harvie Andre among Mulroney's top half-dozen ministers and filling Alberta's quota, no other MPs from that province have a chance. Thus hard-working Tory loyalists such as Jim Hawkes have to settle for the pay and power of lesser offices. The Calgary West MP sits directly behind Mulroney in the House (and on TV), boasts of authority comparable to that of a minister and reminds his constituents at every opportunity that he is chief government whip. The job means he is the one who rounds up Tory MPs to vote like sheep for such things as the Goods and Services Tax – a function that does not necessarily endear him to his electors.

In announcing his 1991 cabinet changes, Mulroney emphasized that it was a "tribute to the great quality of the Alberta deputation" that it contained so many remarkable MPs. Added *Ottawa Citizen* columnist Robert Lee, "all of them, apparently, becoming more remarkable as each passing day swells the Reform Party's membership rolls." In taking an even clumsier swing at the Reformers, Mulroney clouted about twenty Alberta Tories who are not in the first rank. "Albertans will have to decide whether they want this [cabinet] or some back-benchers."

There are junior ministers to satisfy every interest group and lobby: youth, sports, tourism, housing, foreign aid and French-speaking Africa. Many have less-than-critical roles to play in the nation's business. When the minister of state for the environment, Pauline Browes, was appointed in April, she gushed, "I'm the new minister for the Rouge River." The jest clearly explained the political purpose of her appointment, where clean-up of Toronto's Rouge River Valley and related environmental questions could be a key to re-election.

That round of changes seemed to be the last straw for Don Blenkarn, the sometimes fractious but competent veteran from Mississauga. He called it a "no-name" cabinet. Blenkarn stormed that he might have continued to make an extraordinary effort, "if somebody had given me a decent cabinet position." He resigned as the high-profile chairman of the Commons Finance Committee and is not expected to run in the next election.

Since 1984 Mulroney has added six junior ministers to satisfy regional concerns and public-interest groups. There are now sixteen ministries of state headed by cabinet small fry. Some of them relieve senior ministers of political or departmental chores, but they have little money to spend, and therefore little power. "Constrained by the bureaucracy, often mistrusted and ignored by the senior minister, unsure of a mandate and lacking resources, the position of ministers of state to assist is often not an ideal role," concludes Carleton University professor John A. Chenier. Appointing lots of ministers does have its benefits, although not for the taxpayers. It helps keep Mulroney's large caucus happy. The larger the cabinet, the greater the hope that an incumbent will stumble, opening a spot for someone else.

There is even a training group between ordinary members and junior ministers, composed of thirty parliamentary secretaries, each with an extra secretary and $10,500 in additional pay. Some in this category are given real work; others are totally ignored by the minister whose bidding they do, although the appointments themselves are made by the prime minister. Under the latest rule changes, parliamentary secretaries will be included in Commons committees, giving the minister a closer handle on their "independent" work. Parliamentary secretaries also get to read answers at the end of the Commons day to questions where notice has been given in advance. And they get to ride in the minister's limo if they are good. A delighted John McDermid spent hours being driven on and off the Hill in the back seat of Pat Carney's limo when she was away on trade minister's business. Now he has his very own car and driver as junior minister for finance and privatization.

Parliamentary secretaries were invented by Sir Robert Borden to help him during the First World War. None was appointed from then until the Second World War, partly because most cabinet ministers did not want upstarts nosing around and possibly reporting back to the prime minister. The practice was finally entrenched by John Diefenbaker. He said the job was "to make provision for assistance in many of the phases of a minister's life and thereby lighten the load of responsibility which rests on those who occupy the treasury benches." Diefenbaker, of course, was more interested in finding a role for members of his huge caucus than in training potential cabinet appointees. The extra pay of $4,000 a year also helped to silence mischief-makers.

Today the positions are still used to reward loyalists or to keep trouble-makers at bay. In his first term Mulroney kept anti-French Manitoba MP Dan McKenzie quiet as a parliamentary secretary. He stripped the veteran of that role when McKenzie voted against Mulroney's cherished Official Languages Bill. In his second term Mulroney has used the posts to keep Quebec nationalists such as Lise Bourgault and Suzanne Duplessis from bolting to the Bloc Québécois. The extra cash helps some MPs pay the bills, too. Jack Shields, a loyal cheer-leader from northern Alberta, has been a parliamentary secretary since 1984, a job that helps pay the rent on the apartment he shares with Mazankowski and agriculture minister Bill McKnight.

Most cabinet ministers today, not just the junior ones, play little part in key government decisions. Those excluded from "P and P" – the Priorities and Planning Committee (not pay and perks) of cabinet – are outsiders when the real business is being done. Even that twenty-four-member "inner cabinet" is overshadowed by an inner-inner clique of senior ministers. "Cabinet as a whole is more and more just a rubber stamp," says Carleton University professor Robert Jackson. "Mr. Mulroney has made more than half his cabinet into cunuchs." The country is run by a few key ministers and by "cronies and mandarins" in Mulroney's office, he says.

One of the fundamentals of our parliamentary system is the principle of ministerial responsibility. It is clear and simple and increasingly flouted by members of the federal government. As Peter W. Hogg wrote in *Constitutional Law in Canada* in 1977, a "minister is supposed to resign if a serious case of maladministration occurs in his department." Conservatives were outraged at that time when Liberal supply and services minister Jean-Pierre Goyer blamed departmental officials for bungling an aircraft-purchase contract, costing taxpayers $16 million. Opposition leader Joe Clark assailed him in the Commons for attempts to "transfer blame for this government's gross incompetence . . . to a middle-ranking civil servant." Some fifteen years later it was Clark himself who blamed officials in External Affairs for enabling a top Iraqi diplomat to immigrate here in a speeded-up process. External affairs minister Barbara Mc-Dougall and immigration minister Bernard Valcourt also singled out two officials for special criticism and "serious errors of judgement" in the case. The government later set up a committee inquiry to examine the details of how Mohamed Al-Mashat, a close confidant of Iraqi dictator Saddam Hussein and Iraq's ambassador in Washington, got special treatment while thousands of others waited a year or more to have their papers processed. Harvie Andre later ordered Tory chairman John Bosley to close down the committee to end the growing embarrassment it was causing the government.

The way cabinet works has changed dramatically since Sir John A. began with thirteen ministers in a 181-seat House of Commons. Then, as now, all regions and both French and English were represented, but cabinet was small enough for free-wheeling discussions and group decisions. Strong regional ministers had a say in matters affecting their areas, but no major decision could be made without full cabinet approval. Ministers acted as a check on the prime minister. As academic W.A. Matheson says, "the Prime Minister had to carry his cabinet with him on policy matters, especially when many members of the cabinet have their own personal power bases." In those days there were certainly no ministers of oilseeds, tourism or seniors.

At the start of the Second World War the "cabinet was still a manageably small body of fifteen experienced politicians whose method of doing business was leisured and relatively informal," says scholar J. R. Mallory. During the 1950s it grew to only twenty-two members despite the huge expansion and increasing complexity of government activity. Powerful ministers such as Jimmy Gardiner from

Saskatchewan, Ontario's C.D. Howe, and Newfoundland's Jack Pick-ersgill acted as regional power-brokers. But virtually all ministers played a part in thrashing out issues around the cabinet table.

In 1968, Lester Pearson created the Priorities and Planning Committee of key ministers to develop government priorities in relation to overall fiscal concerns. Before that, especially during the Diefenbaker years, decision making was influenced more by powerful ministers than by what was fiscally prudent. While P and P put order into the process, ministers still got to speak their minds. "I always encouraged cabinet ministers to speak up, argue their case to their colleagues, who were encouraged to speak," Pearson wrote later. "My philosophy was to let a cabinet minister, as far as possible, run his own show and that it was not my job to be interfering in details." According to former Privy Council clerk Gordon Robertson, P and P did not make decisions, just recommendations that had to be considered and ratified by cabinet.

The system began to change radically under Pierre Trudeau. He appointed twenty-nine ministers, then the largest cabinet in Canadian history. The growth forced him to set up cabinet committees to decentralize decision making on issues such as foreign affairs, defence, social policy and economic management. In the committees, small groups of ministers would discuss issues and make recommendations to cabinet as a whole. Beginning in 1971, Trudeau also created junior ministers to improve the machinery of government and to free senior cabinet members for critical work. Most were complete failures because they had no real power to deal with other departments or central agencies.

Trudeau's big cabinets were clumsy at decision making. The system caused "intolerable delays and frustrated the initiatives of ministers and senior officials," observed Ottawa-watcher Richard French. To overcome this, Trudeau concentrated power in the hands of a trusted and talented inner circle of unelected advisers. Bureaucratic czar Michael Pitfield, power-broker Jim Coutts and party boss Keith Davey had as great an input as heavyweight ministers like Allan MacEachen, Marc Lalonde and Jean Chrétien. Trudeau broke the traditional lines between deputies and their ministers. He shuffled top departmental officers frequently and ensured that all policy flowed through his inner circle. At the same time, federal-provincial conferences made such premiers as Alberta's Peter Lougheed and Newfoundland's Brian Peckford more potent spokesmen than Liberal ministers for their regions.

When Joe Clark got a chance to govern in 1979 he appointed a thirty-member cabinet, and the committee system gained strength. Committees set policy and allocated money under predetermined budgets called spending envelopes. But the key decisions were made by an inner cabinet of twelve senior ministers who worked closely with Clark. There was a substantial reduction in the authority of the full cabinet, with the inner group becoming the decision-making one. Trudeau retained that system when he returned in 1980, although he expanded the inner cabinet and renamed it P and P. By the early 1980s the full cabinet existed in name to rubber-stamp decisions. "It is incapable as a decision-making body to cope with the demands on government in the modern age," concluded University of Waterloo professor Terrence Downey.

Before he won power in 1984, Mulroney vowed to make cabinet trimmer. As with so many of his promises, he did the reverse in office. Cabinet membership increased to forty, the highest ever and the largest in any parliamentary democracy. He did reduce the number of committees to nine from thirteen and cut the number of budget envelopes. But his plans failed. The inner cabinet spent endless hours in debate over issues before reaching decisions. Near the end of his first term the envelope system had collapsed (it was abandoned in 1989) and cabinet committees had grown to twelve. The inner cabinet was too big, its seventeen members often deadlocked over spending. Despite Michael Wilson's attempts to keep a lid on expenditures, other members who could argue about political benefits often won Mulroney's support.

Having surrounded himself with an odd combination of pals, old-timers, novices and some obvious misfits, Mulroney found himself in desperate need of new direction and better control of his chaotic agenda. To prepare for a second run he purged the PMO and cleaned up the ministry in 1986. He got rid of Erik Nielsen who had a tendency to shoot down everything in sight. Perhaps his days as a Second World War fighter pilot were hard to put behind him. Mazankowski, the hard-nosed but respected farm-implement and car dealer from Vegreville, Alberta, took his place. An informal operations committee of top ministers was set up under "Maz." Control over policy and political strategy was shared between the PMO and "Ops."

The new system began to do what P and P had failed at. It set the cabinet agenda and decided how to spend Canadians' money in a bid for re-election. All proposed bills, major government communications strategies, political planning and damage control flowed through Ops. Individual ministers and their departments could develop whatever schemes they wanted, but these would not get to inner cabinet if Maz and the palace guard of eight said no. There were some problems. Ops became the target of some bitter ministers who found themselves frozen out. Ops had little regional balance. But the bottom line is that it worked. Order was restored. The Tories picked themselves out of the political ditch and roared back to power on the free-trade bandwagon in 1988.

The friends of the first PMO also went on to rich rewards. With their contacts and access to Mulroney himself they became favored lobbyists for big corporations willing to pay big money. Former communications director Bill Fox joined former ministerial aides Harry Near and Elizabeth Roscoe to establish the Earnscliff Strategy Group. Former chief of staff Fred Doucet set up his own firm. Mulroney school-days buddy and political fixer Pat MacAdam moved into the plush offices of Government Consultants International, a firm headed by another Mulroney buddy, former Newfoundland premier Frank Moores, and loaded with Tory insiders. For MacAdam, Doucet and Fox, it was just a short walk to the old quarters in the PMO.

Former principal secretary Bernard Roy also enjoyed amazing good luck when he returned to legal practice. He was hired to recommend pay hikes for federal judges. He also got over $140,000 for his unsuccessful negotiating role during the Oka stand-off. And his Montreal firm landed a lucrative contract to arrange the move of the National Energy Board from Ottawa to Calgary. Meanwhile the government system began to hum without Mulroney's friends.

Mulroney formalized "Ops" when he returned to power in 1988. He recognized that his inner cabinet was too large. P and P was bigger than John Diefenbaker's entire 1957 cabinet. He could have reduced the size of P and P or his thirty-nine-member cabinet. Instead he created a powerful new spending watch-dog that, along with Ops, would run the government. As one insider told veteran *Ottawa Citizen* reporter Greg Weston, Mulroney learned quickly that "committees discuss problems but they are a lousy way to solve problems. When it comes to decision-making bodies, in the prime minister's book, small is beautiful."

In the new regime, power was tightly held by a few players. The committee structure reveals the heavy hitters in cabinet. In addition to Mulroney, they are Mazankowski, John Crosbie, Michael Wilson, Joe Clark, Gilles Loiselle, Harvie Andre, Senator Lowell Murray, Quebec lieutenant Benoît Bouchard, Bernard Valcourt and Kim Campbell. All but Andre and Campbell sit on both Ops and Expenditure Review.

Other ministers have major departmental responsibilities and the appearance of top rank but lack policy and spending clout. Nevertheless their authority is ample to maintain the first-class style appropriate to a position on the second-to-top rung of Canada's political ladder. Conspicuous consumption, a constant swarm of aides surrounding them like fruit flies and personal touches like the gaudy ring Doug Lewis fashioned from his MP's ID pin tell others they have arrived. Office empire building remains as much a part of the game as the cabinet system itself.

Mulroney put a fresh face on cabinet in 1991 in the largest juggling of ministers ever. There were twenty-three changes, but only two players made it up from the minors, Pauline Browes and Jean Charest. For Charest, the new Environment portfolio was far better than the one he lost as sports minister two years earlier for phoning a judge. He not only sat in P and P but now had control of some money and a say in policy.

Within weeks of his return, Charest demonstrated his qualifications for cabinet office with a goofy publicity stunt. Joined by his new junior minister, Browes, and Indian and Northern Affairs chief Siddon, he announced a $100-million Arctic Environmental Strategy. Looking every bit like the three stooges, the trio surrounded themselves with Inuit school children in Iqaluit, N.W.T., and held a news conference by satellite with reporters back in Ottawa. The conference featured a tape of the three ministers travelling by dog-sled to a toxic waste dump. Their silly stunt cost $10,000 and was described by Liberal critic on Native affairs Ethel Blondin as turning a "serious issue into a dog-and-pony show for Charest and Siddon."

About a month earlier, then-finance minister Michael Wilson had demonstrated an equally deft and sensitive touch as he accepted a cheque from a twelve-year-old. The child had sold his toys for $168 to help retire the country's $400-billion debt. The touching display took place at a conference on debt freedom in Ottawa. The previous fall Wilson had told a startled Commons that he had personal experience of financial sacrifice, having taken a cut in his $100,000 Bay Street pay cheque back in 1973.

The 1991 shuffle relieved Mazankowski of his Agriculture portfolio, gave him Finance and kept him as deputy prime minister. Michael Wilson traded Finance for a new super-ministry of Industry and International Trade, and Joe Clark was made minister responsible for trying to hold Canada together. Maz's roommate McKnight took over the Agriculture job, handing Defence over to gadfly Marcel Masse. That was regarded as a cruel Mulroney joke, placing the Quebec fop and lover of opera, travel and self-indulgence at public expense in charge of the Armed Forces just before huge cuts in funding and personnel were imposed. Harvie Andre remained House leader responsible for pushing the government's programs through Parliament, but also became chairman of Ops where he could control the government's agenda and discretionary spending. In general, the shuffle was meant to reassure English Canada, particularly westerners flocking to the Reform Party, that they remained close to the prime minister's heart and the public pocket-book. "The West wants in Canada. . . . The West is in Canada," Mulroney told reporters after the swearing-in ceremony at Rideau Hall.

It was a lot of movement but little change. Apart from Clark's new role, the changes in the senior ranks left government policy making in the same hands. For instance, Senator Murray formally lost the federal-provincial responsibility to Clark but stayed on the two key committees that control policy and spending. He also won a place on a new eighteen-member National Unity Committee, which Clark chairs. Similarly, Crosbie's apparent demotion from International Trade to Fisheries was just an illusion. The Newfoundland minister remains a powerful voice on all major committees – Ops, Expenditure Review, Economics and Trade, P and P, and National Unity. He also got control over the Atlantic Opportunities Agency, becoming patronage king for the East coast.

The panels of key ministers give Mulroney control over every aspect of government. Final decisions are no longer taken by the total cabinet, which reflects the federal and pluralist nature of Canada. There is not one women on Ops, the most important committee in government. Kim Campbell is the only female among the nine members of Expenditure Review. Canadians know little of these important bodies because they huddle in secret, publish no reports or agendas and are even reluctant to say when they meet. That makes newspaper coverage rare, television exposure non-existent.

Much was made of the Expenditure Review Committee when it was created in 1988. It curbed some programs, notably child-care, the Polar 8 ice-breaker and the $9-billion nuclear submarine project of aging boy-wonder and then-defence minister Perrin Beatty. Clearly it blocked many costly plans of ministers outside the power loop.

But the ministers with committee clout did not practise the self-restraint they preached for others. Some observers, such as Jeffrey Simpson, felt that Agriculture was ripe for cuts – either through bureaucratic lay-offs or reductions in Farm Credit Corporation funding. But then-agriculture minister and vice-chairman of Expenditure Review Don Mazankowski chose not to take the axe to his own department. Instead, Agriculture enjoyed one of the largest increases of any department. More than $4 billion, or $30,000 per producer, went to western farmers after 1987. Another $3 billion is on its way between 1991 and 1994 under federal-provincial programs, for which Ottawa pays the lion's share. Similarly Crosbie bullied the $5.2 billion Hibernia offshore oil project through at a time when oil prices and potential returns on the investment are at rock bottom.

Despite some painful spending cuts and tax hikes, the country is far deeper in hock than it was in 1984 when Michael Wilson became finance minister. Seven years ago he pledged to wipe out Canada's $233 billion national debt. It will hit $419 billion in late 1992 and climb to $470 billion by 1995. Today we pay interest charges of $40 billion each year on this monster debt.

Wilson had some success at deficit cutting during the country's prosperous 1980s. Using tax hikes and cuts in social spending, he got it from $38 billion in 1984 to $30 billion in 1991, largely at the expense of the poor and the middle class. A dogmatic preoccupation with inflation caused the worst recession in a decade, tossing hundreds of thousands of workers into job lines, bankruptcy and foodbank queues.

In the last budget Wilson placed a 3 per cent cap on program spending and froze public-service wage hikes at the same level. As a symbolic gesture he placed a one-year freeze on salaries for Mulroney and his cabinet. It was a fraud. Mulroney's gang had already taken a 3.74 per cent hike in January and added $6,000 to their extravagant tax-free expense allowances in the fall of 1990. Mulroney, Jean Chrétien and Speaker John Fraser are not entitled to collect the $6,000 housing allowance, since they live in government residences. But they can claim the allowance for travel to their ridings. (Fraser's communications director, Jim Watson, says none of them has yet claimed any of the additional $6,000 allowance.)

No amount of cutbacks in MPs' personal spending will significantly reduce the national debt. But a real pinch on parliamentarians themselves would show Canadians that restraint applies at the top. Today's double standard just adds to public cynicism. On the May day that Defence department cuts of 1,000 jobs were announced, Pauline Browes was looking for an executive assistant, a media assistant, a policy adviser and a special assistant – possibly to ride around with her chauffeur to look for holes in the ozone layer that the Environment department had missed.

The cocoon surrounding crown princes shelters them from the real world of their subjects. Limousines, armies of aides, plush offices, private jets and non-accountable expense allowances distort the vision of even those who entered public life with the best intentions. They become annoyed with critics of their privileges – oblivious to the double standard that is so clear to other Canadians.

Their insensitivity often produces classic political gaffes. In December 1989, as Michael Wilson was about to smack taxpayers with the 7 per cent GST, he appeared in glossy color on the front page of *Toronto* magazine. Wearing a basic Bay Street tuxedo and smiling, as a luscious Ziggy Lorenc caressed his chin, Wilson was a willing prop for a magazine feature titled, 'Christmas Gifts for the Characters on Your List.' What did the magazine say he should get for Christmas? Just a Mont Blanc fountain pen at $290, an accessory pin at $499.95, a $2,000 bottle of cognac and a $9,000 home computer. That is probably what the folks at the food bank were lined up for too.

Just what hard times mean to a finance minister was revealed the evening of his tough 1991 budget. Wilson held a private party, at taxpayers' expense, in his fifth-floor Parliament Hill office. He brushed off questions about the propriety of a "by-invitation-only" bash after telling Canadians of the urgent need for belt-tightening. "Look this is a private party," he snapped at *Sun* reporter Peter Stockland who had slipped in to take a peek at the Queen Anne scotch, canapés and fat, fresh fruit. White-jacketed waiters kept drinks topped up as guests congratulated the host for his "hard-times economic blueprint." Stockland reported that one guest gushed, "Wonderful, Mike, wonderful," after learning of his threat to lay off public servants if they refuse to accept wage curbs.

For simple extravagance, one need only look skyward to see VIP Challenger jets whisking ministers around, immune to the fare hikes and cut-to-the bone services of Canada's struggling commercial airlines. Ottawa spent $2.5 million in six months of 1990 to keep its executive fleet aloft. Another $876,844 vanished on hotel-rooms, meals and commercial flights by ministers. The figures do not include the cost of other aircraft, such as the Boeing 707 the prime minister takes on foreign trips or the Defence department freebies to Lahr, Germany. Treasury Board president Gilles Loiselle noted that the use of the Challengers had dropped by 40 per cent since the Liberals were booted out of office in 1984.

First-class travel might be adequate for most Canadians, but not for those who represent them in cabinet. The top Challenger users in the period between April and September 1990 were: the prime minister (twenty-five trips at a cost of $296,528); Clark (eleven trips, mostly overseas, at $436,192); and McKnight who controlled the six-plane VIP fleet (fifteen trips at $402,136). While in the Defence portfolio, McKnight flew home to Saskatchewan on four successive summer weekends. He was the only passenger on three flights. On the other one, junior defence minister Mary Collins took the jet on to her home in Vancouver after McKnight was dropped off. Other frequent fliers were Bernard Valcourt (seven trips costing $190,972); Siddon (five for $176,472); and small business minister Tom Hockin (six for $150,672, including two home to London).

The reports of ministerial travel were released after then-auditor general Ken Dye blasted the government for refusing to release the information. But the response fell well short of Dye's demands. He wanted copies of minister's receipts for expenses incurred while travelling and letters to show that use of the Challenger jets was proper. "I guess the federal government's going to stay with the honor system," complained Dye, who flew economy class during his decade as Canadians' financial watch-dog. "Being an accountant, I prefer to have documentary evidence for claims. It's somebody else's money they are spending." He estimated that ministerial travel costs were underreported by as much as $10 million a year.

Loiselle dismissed Dye's complaint that the honor system was not good enough: "Your choice is to take his word against our word." Given the record of sleaze and goofs in high places it is a fairly easy choice to make. The Commons Public Accounts Committee also was not willing to take Loiselle's word. In a unanimous all-party report in December 1990 it issued an unsuccessful plea for an audit of ministerial travel. The committee described government refusals to give Dye receipts as a "most serious infringement of the rights of the

Auditor-General." Liberal Len Hopkins, who chaired the committee, said no one knows for sure if ministers are cheating on their travel. "We've never had an audit," he said. "Every province in Canada does it. Today the public are demanding accountability, not only of the prime minister and the cabinet but of MPs."

No minister flies higher than Marcel Masse, the ego-obsessed high-school history teacher whose contempt for ordinary Canadians, particularly anglophones, has become legend in Ottawa. When he cut $108 million from the CBC budget, a cut that meant 1,100 lost jobs, the laid-off workers appealed for reconsideration. "The minister of communications must turn a deaf ear to this begging," he responded. At the same time he announced plans for a $45-million Canadian Institute for Research on Cultural Enterprises to be headquartered in Montreal. Even the Quebec government and cultural community condemned that expenditure at the height of the 1991 recession. The backlash was strong enough to cancel the plan. When he took over as defence minister he had a memo sent out insisting that every piece of paper that lands on his desk be perfectly bilingual. "The minister expects the quality of French or English to be impeccable in terms of writing, grammar or spelling," according to a memo signed by J.M.D. Henrie, director-general of the executive secretariat at DND.

Masse has the habit of wearing his coat like a swash-buckler's cape, dropping it as he enters a room so flunkies must scramble to catch it. He once humiliated newly appointed parliamentary secretary Jack Shields and deputy minister Arthur Kroeger by forcing them to wait in a Hull restaurant while he listened to an opera on his office stereo. "You should learn to like opera," he reportedly announced to his subordinates as he waltzed in an hour late. "It would help you relax." They were not amused.

As energy minister in 1986 he disappeared for nearly a week after the Prime Minister's Office refused to let him use the Petro-Canada jet to attending meetings in Mexico and Venezuela that were later described as "disguised vacations." Nobody, including his staff, could find out where he had gone to sulk. One of his most famous expenditures was on a costly book he had printed at the same time as 110 scientists were chopped from his department. Photographs of Masse were prominently featured in the glossy book Supply and Services published for him at a cost of $191,000.

The public money Masse spends to feed his own vanity has equipped his former Chrysler LeBaron with a fax machine, two cellular phones and so many other expensive gadgets that it short-circuited and caught fire in the autumn of 1990. His present vehicle, a $27,408 Mercury, is the most expensive one in the ministerial fleet. When he was first made communications minister in 1984 he ordered $105,783 worth of office renovations and furnishings, including a $2,788 credenza, a $2,030 pneumatic chair and a $2,153 stereo system. His famous trip to Hollywood to "snare" an honorary Oscar that was being passed to the acting head of the National Film Board in 1989 cost taxpayers more than $16,300, including a $2,500 luncheon, rental of a stretch limousine and a side trip to Boston on the way back.

That such gross indulgence is wrong can be seen by everyone but Masse himself. Personal excess is not, however, the most serious flaw in a system that installs a few hand-picked princes in an all-powerful king's court. Parliament should act as a curb on government, but it does not because of rigidly enforced party discipline. Back-benchers on the government side are compelled to support every cabinet initiative regardless of their personal views or the interests of their voters. Those who act otherwise are blackballed or exiled to opposition. Thus our system under a majority government has evolved into an executive dictatorship with absolute power. Even that is concentrated in fewer than a dozen hands, an arrangement that denies Canadians democratic representation between elections. The government admits that reforms are necessary to restore Parliament as a counterweight to cabinet, but few believe the elite team at the top will give up the power it has so carefully concentrated in itself.

5
THE ROYAL COURT

*"It's very feudal. This place is a castle and MPs think the
peasants don't know what's going on. The peasants are
expected to bring corn and root crops to cover the costs but
what [MPs] don't know is that the peasants are ready to
put MPs in the moat."*

JIM FULTON, NDP MP, APRIL 1991

NOBODY WOULD ESCAPE. THE GOODS AND SERVICE TAX
would slap 7 per cent on books, children's clothes,
cab fares, rent, even postage stamps – with the prospect of a hike every time the government wanted a few
billion more. Only groceries escaped, at the last minute.

The tax was clearly going to raise two things: buckets of money
and public outrage. With the government sliding down a deepening
recession to the lowest popularity rating ever recorded, it was not
hard for the opposition to figure out what to do – fight. Just as they
had over free trade, Liberals and New Democrats attacked not just
the government but one another over who hated it more.

There were fiery displays of indignation as the tax that punished
us all was pushed through the Commons in the spring of 1990 and
began its tortured trip in the Senate. Near year-end, with the spotlight
focused there as never before, both Liberal and NDP MPs tried to
muscle their way into the action at the far end of the Centre Block
corridor. Liberal senators flung open the oak doors to their august
chamber so TV crews could join the pandemonium. Among those
who briefly grabbed attention in the upper chamber was Nelson
Riis, House leader of the NDP, which is devoted to abolition of the
Senate itself. Riis proved again that a politician will venture into
hell itself if it means a ten-second clip on "The National." Both
opposition parties vowed to abolish the hated universal tax if they
ever came to office.

While the battle raged in public, agents of all three parties were meeting in a private Commons clubhouse to plot their own escape from the tax trap. Otherwise it would add 7 per cent to the millions of dollars MPs spend from their operating budgets each year for equipment, supplies and constituency-office rent. Vowing that the tax would never pass, opposition members, including Riis and Liberals Dave Dingwall and Jean-Robert Gauthier, were planning what to do when it did.

On December 12, one day before the tax legislation cleared the Senate, a secret session of the Commons Board of Internal Economy (BOIE) decided that parliamentarians should not pay GST from their handsome allowance for office purchases. A special extra fund would cover the tax on such items, including the levy on constituency-office rents.

The nine MPs who made that decision form the most exclusive and powerful team of "fixers" on the Hill. They have absolute control over Commons spending of nearly a quarter of a billion dollars annually. Details of their discussions are never made public. The "commissioners" who sat on the nine-member board at the time were Speaker John Fraser, serving as chairman, Deputy Speaker Andrée Champagne, government House leader Harvie Andre, government whip Jim Hawkes, Treasury Board president Gilles Loiselle, Conservative caucus chairman Bob Layton, Liberal House leader Jean-Robert Gauthier, Liberal whip Dave Dingwall (now House leader) and NDP House leader Nelson Riis. The board meets on Wednesdays for a long dinner and short business session in the speaker's elegant Centre Block dining room. (Meetings are pleasant affairs. The wine steward plays a major role, and conversation rather than argument is the norm.) The board is accountable to no one. All that is ever released about its decisions is a brief summary at the start of the following parliamentary session, often two or three years later.

The decision on the GST was typical. The club simply decided, without input from the public or any outside debate, to give parliamentarians one more benefit that no other Canadians enjoyed. Those in other businesses either had to seek extra money and account for it on personal office budgets, or cut back on purchases because of the new levy. MPs' cosy deal to shield themselves from the pernicious tax was not revealed by the BOIE. The folks back home might have found it a bit hard to swallow.

The public found out only when the *Sun* newspaper chain ran the story. Its parliamentary bureau had learned of the exemption from NDP MP Jim Fulton. He found it disgusting in view of the self-righteous assault opposition parties had made on the universal tax. "It's rotten. The House of Commons passes a law to replace an existing tax and then sets up a a slush fund to exempt themselves from it." Except for Fulton, not a single MP on either side came forward to criticize the exemption.

Instead, a damage-control campaign was instantly mounted, using the Big Lie technique. Fraser's press secretary, who bears the title "Director of Communications for the House of Commons," denied that MPs would escape the tax on office purchases. "All members pay the GST. They're completely subject to it," Jim Watson told reporters on January 9. That line ran directly counter to the one provided by Commons accounting director Guy Jodoin who had told the *Sun*: "The GST won't be charged to their budgets. It will be charged to Treasury Board." In issuing his denial, Watson said that Jodoin was mistaken. Thirteen days later, Fraser sent a confidential memo to MPs explaining how they could avoid the tax. "When the amount of the GST is easily identified, the cost of the GST paid by Members for the purchase of goods and services for their offices will be charged to a special account and not the Members' operating budget."

MPs see the special exemption as a mere bookkeeping item. They say they are simply following the example of government departments, which are reimbursed for the 7 per cent tax from a central treasury account. The then-chairman of the Commons Finance Committee, Don Blenkarn, said it did not matter which pocket the money came from. The treasury gets the tax one way or another, but MPs preferred to see it taken from a central fund rather than from their own $165,000 annual office budgets.

But Fulton and most Canadians outside Parliament see the tax-free office purchases as a disguised subsidy, another parliamentary perk that sets MPs apart from the rest of taxpayers. For instance,

Fulton bought a $3,000 computer in 1991 from his office allowance. He was reimbursed $210 for GST from the outside fund. Using that example, it is easy to see how MPs, who invariably exhaust their entire office funds, actually cost taxpayers substantially more than the figure shown on the books. Comparing the GST to a skunk, Fulton says, "Everyone else has to deal with the stench . . . but not cosy Parliament Hill."

It's the huge office allowance that tempts many MPs into questionable or criminal misuse of public money. With substantial amounts lying in the pot unspent, many find a sudden need to hire "contractors" for research, speech writing, preparing Christmas-card lists and assorted other duties. A change in the rules has made it illegal for them to hire their own spouse or children, but friends, associates and the relatives of other MPs often make their way onto the pay-roll. Members charged with offences are usually suspected of taking kickbacks from the people they paid or of having cheques issued for work that was never performed.

The board's genius for creating comfort amid chaos was demonstrated just before the summer break of 1990. The Meech Lake clock ticked off its final minutes and the word "recession" was on the lips of everyone but the finance minister. Times were tough for Canadians. Despite it all, the commissioners had cooked up a CARE package for MPs as they headed off on holiday. It was a $6,000 increase in each member's expense allowance. The money was on top of the $20,600 (now $21,300) that all members get to cover unspecified costs. That tax-free allowance began years ago for such things as accommodation and meals for parliamentarians who had out-of-pocket costs both in Ottawa and back home. The additional allowance was for much the same thing, although members would have to produce receipts to collect it and could use it to pay rent or mortgages.

Reporters who gathered outside the caucus doors one Wednesday in late June believed that the MPs within were wrestling with the economy and the Meech Lake count-down. Instead they were arguing about how best to tell the public about this new gift or, better still, avoid telling them at all.

They chose the latter course, but a disgruntled staffer of one MP told the *Sun* about the $6,000 bonanza. The board had approved it "in principle," to be paid only if the $1.8 million cost could be saved somewhere else in the Commons' nearly-quarter-billion-dollar budget. To no one's surprise, the board hacked and chopped enough spending elsewhere to begin the payments in October.

Tory House leader Harvie Andre was dispatched to justify the cash award at a time when the government was preaching restraint. "It helps a little bit," Andre said, proclaiming at the same time that MPs' salaries had fallen behind those of other professions over the past eighteen years. "Members are coming to us and saying: 'Look, since 1984 industrial salaries on average have gone up 31 per cent, our remuneration has gone up 15 per cent – we're falling behind.' " New Democrat Riis chipped in that "what this does is bring the House of Commons in line with what provincial legislatures have been doing for years."

Their defence of the pay-off did not convince many outside the MPs' castle. Today the new allowance, coupled with the non-accountable $21,300 already provided, gives them a tax-free package equivalent to taxable income of at least $45,000 in 1991. When added to a basic salary of $64,400, it gives MPs the equivalent of $110,000 annually. Despite angry editorials from coast to coast, MPs never wavered in their determination to pocket the bonus. Some critics saw it as a way to hike income to insulate MPs from the recession and the GST. "The House of Commons is becoming the House of Hypocrisy," fumed David Somerville, president of the National Citizens' Coalition. "On the one hand Prime Minister Mulroney's government tells us to tighten our belts to help battle the federal deficit and inflation. On the other hand, however, government – and opposition MPs – give themselves huge, tax-free raises."

Much of the original tax-free allowance was used to pay for travel for MPs and families, telephones, research, printing, subscriptions, office costs, constituency assistance and other expenses incurred in the game of winning office and staying there. Today those items are almost entirely paid for from other budgets, not from the tax-free allowance, which members now simply regard as pay.

A month before they hiked expense allowances, members of the

Board of Internal Economy added another rich perk by extending the Commons' travel provisions to give spouses exactly the same free flights, with taxis or limousines at each end, as MPs. A total of sixty-four free flights is allowed so an MP or spouse can jet somewhere and return more than once a week. There are no longer any restrictions on where they can fly with their first-class domestic air tickets. Previously only twenty return flights could be used for destinations other than the home riding. Family and staff can also use some of the sixty-four points. The tab for all that first-class jetting around runs to $7.2 million. Several million more is spent for travel in constituencies, such as hiring an aircraft or helicopter to fly MPs to remote parts of their ridings.

Members who book through the Commons travel agency have their frequent-flier points saved to pay for later trips. Many book their own trips, save the points and use them for holiday travel anywhere in the world. MPs or family members who want to hop around the country or overseas without using their commercial travel allowance can do so on military flights.

In addition to BOIE members, others who attend the meetings are the top officers of the House: Commons clerk Robert Marleau, Sergeant-at-Arms Gus Cloutier, House administrator Ed Riedel and Fraser's principal secretary, Dr. Stephen Ash, a former professor of business who likes his academic title to be used. One other diner makes up the list of regulars, committee clerk Mary MacDougall. For years, she doubled as clerk of the Commons Committee on Management and Members' Services. This committee conducted most of its meetings in secret, often recommending actions to be followed up by the board. It has been replaced by a new committee with expanded powers and a vow to open up its meetings. The House leaders and whips who sit on both probably know more about the inner workings of the House and the wishes of members than anyone else on the Hill.

There is no end of problems to deal with. Some members persist in smoking in their offices, contrary to a legal ban and the protests of non-smoking employees. Other workers and some MPs indulge their addiction with furtive puffs at the freight entrances to the Parliament

Hill buildings. Smokers appear to have lost the battle in Commons lobbies and committees. The smashing of ashtrays in a committee room by anti-nicotine crusader and former NDP member Lynn McDonald was said to have been a highlight of the long-running conflict. Another ticklish issue was that of the special telephone calling codes that MPs use to call free anywhere, anytime. So many members pass their codes on to outsiders that the bills grow tremendously each month. The accountants discovered that each time the codes were changed, the cost of calls dropped by up to 40 per cent. One code made its way to Carleton University, where students ran a single account into the thousands before the magic number was scrapped. Now codes are changed about every six months.

BOIE decides matters big and small, from how to beef up security to the price an MP should pay to replace the gold ID pin each receives upon arrival. The first one is free. The second one costs $275. The special pins issued to spouses can be replaced for $150. Their purpose is to ensure that no security guard fails to recognize the wearer as a special person who should not be questioned at parliamentary entrances. It has been said that the worst mistake a guard can make is to confuse a cabinet minister with an ordinary MP, or an MP with an ordinary Canadian. One other item members can buy before waving a final goodbye to the Commons chamber is the green leather chair they occupied (more or less) during their term in office. The cost is $900. The chairs are not big sellers.

The Senate has its own board, which functions in the same secret way. Every administrative issue and expenditure in Parliament is funnelled through the two committees, although the Commons board is more powerful, controls the "parliamentary precincts" and has a bigger budget. A current initiative is a green plan for the Commons, including the speaker's very own "environmental officer." The plan has set a national example by banning styrofoam cups in its four cafeterias and distributing a variety of wastepaper baskets into which different kinds of unread Commons documents and reports can be thrown by the thousands each day. Among press secretary Jim Watson's key jobs are ensuring that Fraser never has his picture taken with a styrofoam cup in hand and keeping the ashtrays in his chamber hidden from prying eyes. Watson has other duties. He rounds up guests so that visiting delegations will feel welcome at receptions, often conscripting staff and other innocents with the veiled advice, "the speaker really wants to see you." The young bachelor's responsibilities – and taxpayers' money – have taken him abroad with his boss, to Washington on his own and to the Calgary Olympics as chauffeur/social convener/aide to friends and fans of the Frasers' daughter, who competed in free-style skiing events.

Speakers before 1985 had far more individual authority than Fraser has today, although his power remains great. Until then BOIE consisted of the speaker and four cabinet ministers. That tightly closed shop was expanded to include opposition representatives, the government whip and the caucus chairman in reform-minded recognition that Parliament belonged to all members. The effect was to draw all parties into the schemes for divvying up money, perks and power.

The eight "old boys" and NDP member Joy Langan who make up the Management and Members' Services Committee helped with that task. That committee was begun in 1975. Veteran Tory Robert Coates, who well understood the meaning of self help for parliamentarians, was the longest-serving chairman from 1976 to 1984. With an opposition chairman, the goodies are spread around. All parties are at the trough and none can point to the others as the recipient of special treatment. Coates was succeeded by Liberal Marcel Prud'homme, first elected in the Montreal riding of Saint-Denis in 1964 and returned ever since. Most meetings of his committee are closed to outsiders.

The two committees treat Parliament as a private social club, a type of club quite distinct from service clubs and characterized by what Peter C. Newman describes as "the heavy hush of privilege that intimidates even the most self-confident regulars." The people who run it do their best to keep members content with the meagre rations the taxpayers provide.

The trio of deputy minister–level officers at the top of the Commons administration enjoy pay and power befitting senior executives in any multimillion-dollar business. Cloutier and Marleau occupy magnificent oak-panelled offices in the Centre Block just steps from the speaker's suite across the marble hall from the Commons chamber. Riedel has a huge, deep-carpeted, richly appointed corner of the newly renovated South Block across Wellington Street from the Hill. These three officers' pay is about $140,000 each, with the annual wage of those next behind them on the Commons ladder at more than $110,000. (Federal salaries are hidden in wide ranges – for example, from $113,600 to $138,300 – to conceal the precise figure for any individual. Basing our assessments on seniority, responsibility and the boss's view of the person's importance, we have shown pay figures at the top of the known range wherever the exact number is not available.) The closest of all aides to the speaker is his portly gatekeeper, Dr. Ash. His title, "principal secretary" disguises the control he has over access and the agenda of the BOIE.

By an odd coincidence one of the biggest shake-ups in Commons administrative history took place in March 1991, just as the auditor general began his first examination of the place in twelve years. Virtually all Cloutier's responsibilities were shifted to Riedel and Marleau, leaving the sergeant-at-arms with authority over little more than security and cleaning. What he lost was control over office space, telecommunications, messenger service, the Hill's fleet of trucks and buses, parking and provisions of the Press Gallery.

Mindful of the auditor general's charges of a year earlier, that the Senate was rife with waste and patronage, the Commons seemed to be shuffling responsibilities to give at least the appearance of an administrative house-cleaning. The last such report in 1979 had showed "serious deficiencies in general and financial administration." It said that taxpayers' money was poorly spent and that there was a real risk of "inconsistent administrative practices, unauthorized use of inventories and equipment, overcharging by suppliers and other irregular and fraudulent practices." Stories were everywhere about missing hams, liquor, furniture, office equipment, even a grand piano, and about employees who rarely showed up for work. The changes that followed included the appointment of a tough administrator, Art Silverman, with new powers, the use of transparent garbage bags for everything leaving the Hill and several sudden resignations. Silverman was the first professional adminis-trator hired since 1867, and he is largely credited with cleaning up the mess and introducing proper accounting procedures. He returned to the civil service in 1986.

In explaining the recent changes, Jim Watson said that security demands are becoming particularly "prominent," requiring the full attention of Cloutier who retains his military rank of major-general. Veteran Liberal member of the BOIE Jean-Robert Gauthier said that the changes would help in co-ordinating security services with the Senate. He added that no wrong or punishment was implied by the moves, that implementation of modern techniques was the sole reason for them. It just happened to put a convenient scapegoat in place for the upcoming auditor general's report. Former auditor general Ken Dye made his first request to the BOIE for permission to conduct an audit in the spring of 1989. The board took nearly two years to agree, doing so only after Dye had protested so loudly about Senate stone-walling that he was allowed into the upper house. In both cases parliamentary officers placed strict limits on what the auditor could look into. Watson explained that the Commons audit "will deal exclusively with the adminis-tration of the House of Commons as well as practices and controls governing the provision of support to the offices of members." It will also examine the relationship between the administration of the House and BOIE. It will not deal with members' pay, allow-ances, travel, committee spending or the operations of the BOIE itself. The clubhouse remains safe.

When senior officers leave on handsomely indexed pensions they usually take fat severance payments with them. These ensure, among other things, their silence about intimate details of the parliamentary club and its members. Cloutier's predecessor, Col. John Currie, and former clerks Alistair Fraser (a losing Liberal candidate who won the clerk's job in 1967) and Bev Koester have all kept their clubhouse secrets to themselves. The Commons long-time chief law clerk, Marcel Pelletier, resigned precipitately in late 1990. He has sued the prime minister and Marleau for wrongful dismissal from his $125,000-a-year job and has been negotiating a settlement ever since. No explanation was given for the firing.

Power and privilege begin to work their dreadful magic on members the moment they arrive, flushed with their first election victory, to do the nation's business. There is an immediate scramble for secretaries and assistants. Many members bring favored aides from home, only to realize that it takes years for staffers to master the details of such things as ordering supplies, getting on exclusive invitation lists, preparing a private member's bill or joining a luxury trip overseas. The newcomers get a briefing on the legislative process, the host of services, equipment and personnel available to them and their special privileges as MPs.

They learn that MPs cannot be arrested within the precincts of Parliament for civil offences and need not appear in court as witnesses or jurors. Any attempt to bribe them is a criminal offence, and threats against them or intimidation constitute contempt of the highest court in the land. The rules for playing the parliamentary game make it clear that MPs are no longer like other Canadians.

Most start enthusiastically at the business they came to do. They soon learn that what their leaders want most is for them to vote when and how they're told and to fill committees and Commons seats on "duty days." They learn that most committees are tame servants of majority masters and that innovative reports get shelved. They learn that advancement has more to do with luck, geography, sex, ethnicity and unknown intrigues than with simple merit. And they learn that the nation's course is determined not under the picture-postcard Peace Tower but across the street in the undistinguished-looking Langevin Block, lair of the prime minister's powerful planners. Members who accept the clubhouse traditions of secrecy, hypocrisy and greed get along fine. Critics of the system will find life on the Hill distinctly difficult.

It has been an exclusive club since 1867. Creature comforts grew from the two original dining rooms to as many as seven restaurants, cafeterias and canteens just a few years ago. (Two cafeterias were closed in 1990.) With a liquor store, gym, showers, barber-shop and cheap meals on the self-contained site, many members rarely need to leave the precincts. Many know little of Ottawa but the cab ride from the airport to a shared apartment nearby, good enough for their Tuesday-to-Thursday attendance.

Parliamentary jobs, from senior officers to pages, have traditionally been filled through political connections. Some were even passed on from father to son. Changes have come only in the last decade. For a century the very top job, Commons clerk, was awarded to defeated candidates or other political favorites of the government. When he was promoted to the post in 1979 after four years as deputy, Professor Koester was regarded as the first "outsider" to win the key procedural and administrative job. His successor, Bob Marleau, has spent his adult life in Commons service, starting with committees and developing an intimate knowledge of members and their secrets during seven years of international travel with parliamentary delegations.

One of the special privileges membership confers is use of a special medical clinic. Ottawa's ruling class – MPs, senators, cabinet ministers, senior military officers and bureaucrats – receive medical care at the National Defence Medical Centre (NDMC). There are no crowded waiting rooms or delays for surgery that patients in the real world face. "It's a special deal for special people," says Major-General Jean Benoit, surgeon-general for the Canadian Forces. The hospital had been providing health care to the elite since the late 1970s, but the special clinic for the exclusive use of 1,200 select politicians and bureaucrats was created by special cabinet order in 1987. Since then politicians have no longer had to mingle with the country's war veterans. The special medical facility was provided at a time when the government began reducing transfer payments to the provinces for health care and education.

The hospital's "Senior Officials Clinic" was exposed by then-auditor general Ken Dye in his 1990 report to Parliament. "NDMC patients also include members of the RCMP, members of Parliament and senior civil servants," Dye reported. "In fact, 61 percent of NDMC's 1987-88 patient days were for non–Canadian Forces patients." According to Dye the cost per patient day at the hospital was $472 compared to $286 a day at an ordinary hospital in Ontario.

The 244-bed hospital had an occupancy rate of only 76 per cent, but its special service precluded any cutback.

An MP with a sniffle or tummy ache also has a special physician awaiting his call. Dr. Mark Walter, the family doctor to Canada's 295 MPs and 109 senators, sees an average of eight patients a day compared to about forty or fifty for private practitioners. Walter sees nothing wrong with such an exclusive clinic, which is similar to those for elite Soviet officials. "The people I take care of are under a great deal of pressure because they have very special responsibilities and, as such, may require special attention," he says. "Any high-profile character gets better care, whether it's a movie star or a politician."

Opposition MPs, who had never uttered a critical word until Dye's public revelations, suddenly exploded with outrage. They denounced the clinic as disgraceful evidence of a two-tier medical system: one tier for the elite, the other for the peasants. "All citizens should be treated equally," cried Liberal health critic Dr. Rey Pagtakhan. "It's a misuse of taxpayers' dollars." He either did not know or failed to mention that Liberal MPs and senators had made more than two-dozen visits to the clinic in 1990. "I don't want them [MPs] setting up an elitist medical system for themselves," thundered NDP health critic Jim Karpoff. "We've never asked for special service," added his leader, Audrey McLaughlin. The NDP may not have asked for such treatment, but they did take advantage of it. NDMC records showed that New Democratic MPs made eighteen visits to the clinic in 1990. Tory members dropped by fifty times.

The club showers benefits on its members. Among them are four free "householder" mailings each year to every voter in an MP's riding. The privilege is extended for a final newsletter up to a week after Parliament is dissolved for an election. The MP does not have to show that as a campaign cost, although it clearly gives members of the parliamentary club an advantage over their opponents. Mail is a pretty big item for the House of Commons and a multimillion-dollar cost to taxpayers. It is delivered and collected six times a day from each MP's office, a total of eleven million items in 1989-90. Nearly forty-three million "householders" were sent that year, at up to sixteen pages apiece. Most Canadians should have received at least a card from their MP at Christmas. That December 7,733 "surface bags" of mail were sent out at sixty pounds each and 6,554 "air mail bags" at forty pounds. Commons mail for the year filled just under 100,000 bags.

While North American phone calls are free, overseas ones are not necessarily covered. Just before the 1984 election, however, the BOIE wrote off $92,445 in telephone tabs for a number of members. They also sweetened the car-mileage allowance by over 7 per cent just when MPs would be hitting the campaign trail. The board also gave members one free first-class airline ticket for each week of the campaign, another clear advantage incumbents bestowed upon themselves. For those who could not win even with that help there was a candy-coated consolation prize. Taxpayers would cover their moving expenses to get out of Ottawa. The original period for this service was six months after resignation or defeat. In 1986 it was increased to a year and then to two years. The BOIE has since cut that back to one year, a time in which job counselling and readjustment assistance is also provided. Recently the BOIE also agreed to pay real-estate and legal fees.

Today the most famous parliamentary perk is probably over-rated. The private sixth-floor dining room with its splendid red carpet, marble pillars, art collection and friendly efficient service is a great place to show off for visitors, who may even meet a cabinet minister or two. But the food is only fair and the legendary give-away prices are now up to about half of what you would pay in commercial restaurants. The day of the $4 dinner with wine is long gone and with it the speaker who dared to raise prices, John Bosley. Even the BOIE, when it subsequently gained more powers, resisted pleas by some members to drop prices. Still, at the current level, the restaurant and four cafeterias lost nearly $4 million last year. Some services have been cut back, but it is expected that taxpayers will have to make up the $3.4 million shortfall this year. Restaurant privileges are extended to MPs, senators, Press Gallery members, senior parliamentary officers and spouses. The cafeterias are open to more than 3,500 Hill employees.

Haircuts for the privileged have also gone up to $6, plus GST. A shampoo is $3 and a facial or head rub and massage $2. Just 100 feet from Parliament Hill Carmine Canonico's commercial shop charges $18 for a haircut, $12 for a shampoo and $30 to $35 for a facial. Canonico has to pay himself, staff, his rent and his overhead from customer receipts. The Hill barbers, hairdresser, masseur and shoeshiners are salaried employees, not regular business operators. "We're always getting taxed so we can pay for their haircuts and facials," says Canonico. "The prices they charge are more of a tip. What a joke."

Garth Turner is an example of an outsider who, having joined the club he used to squawk about, finds he now likes it just fine. He was a champion of the little guy against the privileged establishment when he wrote a column for the *Toronto Sun*. Today he says that MPs deserve the cut-rate services because they work so hard. "I tell you, I expected better services than they have on the Hill," says the rookie Tory MP. He complains that the equipment in the three barber-shops (two for MPs, one for senators) is old and that the gym (there are four) for the exclusive use of MPs is small. "I also know with an MP's schedule that it's hard to get a haircut and, if we get to the point where we eliminate services it will be less time for their work." When questioned about such perks, MPs are never at a loss for an explanation, usually one based on some claim to hard work and personal sacrifice.

A naive outsider might expect a new MP to rush right in to work in the office of a defeated predecessor, with little more than a fresh coat of paint to mark the transfer. That happens seldom, if ever. Painting, refurnishing, recarpeting and installation of new office equipment is a big and constant business. Members get a hefty initial allowance to furnish Ottawa and constituency offices, then an ongoing annual one for replacements and upgrading. Confidential figures show that between 1980 and 1985 the Commons spent $4.6 million on office furniture, $1.6 million for carpets, drapes and upholstery, and $6.1 million on office renovations. In 1990-91 it spent $2 million on office furniture and equipment. In the two previous years the Commons spent half a million dollars on carpets, drapes and upholstery and nearly $2 million more on stationery and office supplies.

The Commons has its own in-house crew working full-time on furniture repair and upholstery. So does the Senate. The Commons workshop is in the basement of the Wellington Building. It employs forty-nine people – painters, carpenters, cabinet makers, picture framers and furniture refinishers. There is a master carpenter on the pay-roll for special projects. Wolf Bartsch's artistic work graces the prime minister's office, the speaker's oak-panelled dining room, and Joe Clark's sumptuous East Block office. It can also be seen in the cabinet and fine furnishings of the offices of dozens of lesser members. Bartsch produced a TV and stereo cabinet to match two doors in the corner of Mulroney's office that enclose his so-called hot lines. Little TV monitors are beautifully enclosed in discreet wood-work on the clerk's table in the Commons chamber. The oak ballot-box that we glimpse every few years when the Commons elects a speaker is another Bartsch work of art.

An MP wanting a new look for the office need only dial Commons interior decorator Tony Machiado. He is paid $54,000 a year to advise members on the style of paint, carpeting, furnishings and wallpaper best suited to their taste. A member who wants to look at decorating options is encouraged to visit the aptly named "Enterprise Tower" at Minto Place, a few blocks away. The Commons show-room there boasts a wide selection of top-of-the-line drapes, carpets ($48 per square metre), couches, chairs, paints and fabrics. "There is a lot of choice – and I mean a *lot* of choice," says one insider. "Everything is expensive. It's top quality."

After each election, painters and carpet installers work almost around the clock renovating offices. A decade ago only five standard colors and standard furniture were available. Now MPs can have any color they choose. It has meant a tremendous cost increase. If a new-comer to office objects to the pink couch and chair already there, they are replaced at once. Furniture is no longer easily shuffled somewhere else, as were the old beige, white and light-blue furnish-ings. Those sent back now are either recovered or sold at distress prices in government-surplus auctions.

One long-time employee says that the decorators get some odd requests. One MP's secretary called to have his day-old beige couch replaced because it had acquired some conspicuous love stains in a trial run. A Commons insider tells of another instance when a female MP had her office repainted peach over a weekend. She returned, "said it was too dark and had them do it a paler peach. One of the guys felt like throwing a pail at her."

MPs make sure they use up their $400 allotment each year for framing. Most of their prized artworks are photos of themselves with party leaders or other political stars, complete with inscription and autograph. But the framing shop also gets orders for pictures of MPs with their dogs or cats or horses. MPs have also had children's drawings, running shoes and even a rock from the West Block framed. Pictures and posters of Boy George, E.T. and Teenage Mutant Ninja Turtles have all been framed or laminated. "They have their $400 and they can do what they want," says a long-time employee. "If they want to frame Boy George, what can you do about it?" Special cases are custom-built so MPs can ship such artwork home, free of course.

About the only place on the Hill where things cost more than off it is the parliamentary liquor and beer store. To discourage staff from shopping there, it charges a 50-cent premium per item. Rarely do MPs pick up their own booze, though. A staff member or one of the 150 green-uniformed messengers on hand for "urgent personal services to members" is usually sent.

Messengers do not form the largest job category in the Commons. There are more aides, assistants (secretaries), researchers and clerks spread through both the Commons overall and MPs' personal staff lists. There are 236 guards in the 1990-91 budget, which shows security costs of $9 million. Cleaning used 178 "person years" in a budget of $4.3 million; post office and distribution used 87 for a cost of $2.8 million. Preparation of Commons publications (*Hansard*, committee reports, statistics, etc.) employed 194 people and cost $7.8 million, and the printing of such documents used 76 people and a budget of $4.1 million.

There's only one bell-ringer. The Dominion carillonneur in the Peace Tower rang up a 1990-91 bill of $95,000. Eleven persons fell into the $2.4 million budget of the office of the director of parliamentary accommodation, who is "accountable for the planification and administration of major and minor construction within the precincts of the House, of space utilization and curatorial services." The secret document does not say how many person hours were required to write the job description.

A lot more Commons costs are hidden in the separate $16-million budget of the Library of Parliament. Its research branch of ninety specialists – including an assortment of lawyers, economists, political scientists, sociologists and historians with masters and doctoral degrees – works mainly for the Commons. Many of the experts are seconded almost full-time to Commons committees. Others devote their time to answering specific requests from MPs, writing "everything but the jokes" for speeches and often devoting hours to projects that look suspiciously like school homework assignments. The Information and Technical Services Branch spends most of its time answering Commons queries (although members of the press and Senate are also big users). The branch compiles answers to frequently asked questions, finds answers to others and works overnight to provide a printed collection of news stories, available to members with their morning coffee. It is called "Quorum," and you'll often spot members reading it during Commons debates.

The budget of the House of Commons itself is a top-secret document, guarded by the BOIE commissioners and not even distributed freely to MPs. In fact, few MPs even know of its existence. It provides one of the quickest ways to trace the explosion of perks and expenses that the royal court has awarded its members in recent years. The first entry is in 1913 when secretarial assistance was first made available to members a "few days at a time." Three improvements in office staffing are noted in the next fifty-five years, including the hiring of one full-time secretary per member, in 1968. There are six more increases up to the 1980s, including the establishment of constituency offices and a total budget per MP of $68,000. In the 1980s, there were ten additions of services to bring MPs' "operating budgets" to more than $165,000. The history of constituency allowances, which began in 1973, shows almost annual hikes to cover new equipment, staff and inflation costs. Little-known "constituency travel entitlements," to pay the costs MPs incur while driving around their ridings, eating and staying overnight, were expanded more than once each year through the 1980s.

Presiding over Parliament's royal court is Speaker Fraser. He is paid the same as a cabinet member, which he was before the Tunagate scandal sent him into temporary exile. Some of his responsibilities are similar to those of a minister – managing more than 3,500 employees and a multimillion-dollar budget, for instance. But the office is much grander, the perks and prestige far more magnificent. He is fifth on Canada's Table of Precedence behind the governor general, the prime minister, the chief justice and the Senate speaker. Ambassadors are next, and cabinet ministers are in seventh spot, ranked according to their appointment date. The speaker is the only MP with an apartment on Parliament Hill. It consists of two small rooms, plus a beautiful dining room for formal entertaining, adjoining the sitting room and office. His chauffeur drops him each morning at his private entrance to the Centre Block (marked with a brass plaque). The Senate speaker has a similarly exclusive door at the east end of the building, something even the prime minister does not have.

Fraser has a huge, government-owned estate just a twenty-minute limousine ride away at Kingsmere in the beautiful Gatineau Hills. It is part of the much larger property that was once owned by Mackenzie King and that is preserved for visitors today by the National Capital Commission. The speaker's portion, called "the Farm," was recently renovated at a cost of $430,000. Fraser gets a huge special allowance for entertainment and an office budget of $588,000. A travel budget of $694,000, which he shares with Senate speaker Guy Charbonneau, comes with the job. The two speakers have official obligations to greet and entertain visiting dignitaries and to head delegations abroad. As compensation for being politically "neutralized," the speaker is traditionally given extra funds to travel, entertain and foot other bills that may help with the essential job of getting re-elected.

With the generous assistance of taxpayers, Fraser throws the biggest parliamentary party of the year each June on the huge, sloping lawn of the Farm. The fleet of Commons minibuses ferries many of the 1,500 to 2,000 politicians, employees, diplomats, media and hangers-on to the seemingly limitless spread of food and drink. The event was cancelled in 1991 as an example of restraint. One other little perk for the speaker is a hold-over from the days before the car and driver were provided. He still gets a $1,000 "car allowance." Cabinet ministers and the opposition leader get a $2,000 "car allowance," in addition to their car and driver, but otherwise the pickings are a little thinner than those of the speaker.

Opposition leader Jean Chrétien is still safely above the poverty line, however. He gets the same pay as ministers and the speaker, a limousine and free room and board at Stornoway, a government-owned mansion in the heart of upper-crust Rockcliffe. The Commons spends more than $150,000 a year for such household staff as cooks, maids, a gardener and a chauffeur. Renovations and maintenance are paid for by you-know-who through the Department of Public Works.

The self-described "Little Guy from Shawinigan" moved in six months after becoming Liberal leader but just days after a December 10, 1990, by-election gave him a Commons seat and the title "Leader of the Opposition." The Little Guy, now from Beauséjour, N.B., left his half-million-dollar home overlooking the Rideau Canal because it was too small for entertaining, according to his principal secretary, Eddie Goldenberg. The taxpayers bought more than $27,000 worth of new furniture to make the Chrétiens feel welcome, brightened up the walls with $17,000 worth of paint and provided $11,877 worth of fresh linen as Ti-Jean lambasted Mulroney for the pain and suffering inflicted on Canadians by the Tories' made-in-Canada recession.

Stornoway is one of the more costly residences of the political elite. More than $938,000 has been spent on renovations and maintenance for it since 1983. The house on the huge lot at 541 Acacia Avenue has six bedrooms, plus a family room, formal living room, formal dining room, powder room, sun room, breakfast room, private den and change room. When the Mulroneys moved there in 1983, they spent $150,553 to spruce the place up. During the Turner years, government figures show that taxpayers forked out $224,187 in operating and maintenance costs and $489,599 in capital costs between September 1984 and December 1986. Another $75,000 was sunk into renovations in 1987-88.

The chairman of the Official Residences Council, Hamilton Southam, warned in 1990 that taxpayers can expect to continue to pour money into Stornoway. Apparently it was poorly built and still needs major repairs, including an overhaul of its plumbing and electrical wiring, which were somehow missed in previous overhauls. "It will no doubt be expensive," confessed Southam. "The house is not in very good shape and if it's to be kept on, and we believe it should be, more work will be necessary." Some feel demolition might be a good start.

Chrétien has an office budget of more than $1.6 million. It helps pay top salaries for Goldenberg, policy director Chaviva Hosek, three press secretaries, a Quebec adviser and a host of lesser aides. The activities of the advisers involve far more political than parliamentary work, but the public, not the party, foots the whole bill.

New Democratic leader Audrey McLaughlin is rewarded with $29,500 on top of her MP's pay and the top-of-the-line expense allowance she gets for representing her huge Yukon riding. The total is well over $125,000. There is also a car and driver. That was first given to Ed Broadbent by Brian Mulroney in 1984 to keep the NDP quiet about Mulroney's increasingly opulent lifestyle. McLaughlin also gets a hefty office budget of $1.2 million. Both Liberal and NDP leaders receive $75,000 worth of free translation services.

Clearly not all our 295 elected representatives have to scrape by on a basic MP's salary. Eighty of them get extra pay, including the aforementioned thirty-eight cabinet ministers, the speaker and opposition leader at $49,100 and the NDP leader. There are thirty parliamentary secretaries who draw an additional $10,500. The deputy speaker gets an extra $25,700, the opposition House leader, $23,800; government and opposition whips, $13,200; the deputy chairman, Committee of the Whole (a speaker stand-in), $10,500; the assistant deputy chairman, Committee of the Whole (another speaker stand-in), $10,500; other party House leaders, $10,100; other party whips,

$7,500; and deputy government and opposition whips, $7,500.

A quick count shows that seventy-four Conservatives, nearly half their total membership, pocket premium pay. And Deputy Speaker Andrée Champagne gets to put an extra $1,500 in her purse "in lieu of an apartment" according to confidential Commons documents. In his first term Mulroney's Commons brains trust cooked up a bill that would pay about twenty-five committee chairmen, all but two of them Tory, an additional $9,500. It got approval in the House but was stalled by senators who insisted that their committee chairmen should get the same bonus. The 1988 election came and the bill died before the two houses could work out their differences.

In the Senate, the leaders of the government and opposition, the deputy leaders and the whips, all get additional pay, ranging from $4,700 to $29,900. Speaker Charbonneau is paid $105,800, including a $3,000 residence allowance and a $1,000 car allowance. It is paid the same way as Fraser's, on top of the car and driver, which are at his beck and call twenty-four hours a day.

Cash from the public treasury is also funnelled into party research offices, whose work is clearly partisan. Taxpayers subsidized the three main parties to the tune of $2.6 million in 1990-91. The money was split according to party strength in the House: $1.08 million for the Tories, $1.02 million for the Liberals and $647,000 for the NDP.

The Bloc Québécois saw the rich potential of party designation in the Commons to help its campaign for an independent Quebec. Bloc leader Lucien Bouchard and his sidekick Jean Lapierre vigorously fought for party recognition and the loot that goes with it. So far their appeals have been rejected and their disruptive tactics overcome. If the separatist party's Commons membership reaches twelve (it is eight today), it wins official party status and its rich rewards.

All that party research money comes on top of the services mentioned earlier that are provided under the budget of the Parliamentary Library. Library research experts will even drop by an MP's office to deliver a firsthand lecture on anything from geophysics to parliamentary procedure. Each year the research branch answers

2,000 requests from parliamentarians. It uses computer banks for instant access to 650,000 books, 1,800 periodicals and 4,000 clipping files.

MPs enjoy state-of-the-art technology that any modern business would envy. They have computers, word processors, copiers, TVs, VCRs, and phones too complicated for many members to operate without help. MPs have elaborate printing services at their disposal. They can order instant replays of speeches or questions in the Commons on office TVs; they can also switch to satellite signals from stations back home in Edmonton, Hamilton or Vancouver.

The Commons has an incomparable $6-million electronic information system. "There's no legislature in the world that has as integrated office automation as Canada does," brags Bob Desramaux, the Hill's computer guru. Known as OASIS (Office Automation Service and Information Systems), the system provides a dazzling array of information on eighty different TV channels. MPs can tune into all thirty cable broadcasts, House of Commons proceedings in French and English or "floor" sound, live news conferences from the National Press Building, a selection of network news items from the previous evening, details of all committee meetings, airline information and much more. Minutes after a phone request they can have a recent item from "The Journal," "Fifth Estate," "Canada AM" or other public-affairs program fed into their office TV. They can send messages around the Hill or hold conferences without leaving the office (which raises questions about the need for those 150 messengers).

All these services and operators, of course, require senior managers with their own offices and support. Thus the administration of the Commons has mushroomed in recent years. In 1975 its organization chart showed twenty-nine department heads. Today there are eighty-five managers, many with tidy salaries and benefits.

Parliament's royal court cannot kick out members who fail to conform to its unwritten rules, unless they also commit a crime. Quebec Conservative Richard Grisé, convicted of breach of trust in 1989, resigned before he was expelled from the Commons. Wayward members who are not convicted of crimes can be punished in plenty of other ways.

The royal court has its own code and its own list of misdemeanors. Party servility is prized, independence despised: truth is a matter of political convenience, and secrecy a basic operating procedure. John Turner virtually disappeared from the Commons, but not from its payroll, after he gave up the leadership to Chrétien. No one seemed to recall Turner's suggestion he might quit when his replacement was chosen: "I do not intend to be a John Diefenbaker who had to watch Bob Stanfield lead the Conservative opposition," Turner told his Vancouver-Quadra riding association in May 1989 according to columnist Allan Fotheringham. Two years later the riding remained effectively unrepresented in the House while Turner practised law full-time in Toronto. Complaints were raised only when he bucked the system of party loyalty by backing Mulroney's Persian Gulf War policy. Liberals than carped publicly about his absence from caucus. The day after he broke ranks, the locks on Turner's Centre Block office were changed. His staff was told to pack up and move to the Confederation Building. Having suitably punished Turner, few MPs demanded that he keep his promise to resign so that his constituents could elect an active member.

The same thing happened to David Kilgour, Turner's brother-in-law, when he was thrown from the Tory caucus and fell into the arms of the Liberals. Kilgour had occupied the same Centre Block office since 1979. After his rebellion on the GST vote he was ordered to move to another building. "It seems to me that it demeans the institution and that we're caught in a game of petty revenge," he said. Kilgour was not alone in losing a favored office for a party offence that had little to do with the way he served his electors. Tory and Liberal MPs who left to form the Bloc Québécois were victims of an office shuffle orchestrated by all three party whips. When Bloc MP Louis Plamondon refused to leave his office, the speaker sent in the movers during the weekend while he was away in his riding.

Another thing the system abhors is an MP who questions the lavish perks and services that parliamentarians receive. Conservative Guy St.-Julien caused an uproar in December 1990 when he suggested that MPs and senators should chop 20 per cent from their budgets, including perks and expenses. "I don't think I will become very popular," St-Julien confessed. "But I don't care. I think we should set an example when the economy is in a bad period."

Poor St-Julien was nearly tarred and feathered by his caucus for his breach of its code of self-interest. "I will not support it," roared twelve-year veteran Conservative Bill Domm. "I couldn't live. It wouldn't be profitable for me to stay here. I'd be forced into early retirement." Fernand Jourdenais cried that MPs are having a hard time making ends meet, while colleague Bob Hicks noted that MPs took a $1,000 pay cut in 1987 and Canadians did not seem to care. "If we took a pay cut they'd still think we were overpaid when in reality we are underpaid."

St-Julien stuck to his lonely trail of honor and took more unpopular action. He became the first MP to disclose a detailed list of operating expenses to the 85,000 constituents in his northern Quebec riding. "I open my books for my people and for the people of Canada," declared the backwoods MP, who released a six-page statement detailing $50,000 in expenses for his Ottawa, Val d'Or, Senneterre and Amos offices for the previous three months. "My job is for my people."

The release of the information did not set off a stampede of other MPs to do the same. St-Julien's action was met with seething silence from most colleagues. Conservative caucus boss Robert Layton dismissed the disclosures as a re-election ploy. "All this puzzles me," Layton told the *Hill Times*, a lively weekly that is pulling the secret shroud from Parliament. "I think most of us do our best and use our best judgement [on spending the money], which is a little like motherhood." If St-Julien's actions were simply an election ploy, it is surprising that no other Tories tried it in an attempt to escape their rock-bottom rating in the polls.

When Reform MP Deborah Grey and Senator Stan Waters held a news conference to announce that they would give up 10 per cent of their basic pay, other parliamentarians dismissed their position as shameful grandstanding. They also noted unhappily that the public seemed to like the idea.

Parliament's $291-million budget is a drop in the $159-billion bucket of Ottawa spending. MPs have a legitimate claim to adequate pay and many of the services they receive. But their excessive luxury and perks have made them a class apart from the people they serve. They have totally shielded themselves from the daily pain and suffering that a recession has inflicted on other Canadians. The good life provided by the royal court to its members creates an incentive for seeking office that has nothing to do with public service. The lavish lifestyle behind Parliament's walls sets a disgraceful example for other custodians of taxpayers' dollars and does more than anything else to bring our primary political institution into disrepute.

6
ABOVE THE LAW

"To say that Members of Parliament are like everyone else is nonsense. They are special. They are handed special responsibilities and there is no greater responsibility than the protection of the democratic institution itself."

JIM HAWKES, MP, NOVEMBER 1990

THE GREEN SHUTTLE BUS STOPPED SMARTLY AT THE WEST entrance to the Centre Block on a chilly November afternoon in 1990. Question Period was about to begin, the one event that still draws members into the chamber. Among those rolling off the bus for that day's dramatics was Conservative Bill Kempling, the amiable Humpty-Dumpty MP for Burlington.

Staring at him as he stepped down was a stuffed pig wearing a bib and placard asking, "Where's the Trough?" Beside the porker was a set of foam dice and a large sign screaming "Impeach Lyin' Brian." They were the props of Glen Kealey whose own brand of parliamentary theatre is to stand in the shadow of the Peace Tower decrying Tory corruption at the top of his lungs. He'd done it daily for three years.

Kealey is a former advertising executive and real-estate developer whose allegations of bribes, kickbacks and fraud against top Conservatives are now before the courts. He had left his familiar beat by the MPs' door for a little lunch-time picketing on busy Wellington Street, a hundred yards away. The pig and the signs were Kealey's own creations. The big green dice had been given to him by a Toronto woman. She was responding to Mulroney's boast that he had deliberately timed the First Ministers' Conference in June to "roll the dice" at the eleventh hour of the Meech Lake constitutional negotiations. Kealey had left his valuables in the care of a quiet co-demonstrator, Father Tony Van Hee.

115

The slight Catholic priest with the twinkling eyes and warm smile was an odd foil for the brash, bellowing Kealey. The Jesuit, a classical scholar and long-time pastor on Indian reservations, had maintained an anti-abortion vigil for more than a year. In that time he and Kealey had developed a protective sense about one another and the little protest patch from which they pitted themselves against the establishment.

Kempling, a nineteen-year parliamentary veteran who clearly resented Kealey's daily cries of Tory corruption, grabbed the unattended items and stalked towards the Centre Block door.

"You can't take those. They aren't yours," exclaimed a startled Van Hee as he chased after the rotund MP.

"They don't belong to you," retorted Kempling, apparently unconcerned that the pig, dice and sign did not belong to him either.

Van Hee was trapped outside when Kempling, dropping the pig en route, huffed his way into the Centre Block where entry is restricted to MPs, employees and media with security passes.

"I just took them from where they were and put them in the garbage at the back of the building," Kempling said later. "I didn't take them off the Hill. That's getting rid of pollution. I don't think people can come on Parliament Hill and erect a sign and just walk away and leave it there."

Incensed by Kempling's cavalier disposal of his friend's property, Van Hee approached David Kilgour for help in retrieving the purloined dice and sign. Kilgour, who had recently been booted from the Tory caucus for his anti-GST vote, now had a brand-new case of arrogance to avenge. He stormed into the Commons building. A bemused security guard told the furious Kilgour he could find the missing items in a garbage container behind the building.

If the issue was ownership of a soiled, stuffed pig, it would have ended there. But to Kilgour it was clearly a matter of even-handed justice, of one law for all. When Kealey filed a complaint with Ottawa police, trial lawyer Kilgour supported it with a written statement. "One of the questions in this incident is whether MPs are subject to our criminal laws like other citizens. In the early 1600s, Sir

Edward Coke established for all time in Britain that even kings are not above the law," he said.

Kealey failed to have charges laid against Kempling because police said that there was insufficient evidence. Undeterred, he went to Justice of the Peace Terry Pasch, who ruled that there was no intent to commit a crime. "If we are going to engage the police in silly things like this, then I think it's a waste of time," Kempling complained. In Kealey's view, Kempling's action was at least as serious as the Doug Small budget affair in 1989. He said his stuffed dice were worth $10, more than a thousand times the value of the booklet of budget-leak fame. Pasch reversed his decision in June 1991 and summoned Kempling to court to answer charges he stole the sign and pair of fuzzy dice.

The silly incident in fact underlines a disturbing truth about our elected representatives. MPs and cabinet ministers increasingly act as though there is one law for "ordinary" Canadians and another for themselves. Examples of the double standard are everywhere on and around Parliament Hill. In fact there is a triple standard in both social and legal matters, with ministers at the top, MPs next and ordinary Canadians lagging behind.

Most MPs caught committing an infraction don't plead innocent, they simply plead that they're members of Parliament. The clear message is that other people's rules don't apply to them. This sense of immunity emerges in dozens of daily incidents. Ministerial limousines idle for hours in the fire lanes outside the Confederation Building. Their drivers routinely turn left, illegally, from Parliament Hill onto Wellington Street during rush hour. Speed limits, naturally, are made to be broken.

Former CPR station agent Les Benjamin has learned a bit about special treatment in his twenty-three years as a Saskatchewan MP. He was so offended by a $7 parking ticket a while back that he rose on a question of privilege in the Commons to protest. He was indeed parked illegally on Parliament Hill but as an MP that didn't count. His ticket was cancelled with apologies.

While petty in themselves, such incidents reflect an attitude of indifference or contempt for the laws that govern other Canadians. MPs' belief that they are immune to the rules results in far more serious misdeeds and cover-ups. There have also been troubling assaults on free speech, freedom of association and due process, all guaranteed in the Charter of Rights and Freedoms. The principle of ministerial responsibility has been flouted so often it's rarely cited anymore. In today's world a minister who doesn't have a smoking gun in each hand is clearly innocent legally, and thus morally.

One of the oldest, though not necessarily the wisest, parliamentary traditions is that of budget secrecy. The code of ministerial responsibility requires that a finance minister resign in the event of a leak. Marc Lalonde, the former Liberal minister, allowed a TV crew to shoot a few paragraphs of his budget while he did some pre-release mugging for the cameras. He kept his job by adding $200 million to government spending, thus invalidating the figures on film. As a Trudeau finance minister, he found that a lot funnier than taxpayers did.

In the 1989 budget-leak case, the RCMP were co-opted by the government in a prosecution for which they had no heart and little legal ground. The political objectives were twofold: to let the media know the price they would pay for looking where they shouldn't and to save Michael Wilson's skin. The government won on both points, while losing the legal case.

Doug Small, the zealous Ottawa bureau chief for Global TV, could not know what a legal horror story he was about to unleash when he drove to an Ottawa gas bar in response to an anonymous tip. There, the night before Wilson's fifth budget, Small was handed a "Budget in Brief" pamphlet by a tipster whom he had not met before and could not describe afterwards. John Appleby, who handed it over, and Norman Belisle, who gave it to Appleby's son after taking it from a trash container at the government's Hull printing plant, also had no idea what they were getting into.

Minutes later, when he went on the air with the tiny booklet, worth less than a cent, Small assumed that it could force Wilson's resignation. He could not have been more wrong. Small's scoop did compel Wilson to release his budget twenty-four hours ahead of schedule. But the resignation never came. Instead of asking Wilson to resign, the prime minister took the offensive. Mulroney declared in the Commons that the leak was "a crime. . . . Somebody stole, apparently stole, government documents." To the opposition MPs screaming for Wilson's head, he said, "Honorable members should be concerned about the person who stole the property."

Mulroney's rant set in motion a month-long police investigation, which resulted in charges against all three "budget bandits." It produced a year-long court battle that cost Global TV $100,000 and almost ruined Appleby, a Korean war veteran with a bad heart and little money. The hapless clerk wanted to sell his modest, mortgaged house, but was told that, if he did, the first bill he would have to pay would be $15,000 for legal aid in the budget case. After paying other bills he ran up during the ordeal, he would be broke. Not only did that seem a high price for an innocent man to pay to defend himself against the government, it also demonstrated a clear double standard. Take just one example, that of millionaire Sinclair Stevens. While never charged and convicted, the former minister was run out of office by Mulroney when an investigation showed that there were serious improprieties in how he conducted his dual roles of businessman and cabinet minister. The taxpayers picked up the $300,000 legal tab for Stevens after the inquiry was completed. In the end, legal aid forgave the loans to Appleby, but only after he launched a highly publicized campaign.

In the Small budget case, the charges were thrown out in July 1990 by Ontario Provincial Court Judge James Fontana. In a fifty-one-page decision he said that the prosecution should never have been launched. He scorched the RCMP and Crown attorneys for prosecuting a case "offensive to the principles of fundamental justice and fair play." He accepted the word of Mulroney's then-chief of staff, Stanley Hartt, that the prosecution was not politically motivated, but concluded that it was an "abuse of power."

Staff Sergeant Richard Jordan, a lawyer, had testified that his superiors wanted to teach journalists a lesson while pleasing their political masters. Especially eager to see Small prosecuted, he said, was RCMP Deputy Commissioner Henry Jensen, who then claimed that his surprise resignation in the midst of the furore was unrelated to the Small case.

Although the charges were quashed, the case was hardly cause for media jubilation. Respected Thomson News columnist Stewart MacLeod noted that the Mulroney charges and police action got the budget leak instantly out of Parliament where its damage would be impossible to control. It drew attention away from a second leak, to the business community. In his judgment, Judge Fontana said that Small may have prevented profiteering from a collateral budget leak to Mutual Life of Canada, a leak the government covered up for weeks.

Most important to the government, the police involvement saved Wilson. "Every word was orchestrated," a close aide to Mulroney said about the prime minister's quick reaction to the "crime." "Just remember his primary task was political – to save the hide of Michael Wilson. And the only way was to take the view that the finance minister was the victim of a criminal act for which he could not reasonably be held responsible. The alternative was to accept the leak as carelessness, and if he did this, the finance minister would be dead meat."

To most Canadians the whole thing may seem somewhat overblown. After all the little booklet had simply been plucked from a waste-bin where it had been discarded with hundreds of others because the cover was stapled on upside down. And besides, who could really expect a finance minister to take the rap for a goof-up like that? The Conservatives, of course. Here's a bit of what they said six years earlier when the roving camera picked out those few numbers in Marc Lalonde's budget just hours before he unveiled it in the House.

"Budget secrecy is a basic principle of our traditions of parliamentary government," roared acting opposition leader Erik Nielsen. "A breach of budget secrecy has always and invariably led to the resignation of the minister." After Nielsen, Joe Clark weighed in: "The traditions are well established that there is not to be release, deliberate or inadvertent, of the contents of budget material prior to presentation in the House." Unless, of course, it happens to be by a Tory minister.

The Doug Small affair damaged the RCMP's cherished reputation for independence from government. It certainly left a bad taste in the mouth of Richard Grosse, chairman of the RCMP public-complaints commission. He took the Mounties to Federal Court after their refusal to co-operate with his efforts to launch an inquiry into the case. Grosse's watch-dog agency was trying to determine why charges were laid even though the RCMP knew that no crime had been committed. The appeal was rejected.

The budget fiasco also betrayed the tattered tradition of ministerial responsibility. It clearly demonstrated Mulroney's willingness to use the law and the police for his own purposes. And it casts a chill over the media, whose legal costs for a single legitimate news story can run to $100,000 if the government wants to use taxpayers' money to fight it. The inexhaustible resources of government can clearly scare news organizations away from important stories. Investigative stories often begin with tips provided by ordinary people like Appleby. When the public sees the price exacted for a scrap of waste paper taken out of a garbage can and handed to a reporter, such scoops will be even more rare.

Just how ruthlessly the government wields its power became clear when the might of the law again came down on Kealey and his hapless fellow protester, Father Van Hee.

On a warm day in March 1990, MPs and reporters leaving the Commons after Question Period were startled to see the two protesters engaged in a tense face-off with four RCMP officers. They had just been told that they had breached a new regulation prohibiting demonstrations within 50 metres (160 feet) of Parliament's doors. Under the delighted blaze of television cameras two burly Mounties dragged the frail Jesuit priest to a patrol car from the spot he had occupied for 140 days.

Moments later three Mounties started to do the same to Kealey. New Democratic Party MP Dave Barrett and Liberal Eugène Bellemare grabbed Kealey's arm and tugged, furiously demanding to know why he was being arrested. "We're trying to have a conversation with a private citizen and here you are standing behind us as if you are the KGB in the 1950s," barked Bellemare. The irrepressible Kealey was finally shoved into a police car, hollering from the window as he was whisked away, "Ceausescu, Noriega, Mulroney – two down and one to go." Van Hee and Kealey were charged with being public nuisances, for which they faced maximum fines of $400 upon conviction.

Kealey's protest had gone largely unreported until then. Parliament's many picketers are usually regarded as little more than a kooky adornment to our democratic system. But the arrests made it clear he was getting under the skin of Tory ministers and MPs. His daily shouts of "Buy your Tory MPs here" were becoming more than ribald entertainment for Hill tourists. His loud advice to students on school visits to "check your wallets" before entering the Parliament Buildings obviously rankled. Each day Kealey would bellow, "Resign, resign," whenever Brian Mulroney glided to the west door in his shiny limousine. That so annoyed the prime minister that he shifted his drop-off point to the Peace Tower entrance some thirty yards away from Kealey's prime position. Mulroney then had to walk back to his office on the third floor near the west entrance and listen to Kealey's incessant shouts as he worked at his desk.

One month before the restrictive cabinet order was passed, security guards were sent to attack the snowbank where Kealey parked his placards while shouting at passing Tories about patronage and corruption. The leather-lunged nag simply shovelled the snow back and dished out more insults. Such persistence finally got results in the "Glen Kealey regulation" to limit the path of protest.

Kealey was once a Conservative riding officer in Hull. He launched his loud, lonely crusade after an office-complex deal he was promoting collapsed. He claimed that a former Tory cabinet minister, identified in the Commons as the now-retired head of Public Works, Roch LaSalle, had asked for a $5,000 bribe in 1986, to ensure, Kealey said, that the federal government would occupy part of the building. When he refused to pay up, according to Kealey, his project died and he was forced into bankruptcy. LaSalle called him a liar. The Mounties said that their probe had turned up no evidence that would allow them to lay charges. Kealey went to court.

The arrests of Kealey and Van Hee touched off a storm of outrage both inside and outside the Commons. Government House leader Harvie Andre claimed that the regulation was needed to stiffen Parliament's nuisance regulations because Ottawa taxi drivers had once blocked access to the buildings during a rowdy display by GST opponents. The risk that emergency vehicles would not have access to Parliament during demonstrations was something that the government had suddenly discovered more than a century after Confederation.

Opposition MPs accused cabinet of using an underhanded procedure to stifle protest. Andre tried to hand responsibility off to the all-party Board of Internal Economy, which oversees administration of the Commons. The board had been examining ways to restrict vehicles after the taxi incident. However, cabinet alone amended the Public Works Nuisance Regulations to ban organized protest or "any loud, disruptive noise" within fifty metres of any parliamentary doorway.

The arrests became a fiasco for the government and the RCMP, already tarnished by the budget-leak case. Liberal and NDP members mounted loud protests in daily defiance of the cabinet order as bewildered Mounties looked on. Even a few Tories joined the cause, including Pat Nowlan, who was to leave caucus a few months later. "This is the Parliament of the people," he fumed.

Andre later admitted that the regulation was designed to get Kealey. "The problem is not with the priest. It is with the other fellow who is yelling insults. If he would just walk around silently," lamented Andre, who had been a loud and sometimes violent critic when he felt Trudeau Liberals were guilty of abuse in the past. "Is it unreasonable for me to ask that I be able to access this building without someone calling me names? If I were in a different line of work I'd be tempted to go over and punch him in the nose." Few who know Andre doubted it for a moment.

While he and opposition MPs were duking it out on the Commons floor, Van Hee and Kealey were languishing in jail. They were promised release only if they agreed not to return to the Hill. They refused and were carted off to join the junkies, rapists and robbers who inhabit the cells of the Ottawa-Carleton Detention Centre. They were there for four days. Van Hee, weak after a 126-day fast, was mocked and threatened by young inmates. A bully who had been moved temporarily from maximum security to the fourteen-inmate dormitory menaced Van Hee and squirted toothpaste over his sheets and pillows. Kealey naturally drew a political parallel: "The bully ran the show. He'd grab the soup and dessert at meals and control it, dishing it out as favors. He's like the prime minister who has the goodies and hands out perks to politicians."

The whole sorry event turned into a major gaffe in government public relations. Kealey was no longer just a loud-mouthed nutcase. He was a valiant champion of democracy, not just in his own eyes but in the view of others. Newspaper editorials flailed the government. "It is a bad law, badly made, with sinister consequences," protested the *Ottawa Citizen*. "It is a ham-handed attempt to quarantine the lawmakers from legitimate protest," chided the *Vancouver Province*. Kealey was invited to speak about democracy to audiences as far away as Saskatchewan and British Columbia.

In the face of unrelenting criticism, justice minister Kim Campbell dropped the controversial charges. She said in a statement that it would not be in the "best interests of the proper administration of justice" to continue the prosecution of the self-styled corruption crusader and the philosopher priest.

"I didn't think they'd be stupid enough to go to court," beamed Kealey, who by then had been arrested three more times in Hull for plastering lampposts and parking metres with "Impeach Lyin' Brian" stickers. But the regulation remains in effect, and the two protesters are kept fifty metres away by barricades erected supposedly as a precaution during the Persian Gulf War. Van Hee was charged again in March 7, 1991, for protesting in front of the barricades. Judge Paul Belanger acquitted him in June and slammed the RCMP for laying charges that were "arbitrary, unnecessary and unjust." Belanger said police must realize that protesters have a right to speak their minds. "If freedom of speech is not seen to be cherished there [Parliament Hill], how can it be seen to be cherished elsewhere?"

Free speech is a fundamental but delicate right. In efforts to silence an annoying critic, the government showed the kind of dangerous intolerance that can put it at risk. Apart from noisy statements that may have embarrassed his targets, the unemployed businessman posed no threat. He did not impede access to Parliament. Nevertheless, because he irritated the prime minister, police were empowered to suppress the right of a Canadian citizen to protest on Parliament's doorstep.

In fact, Kealey is not the loudest, the most dangerous or the most bizarre in a long list of Canadians who've unleashed their frustrations on Parliament. Charles Yacoub did it in April 1989 with a gun and a Greyhound bus full of hostages. He fired a few shots out the window at the world in general then settled in for a ten-hour stand-off before he finally surrendered. He was charged, tried, convicted and sentenced to six years in jail. There wasn't much the law could do about Paul Joseph Chartier, who took his protest inside the Centre Block on May 18, 1965. He died in a shattered washroom just steps from the Commons chamber, the victim of a mistimed fuse on his own dynamite bomb.

Most of the others have been as harmless as Kealey. And some have been even more colorful. Top prize for creative flair probably should go to Michael Robertson, a farmer protesting the projected expropriation of land in 1973 for the proposed Pickering airport. With the help of a truck, a towline and a huge orange kite, he took to the air some 170 metres above Parliament's snow-covered lawns. As he glided down, circling between the Peace Tower and the Eternal Flame, Robertson yelled to neck-craning onlookers that such pure flight was the only kind his region would permit. Although he was refused RCMP permission to take his cause aloft, Robertson escaped almost scot-free. His only penalty – a ticket for running a stop sign with the truck that got him airborne. The airport he opposed was never built.

Remarkably few demonstrators have faced criminal charges, although many have been muscled off-stage by authorities. For those who cause a disturbance in the Commons galleries there remains the threat of being taken into custody by the sergeant-at-arms, who can levy a four-dollar fine, a sum that has not changed since 1867. There's no record that anyone ever paid for exuberant self-expression by serving time in the old cell, now gone, that the Centre Block once boasted.

All kinds of things have been tossed down on members to express views much like Kealey's. A cup of human waste splattered a few New Democrats in 1985, and a carton of ox's blood exploded on the centre aisle carpet twenty years ago. In October 1991 disgruntled students showered MPs with dry macaroni and protest cards. Many demonstrators find that the best way to attract attention and TV cameras is to bring a gang. Parliament Hill has seen pork producers with their pigs, food-price protesters beating pots and pans and even, in 1975, a beauty queen, posing in a Canadian flag and nothing else for a magazine layout in front of the Eternal Flame. None of these protests drew the response from the authorities that Kealey has.

In other distressing instances, lawmakers have flouted the law by using "parliamentary privilege" and certain immunities it provides. Parliamentary privilege exists to ensure that the people's representatives are free to work in the public interest. Embodied in the Constitution Act of 1867, the privilege protects the right of a member to speak in Parliament without fear of harassment for what he or she says. It exempts MPs and senators from jury duty because of their obligations to serve the nation's highest court, Parliament. It exempts them from enforced appearances as witnesses for the same reason, and from arrest in civil cases. They do not receive special immunity against criminal charges.

Members rise frequently on questions of privilege that have to do with parliamentary business, but the right is invoked only rarely, and not frivolously, outside.

Prime Minister Pierre Trudeau and his finance minister, Edgar Benson, used it successfully in 1971 when they were being sued by the Roman Corporation for damaging statements made in the House and repeated later in correspondence. André Ouellet was less successful six years later. He was found guilty of contempt of court when he questioned a judge's sanity. As consumer affairs minister, Ouellet was outraged when a Quebec judge threw out price-fixing charges laid by his department. Unfortunately, he delivered his intemperate outburst to reporters in the Commons lobby, not in the House itself. The court ruled that immunity did not apply outside the chamber.

In a couple of cases during the 1970s judges ruled that police cannot enter an MP's office in search of documents without first obtaining the speaker's permission. The members involved – Tory Flora MacDonald in 1973 and New Democrat Terry Sargeant in 1979 – were not suspected of any crime.

The most recent case when privilege was invoked involved David Kilgour, who was subpoenaed as a witness in a libel action. He claimed parliamentary immunity, refusing to appear in court or disclose information he had gained because of his position as an MP on the grounds that it would "be a violation of each and every Canadian citizen's inalienable but unspoken right to deal in a confidential and privileged manner with a Member of Parliament." Madame Justice Patricia Proudfoot threatened him with a contempt-of-court charge. The stand-off ended when the lawyers involved withdrew the request to have Kilgour testify. Commons speaker John Fraser then rebuked the judge for failing to respect parliamentary privilege. In his ruling, Fraser detailed how immunity applies in such cases.

The lecture must have stuck in the mind of Dave Barrett. During his years as a social worker, B.C. premier and hot-line host, "little fat Dave" has prided himself on being a champion of the underdog, an image he tried to parlay into leadership of the NDP in late 1989 after Ed Broadbent stepped down. Barrett's halo slipped soon after that bid failed, however, and he proved he understood power and privilege and how to use them on his own behalf.

David Berman, a graphic artist who had worked on Barrett's leadership campaign, claimed that $5,423.05 of his $10,000 total bill had gone unpaid. Calls to Barrett and key members of his campaign team had proven fruitless. Berman finally launched a civil suit. A court date was set, November 15, 1990, and Barrett was subpoenaed to appear. Incredibly, the passionate David who had taken on a thousand Goliaths invoked parliamentary immunity to avoid appearing.

The Commons legal staff was put to work composing a letter to the Provincial Court explaining why Barrett would not respond to its summons and outlining the legal basis for parliamentary immunity. The letter cited "the paramount right of Parliament to the attendance and service of its members" even though the court date was one on which the Commons was not sitting. As it turned out, Barrett didn't want to appear that day because he was to be the speaker at a conference on pensions in Hawaii.

Barrett insisted that his use of parliamentary immunity was "standard procedure," although Commons lawyers described it as rare. A former law clerk, Joseph Maingot, said he had received only two or three inquiries about immunity during his stint as the

Commons' top law officer from 1976 to 1982. "It was inappropriate," he said of Barrett's misuse of the "medieval" privilege.

"I'm not shirking any responsibility. I'm not hiding behind any parliamentary law. I just made it very clear to Mr. Pelletier [chief parliamentary counsel Marcel Pelletier] that I wasn't available that day," pleaded Barrett to reporters.

To Berman, and to Barrett's fellow MPs, the action smacked of special use of a rare privilege to allow him to go on a cushy trip that had little to do with his work as an MP. "By hiding behind this immunity, Mr. Barrett is showing there are two standards – one for politicians and one for ordinary Canadians," Berman complained.

The case became much messier before it ended. Berman alleged that Barrett's campaign committee had tried to settle part of the bill by giving him tax-deductible receipts for mythical political contributions. In correspondence released by Berman, a campaign representative offered a tax receipt for $1,000 in lieu of payment for some outstanding bills. Such a transaction would clearly be illegal. Politicians are not allowed to issue tax receipts for contributions to leadership races (even when such contributions are made). Donors can receive them only for money they provide to the party. The party can then forward 85 per cent of the total to a designated candidate. No matter how the squirming political agents tried to explain it, the idea made no sense to Berman. He would have had to contribute a cheque to the NDP in addition to the services he had provided to the Barrett campaign.

Berman also alleged that Barrett's workers offered receipts "greater than the value that you can give a person" and at one point even offered receipts to his girlfriend to settle his claim. "They said they didn't have any money because they didn't win the leadership, so they started offering me tax receipts."

New Democrat MP David Stupich, an accountant who was once B.C. finance minister and Barrett's campaign treasurer, at first denied Berman's allegations. Fortunately for the artist, he still had a copy of a letter from another Barrett worker, lawyer David Perry, who was an aide to MP Chris Axworthy. It said "our campaign can offer tax receipts." When Perry's letter was read to Stupich, he retracted his earlier denial and explained that the offer was an inadvertent error. "He's wrong. He's confused about the process," Stupich said. "That's wrong. As a treasurer I would never have entered into this at all."

By this time the whole fishy business was receiving wide coverage in newspapers and on radio and TV. Other MPs quickly closed in for their pound of Barrett's flesh. "This reeks, man. It's sick," opined Conservative MP Felix Holtmann, the husky Manitoba pig farmer who doubled as chairman of the Culture Committee. Liberal Don Boudria, who styles himself "patronage critic," complained that, because the civil suit and Hawaiian trip had nothing to do with Barrett's parliamentary duties, he had misused the privilege principle. Sheila Copps, the feisty Liberal from Hamilton East who never misses a scandal, real or imagined, termed Barrett's use of privilege "outrageous." She said it gave a "black eye" to all politicians.

Five days after Berman's story was published in the *Sun* newspaper chain, Barrett settled the embarrassing lawsuit. As part of the agreement, neither side could discuss the details of the settlement. Barrett accused both Liberal and Conservative critics of "crass smearing" of his reputation, but said nothing about his use of parliamentary privilege or the merits of paying bills on time.

The immunity Barrett claimed was never meant to grant MPs special status in handling their political or private affairs. However, its use strengthened public suspicion that the welfare that parliamentarians are primarily interested in is their own, and that they invoke special rules to protect it. Several Conservatives spluttered briefly about a Commons inquiry into the case. Of course nothing was done. Cooler heads realized that such probes invariably reveal enough questionable behavior and raw greed to damage all MPs. When cornered, the natural reflex of a politician is to fling mud at a rival. Everybody gets splattered. That's why examinations of the ethical and legal conduct of parliamentarians are few and, if possible, confidential.

One of the most fundamentally undemocratic pieces of legislation in Canadian history was working its way through the House of Commons when Barrett was under fire. It was a measure most MPs hoped would escape public notice, and the distractions of

Oka, Kuwait and the GST accomplished that almost until it became law. Very simply, the proposed law would have curbed police investigations of federal politicians. The circumstances that produced the proposed Bill C-79 are a classic example of how the spoiled colony on Parliament Hill considers itself above the laws that apply to other Canadians.

On December 12, 1989, RCMP commissioner Norman Inkster set off an explosion on Parliament Hill with his disclosure to a Commons committee that Mounties were investigating fifteen MPs and senators. Four politicians were under investigation for violations of the Elections Act, eleven for other crimes. Two of those under scrutiny were senators – Mulroney's buddy Michel Cogger and Liberal Hazen Argue, who was later charged with fraud. In answer to committee questions, Inkster said that his officers had investigated more than thirty of Ottawa's political office-holders in the past five years.

Instead of being distressed about the large number of possible miscreants in their midst, MPs expressed outrage at Inkster. They accused the Mounties of engaging in "fishing expeditions" and talked darkly of police vendettas against politicians who criticized the force. "It is no exaggeration to say that we were somewhat angered by the news, given that the conduct of police investigations, whether or not a conviction results, can hinder and, we can appreciate, ruin a parliamentary career," remarked Liberal Jean-Robert Gauthier. In fact the list of parliamentarians who have survived inquiries, criminal investigations and even convictions is a long one. Their survival record after such experiences is as good as that of other Canadians. But the view that careful police scrutiny might help to keep the place honest and reassure the public was never expressed by members.

One should know that it costs some $229 million to keep the House of Commons in business each year. If that is divided by the number of members, 295, a per-member-price of more than $770,000 is produced. Control over much of that spending is in the hands of individual MPs, who get more dollars and more discretion every year. And more temptations to fiddle with such items as office budgets.

For some time members had been concerned that the RCMP did not understand how MPs dispense those burgeoning office allowances of, at present, $165,000 a year. They felt that the Mounties used the complicated *Members Services Manual* as a "bible" to launch trivial investigations. The manual attempts to separate allowable expenses from those considered too partisan for taxpayers to cover. The Mounties had initiated inquiries over the use of travel vouchers and free phone privileges for partisan purposes by officeholders and those around them.

Many members felt that they were entitled to do more or less what they wanted with office funds and facilities. They contended that many political expenses are legitimate costs of running a politician's office. A Quebec judge partly agreed when he dismissed breach-of-trust charges against Conservative Jean-Luc Joncas in March 1990. He chided the Mounties for conducting a witch-hunt. Tory Pierre Vincent fought an RCMP raid on his office by arguing that MPs have absolute discretion over the use of office budgets. He was investigated and later exonerated for paying a university student $10,000 to mail greeting cards and speeches to his Trois-Rivières constituents.

Other MPs grumbled about having their names dragged through the mud over minor electoral violations. Conservative John Reimer said he did not learn he was under investigation for electoral spending irregularities in 1985 until he read about it in his home-town paper, the *Kitchener-Waterloo Record*. He could not obtain details of the allegations for days afterwards, and it took him fifteen weeks to get cleared. Both concerns could easily have been settled by clarifying the expenditure rules in the manual and by changing the Elections Act to prevent the disclosure of investigations. Of course, members generally prefer the fuzzy rules that provide some leeway for interpretation of questionable spending.

Two days after Inkster's bombshell revelations, a special Commons committee was struck, chaired by Quebec Tory Marcel Danis, to study the "duties and responsibilities" of members of Parliament. It quickly became apparent that our elected representatives were concerned primarily about their privileges, not their responsibilities.

The work of the committee was deemed so important by the government that Danis remained its chairman even after he was named to cabinet as sports minister to replace Jean Charest, who was forced to resign in January for phoning a judge. In its February report, the committee proclaimed the right of MPs to use their office budgets and staff, for partisan as well as non-partisan purposes, free from "interference or intimidation" by the RCMP.

After months of hearings, many in secret, the committee gave the draft bill to the Tory House leader for what was supposed to be a quick trip through the Commons. If passed, it would have required the RCMP to consult the Board of Internal Economy before searching MPs' or senators' offices, tapping their phones or laying criminal charges against them for mishandling office budgets. The board could have blocked any investigation for thirty days while preparing its own legal opinion. The committee originally wanted a ninety-day delay, but even the members concluded that was more warning than any parliamentarian needed. Judges would have to review the opinion of the board of MPs before authorizing a wiretap, search warrant, restraining order, summons or arrest warrant linked to an investigation of any member's expenses.

Nothing could have more clearly granted preferential treatment to our representatives in Parliament and created a two-tier justice system than these proposals. The plan was presented the day before the summer recess began, part of the government strategy for getting quick approval without debate.

There was barely a peep of protest. Only then-NDP justice critic Svend Robinson objected. One of the most committed civil libertarians in Parliament, Robinson denounced the all-party deal to give "sweeping and unprecedented powers" to the Commons own Board of Internal Economy. "I believe the public would perceive this as being the old boy's club looking out for themselves," he said in interrupting the bill's smooth progress. NDP whip Iain Angus and colleague Rod Murphy, who had sat on the special committee, felt that the police should consult the board, although they objected to the thirty-day delay before action could be taken. Gauthier also supported the measures. But then-opposition leader Herb Gray was more guarded. He wanted the bill studied by a parliamentary committee before taking a final position. Meanwhile, the legislation was approved in principle in less than ten minutes on June 27. That was the last order of business before the House shut down for three months. Reporters hardly noticed as it zipped in and out of the House.

Certainly the prime minister had good reason to push the bill through. He was under intense pressure from members of his Quebec caucus to get the RCMP off their backs. The Mounties' recent success rate in nailing Tory MPs was quite high. In the past two years Michel Gravel, Richard Grisé and Edouard Desrosier had pleaded guilty to criminal charges after pocketing money from their office allotment. MPs Gilles Bernier and Gabriel Fontaine were charged with fraud and breach of trust. Two Ontario MPs – Terry Clifford (London-Middlesex) and Bob Hicks (Scarborough East) – were under scrutiny for having hired each other's daughters to skirt the prohibition against employing immediate family. The RCMP cleared them of criminal wrongdoing.

To assuage his angry Quebec caucus and stem the flood of desertions to Lucien Bouchard's Bloc Québécois, the prime minister promised quick action on the bill. Angus and Murphy claim that they were approached in June by industry [now health] minister Benoît Bouchard, the newly appointed Quebec lieutenant, for a deal. According to the two New Democrats, "Benny" told them that the Quebec caucus had insisted on having the bill passed without amendments, and Mulroney had agreed. Tory whip Jim Hawkes told a later committee meeting that his caucus had been assured that action would be taken to rein in the horsemen.

When the committee resumed its study of the bill in September, its business drew little media attention. The headlines were about battles on Indian reserves, in the Persian Gulf and in the Senate. Once again it took the RCMP commissioner to draw public attention to the dangerous legislation. In appearances before the committee on October and November, Inkster declared that it would be too easy for members of the Board of Internal Economy to tip off friends who were under investigation. What MPs were attempting was to give themselves a thirty-day warning to clear incriminating evidence from their files and prepare a defence even before an investigation was complete.

"This necessary disclosure could compromise the evidence, breach the confidentiality of sources and witnesses, and possibly jeopardize other criminal processes," said Inkster, adding that MPs needed clear spending rules and insisting that the force was interested in criminal misconduct, not administrative violations.

MPs began back-pedaling. Liberals and New Democrats said they would not support the bill unless the thirty-day clause was removed. The Tories, led by Hawkes and supported by former Tory François Gérin, now a Bloc Québécois member, were determined to send it back to the House unamended.

NDP House leader Nelson Riis could sense which way the wind was blowing. He launched a public crusade to block the bill's passage. At a news conference he attacked the Tories for using their majority on the committee to return the bill for final reading. "It's outrageous. It's disgusting. It's despicable," Riis thundered. Although not a committee member, Riis kept up a daily assault on the bill. Predictably, that led to a whispering campaign to discredit him. A number of Tory MPs (whom he refused to identify) suggested that Riis was trying to stop the bill to gain special treatment himself from the RCMP. "They were saying I was helping Inkster because I was under police investigation, and you know, maybe by helping Inkster they'd back off."

Despite its underlying seriousness, the raging debate produced some moments of comedy. Many of them featured Hawkes, the rotund clinical psychologist from Calgary. Reporters chuckled when he discounted Inkster's fear that MPs could be tipped off by their friends about police investigations. There was no such danger because MPs "very, very rarely" divulge sensitive information. He also made it clear the RCMP should not look to MPs for help. "We have 400 years of history, saying we shouldn't give out information to police forces." At one point, some members, including Gérin, argued that "a member is not a public servant." Hawkes even told the Commons that MPs are not to be treated like other Canadians. "To say that members of Parliament are like everyone else is nonsense. They are special. They are handed special responsibilities, and there is no greater responsibility than the protection of the democratic institution itself."

The ability of members to confuse their own interests with those of Parliament was never clearer. It's obvious that what is needed is proper conduct by the people we elect, not some scheme to prevent investigation of their conduct. If the place has fallen into disrepute, it's not because police are poking around, but because there's so much for them to look into. Ideally, of course, we expect our representatives to be above reproach, not simply above the law.

Faced with pressure from mounting public criticism and raging newspaper editorials, the government revised the bill, abandoning the thirty-day provision. Mounties no longer would be obliged to seek an opinion from the BOIE before starting investigations. However, an MP under scrutiny could request an opinion from that team of fellow members and pass it on to the police or courts. The deletion allowed the RCMP to continue to carry out long-standing police procedures, although the battle certainly showed them that such work lacked the support of most parliamentarians.

On November 30 as the bill passed from the Commons, those who had followed its tortured path were stunned to hear Gauthier announce that C-79 "would put an end to cynicism so apparent in the media and the public toward politics."

It had the opposite effect. In May 1991 the government hastily rounded up the four required ministers to sign a cabinet order proclaiming the bill. That was done one day before Conservative MP Gabriel Fontaine was to appear in court on fourteen charges of breach of trust, fraud and conspiracy in connection with the misuse of thousands of dollars in House of Commons contracts. Harvie Andre had told government officials that it was "urgent" for the law dealing with investigations of MPs to be enacted that day. The next day Fontaine's lawyer cited it to win an adjournment of his client's preliminary hearing. Andre said that critics of his action were "just looking for scandal and unduly harming people's reputations by this excessive desire for scandal." He termed an opposition demand for a probe "absurd." Quebec Tory Maurice Tremblay also wanted the law proclaimed quickly after the RCMP obtained a search warrant for his office. A favorable ruling from BOIE might improve the legal position of both men.

Although MPs were quick to act against the RCMP when threatened, they have proved to be rather slow in adopting rules or a code of ethics to meet public expectations. Deluged with scandals in his first mandate, Mulroney introduced much-needed conflict-of-interest legislation. It was never approved. The proposals would have made parliamentarians and their spouses more accountable by requiring them to divulge their business interests to a conflict commissioner. Details of corporate directorships, shareholdings, family financial arrangements and fees charged for private consulting or other outside work would be required. Back-benchers from all three parties and their spouses objected to the code. "It's got to the point where we'll have to make a statement every time we got to the toilet so that we aren't taken for homosexuals," Montreal Tory Vincent Della Noce fumed. Political wives objected to having to disclose assets. John Crosbie's wife, Jane, and Tory MP John Bosley's wife, Nicole, were particularly incensed. Said the latter: "Nobody told me when I married John that I would have to disclose how much I earn."

The ethics package died when the election was called in the fall of 1988 and, almost two years afterwards, the government has made no effort to reintroduce it. A similar law is proposed by Mulroney from time to time when one of his MPs or friends gets caught in the honey pot, but no action has been taken by this Parliament. Mulroney and many MPs seem unable to realize that workable guidelines are the best protection against abuse and an important step towards improving Parliament's public image.

Still, legal guidelines or rules must be founded on a moral system. We must not be misled into believing, as both the public and politicians often appear to believe, that putting the behavior code into the law somehow eliminates its underlying moral rationale. The unfortunate view of many politicians is that if an activity is legal, it is also acceptable. There must be a code of behavior for politicians other than the Criminal Code.

7
FLYING THE FLAG

"After arrival Thursday morning, February 21st,
the delegation was given a tour of the island,
paying particular attention to the many important
historical sites on the island."

GIRVE FRETZ, MP, FEBRUARY 1991,
DESCRIPTION OF A TRIP TO ANTIGUA

A GLACIAL WIND WHIPPED AROUND THE GOTHIC STONE OF Parliament Hill. Shivering clerks, messengers, secretaries and legislative assistants wrapped in thick coats bent their heads against the Arctic blast as they rushed to take shelter in their offices. A heavy snowfall snarled traffic along Wellington Street and yellow Automobile Association trucks skidded about the city boosting frozen cars back to life.

It was mid-February 1991, the time when reporters note with perverse pride that Canada's capital is either the coldest on earth or in a frigid tie with Ulaanbataar, Mongolia. Escape from dirty snow, dead batteries and ice-encrusted windows lay a month or more ahead for most of those trapped in Ottawa.

Just eight miles away at the capital's international airport, a group of parliamentarians was about to make a break for freedom. Seven beaming senators and MPs, buckled into first-class seats, were fleeing for the Caribbean. There they hoped that the glistening beaches, seaside bar and exotic fare of the Leeward Island chains might help them to bear the pain and sacrifice of serving Canada's often ungrateful taxpayers. They were hardly aloft before the drinks arrived to ease the tension and ready them for their responsibilities in the balmy tourist havens of Antigua, St. Kitts, Montserrat and Nevis.

Members of all parties would share the work-load under the palms. The burden was so heavy that the chairman of the Canadian branch of the Commonwealth Parliamentary Association, Girve Fretz, MP, took on the leadership assignment himself. Others about to do their duty in the sun were senators Bill Doody (PC) and Bill Petten (Lib.) along with a Commons cast of Steve Paproski (PC), Doug Fee (PC), Lawrence MacAulay (Lib.) and Dave Barrett (NDP). It was as congenial a group of Caribbean fact-finders as Parliament could hope to produce.

One week earlier, another high-powered parliamentary team had soared into unseasonably mild Ottawa skies en route to Cuba. At the controls of that delegation, the first from Canada to the sun-soaked Communist island in ten years, was rookie Quebec Tory Charles DeBlois. While trade and tourism might seem logical topics for discussion on such a mission, its members had other business in mind. In a brief exchange with Cuban foreign minister Isidoro Malmiercag, they deliberated on the role our two countries "might play in bringing an end to the Persian Gulf conflict." Cuba, they learned and later reported, had no links to the combatants and thus could play a limited role indeed.

Having determined that, our representatives headed for further enlightenment at such points as the famous La Corona cigar factory in Havana. Their schedule included four days in the Cuban capital, a stop at San José to visit "livestock facilities" and further surveys of points critical to Canadian interests such as a sugar refinery and the site of the Pan-American Games. Fortunately a first-class flight was able to whisk them to the world-renowned seaside resort of Varadero before the pressure became unbearable. Even there it was not all fruity rum drinks and splashing in the sea. Their report notes that our ever-diligent parliamentarians managed to "tour hotel facilities" and meet with representatives of the local tourist office.

One amazing aspect of Canada's effort to learn about the world's equatorial zone is how urgent it becomes each winter. Fact-finding trips south are scheduled for the first three frozen months of each year, while the need to study Britain and Europe becomes more pressing in the spring and summer. Asia and the South Pacific are more often the chosen subjects for investigation in the fall.

Oddly, the places where starvation, strife and disease are daily realities and foreign aid is essential, warrant little attention from Canadian parliamentarians. The list of "fact-finding" missions shows that there is far more to be learned in, for example, Bermuda and St. Lucia, than in Bangladesh, Ethiopia or Somalia. (A delegation of four MPs that visited famine- and war-torn Sudan in January 1991 confessed on their return to confusion and discouragement about how to help. Three months later the government added $15 million to its famine-relief program, mostly in the form of surplus Canadian grain.)

Most winter travel, however, is to relatively untroubled sun spots. Many of Canada's politicians and their spouses consider a free trip every year or so to be a basic entitlement of the job. Such travel perks are seldom noticed or reported in the media, unlike the higher-profile exploits of ministers or top bureaucrats, which sometimes burst into the headlines. MPs and senators prefer to keep it that way, although the rule changes in the mid-1980s now require the filing of reports in the Commons.

We now know where our parliamentarians have broadened their horizons since 1989. The list is impressive and diverse: Uruguay, Mexico, Guatemala, Bermuda, St. Lucia, Dominica, Tunisia, Turks and Caicos, Trinidad and Tobago, the Philippines, Spain, Egypt, Yemen, Saudi Arabia, Switzerland, Iceland, Cyprus, Britain, Austria, Germany, Belgium, the Netherlands, France, Italy, Czechoslovakia, Poland, the Soviet Union, Hungary, Romania, Bulgaria, Yugoslavia, Morocco, Sénégal, India, Hong Kong, Japan, Australia, Singapore, Malaysia, Zimbabwe and New Guinea.

In 1991-92, MPs and senators budgeted $3.5 million for junkets abroad and to entertain foreign visitors here. The figure does not include trips parliamentarians take as members of ministerial delegations or with committees that have a specific job to do. Recent examples are a trade delegation headed by Michael Wilson that visited Saudi Arabia in May 1991, and a tour of European capitals in the fall of 1990 by the Commons Fisheries Committee to discuss overfishing off our east coast.

Such expeditions can indeed help to meet a particular need. Sometimes, however, MPs on these assignments stray from the official itinerary. The dalliance of defence minister Bob Coates at a West German strip-club won him headlines and cost him his job. In fact,

Coates was doing no more than dozens of Canadian parliamentarians have done before and since.

While on their European tour, some members of the Commons Fisheries Committee conducted an extensive study of the international flesh-pots. One MP later bragged that he and his Tory counterpart knew "where all the prostitutes are at a cost of anywhere from $400 (Cdn) to $500 to get laid and a blow-job."

Such incidental expenses were paid from the public pocket, not the parliamentarians' own. The MP also boasted that many particularly well-informed and well-travelled MPs have phone numbers for hookers in Paris, London, Hamburg, Sochin-on-the-Sea in the Soviet Union, Leningrad, Copenhagen and the Hague. On one night out in Paris, a duo paid $100 to get into a basement brothel in the Latin quarter where they were seated near the strobe-lit stage. They bought drinks for two hostesses in black leather and sat back to enjoy the show. "The girl comes out and she takes off her clothes," the MP recounted (on the condition that his name and that of his buddy not be revealed). "All of a sudden the two of us say we are leaving because we don't like the look of the place. Three big guys are standing there. They won't let us leave. 'No, no, pay the bill,' and they give us a bill for one thousand [dollars] apiece for a glass of wine or they'll call the police. Christ, we're MPs." One had to run up $1,000 on his Visa and the other paid $1,000 out of his own pocket. "And," the tattle-tale MP lamented, "we got nothing out of it."

A trip to Yugoslavia in April 1991 produced some embarrassing moments for the companions of an MP who spent most of his time drunk on buses and in meetings. During his waking moments he managed to insult the religious and political leaders with whom the delegation met. Another member of the group, Tory Geoff Scott, accomplished one objective, which was to have his picture taken with both Serbian and Croatian leaders. The shots would come in handy when he campaigned among Serbian and Croatian voters in his Hamilton-Wentworth riding.

Of course, many parliamentary trips provide relatively little excitement. For the most part our MPs and senators simply take their spouses to see the sights on the taxpayers' tab and keep a low profile.

After all there are few votes to be gained in the whore-houses or museums of Europe or on the balmy beaches of the Caribbean. MPs see no need to publicize such work. Electors fighting debt in Saskatchewan or snowdrifts in New Brunswick don't need to know everything their MPs do.

They are more likely to visit the capitals of the world than of the other nine provinces and two territories. In their own country, whose survival is at risk because its regions neither know nor care much about one another, MPs stick close to familiar turf. The thought that members from Halifax might spend time on prairie farms, that British Columbia members should switch places for a week with those from Quebec's north shore, or that an Edmonton MP might undertake an exchange with one from Newfoundland's rocky coast is too bizarre to contemplate. Far better that they should all get together in Ottawa to plan a trip to London, Taiwan or Bermuda.

Their need to see the world grows constantly. MPs and senators, often with spouses or even sons and daughters, now take some 400 first-class trips every year as members of delegations using travel as, "an important educational tool, essential to the understanding of issues."

Keen observer and former MP Doug Fisher calls that "mostly nonsense." He says the trips are usually just holidays, "an integral part of the system of perks for MPs and senators." He recalls one New Democrat who went overseas twice a year just to appease a nagging wife and a second who was regularly sent abroad because he was "a drunk and a womanizer" whom his colleagues "couldn't stand to have around."

Top travellers resent such suggestions and shun the label "junket." Liberal Jesse Flis has taken twelve trips in two years and says every one has been marked by long days and hard work. Tory whip Jim Hawkes told Bill Gillespie of CBC's "The House," "I've never been on a single parliamentary trip where I didn't come back absolutely exhausted." He says wives and children have actually provided a relaxed atmosphere for doing business on some trips, leading to better results. Doug Fisher responds that it also produces better family pictures in front of the Eiffel Tower.

Such official travel leads to some complaints from the MPs who are left behind. Tory René Soetens complains that they must expand their work-load, sit on unfamiliar committees, and cut visits to their ridings while filling in for absent colleagues.

None of that should discourage trips or make MPs ashamed to talk about them, says frequent flier Marcel Prud'homme. He says, "a federal member who ducks and pretends he or she has no international preoccupation should run for school boards, municipal elections or provincial elections." In the spring of 1991 the twenty-seven-year Commons veteran was appointed by the House management committee to review and report on the associations and "friendship groups" that promote parliamentary travel.

Their first travel club was the Empire Parliamentary Association, set up in 1911 by Sir Wilfrid Laurier to foster closer ties among members of the vast and diverse British Empire. It has since become the Commonwealth Parliamentary Association (CPA), with members from 115 national, state, provincial and territorial parliaments scattered across the globe. The locations of its last dozen or so annual get-togethers include India, Zimbabwe, Barbados, Australia, Malaysia, the United Kingdom, Saskatchewan, the Isle of Man, Kenya, the Bahamas, Fiji, Zambia, New Zealand and Jamaica. Between those big meetings, delegations from among the 9,000 members worldwide drop in on one another. It is a good way for an MP from Mississauga to learn about Mauritius, if not North Battleford, Saskatchewan.

In the early days CPA travel was limited, its spending minimal. Much information was exchanged by post. As late as 1946, Prime Minister Mackenzie King, a renowned penny-pincher, set aside only $2,000 for MPs to go abroad. That usually meant Westminster. A second travel club, the Canada-NATO Parliamentary Association, was created in 1958 with a $10,000 grant from taxpayers. The Cold War was on and it was felt that Canadian parliamentarians must learn more about it from their European counterparts. Formation of that group spawned two new associations: the Canada-U.S. Inter-Parliamentary Group and the Inter-Parliamentary Union, a large cumbersome social club where politicians from around the world trade little-read papers on the intricacies of their work.

Until the early 1960s, the cost of all four associations averaged less than $60,000 a year. That budget paid to send two or three parliamentarians to conferences of the four international parliamentary bodies. By the mid-1960s expenses began to soar into the hundreds of thousands of dollars as more MPs set their sights on destinations far from home. They had discovered the need for "firsthand knowledge and experience" in international affairs through increased travel, person-to-person contact and an "open exchange of views" with their counterparts in other countries.

By 1967 taxpayers were footing a bill of over $460,000 to send representatives abroad. Each year the cost jumped. MPs found new places and formed new clubs to plan visits. In the early 1980s the travel budget neared $2 million as delegations set out to swap yarns with their counterparts around the world.

Globe-trotting increased and budgets grew so much that Parliament created its own travel agency to send our representatives abroad and bring others here. It hired Ian Imrie in 1964 to help organize excursions. Today his title is "Secretary General of the Parliamentary Associations Secretariat." He is a discreet, powerful guardian and dispenser of travel goodies and wise counsel to those venturing abroad.

"Each of the Parliamentary Associations has increased its activities and the Parliamentary Relations Secretariat has grown to a full-time organization comprised of nineteen staff members, some directly responsible for the various associations and groups, others working in administrative, financial and logistical areas of organization," he wrote in 1979. Today the combined operations of the renamed Parliamentary Associations Secretariat and the separate Parliamentary Exchanges and Protocol Directorate occupy the eleventh floor of an office tower near Parliament Hill and take up a column in the government phone book. Among their little-known responsibilities is keeping track of the $22,000 taxpayers provide for get-togethers of the Parliamentary Spouses Association of Canada.

There are now eight official parliamentary associations – Canada-

NATO, Canada-Europe, Canada-France, Canada-Japan, Canada-U.S., Commonwealth, the Inter-Parliamentary Union and the International Association of French-Speaking Parliamentarians. The associations are controlled by MPs and senators, who are responsible for organization and budgets, while staff handle the confidential paperwork. These individual travel clubs set up meetings between Canadian parliamentarians and their counterparts around the world. Their rationale is to assist parliamentarians to broaden their knowledge and gain an international perspective. Quite naturally, more of the work is done over cocktails and dinners than in meeting rooms. Among Jim Hawkes' tasks as Tory whip is that of picking members for the dirty jobs that somebody has to do. "Certainly they are worthwhile," he says of the trips. "They help the nation, or Parliament wouldn't be spending the money." Part of the money includes the expenses for their spouses and lovers, including a per diem of up to $100, according to a well-informed source who has handled the transactions. It was 1986 before the Commons adopted the rule requiring the head of an inter-parliamentary delegation to present a report after each trip. That threw an additional writing burden on the aides who are along to help with bags, flight and hotel bookings, wake-up calls and other duties. The deadline for reports was later extended from ten to twenty days. The reports themselves can be as little as a page or two. Presentation in the House is a ten-second routine, unless the delegate chooses to elaborate on the trip. Few do.

The travel budgets of parliamentary associations were once publicly detailed in the government's annual spending estimates. As the number and cost ballooned, both the bills and the itineraries became carefully guarded secrets. Secretary General Imrie has strict instructions not to release budget details or to say in advance where MPs are going. Access-to-information laws, which can be used to get the travel documents of cabinet ministers, do not produce details of the activities of parliamentary associations. The auditor general is stymied too. He can't see the books unless invited to do so by the speaker. The invitation never comes. Travellers themselves, particularly chairmen of associations, seem to suffer memory loss when queried about spending. Since January 1986, MPs must report that such trips have taken place but need not say why, or how much they cost. We can only guess what makes it necessary for them to visit Bermuda on two successive Februaries, but almost never to look in on Port-aux-Basques, Newfoundland, or Chapleau, Ontario. The public, of course, has no access to the secret meetings in which MPs decide travel destinations.

Despite the shroud of secrecy, a confidential Commons document shows the 1990-91 cost of each travel association. Their total budget of almost $3 million does not detail Senate contributions. The figures that follow are for the Commons only. Also not included are figures on the cost of staff in charge of the travel or the price-tag of incoming parliamentary delegations and trips sponsored by the speakers of the Commons and Senate.

Travel association costs, 1990-91

$342,614	Commonwealth
$330,522	NATO
$247,492	IPU
$222,785	IAFSP
$139,814	Canada-Europe
$113,616	Canada-U.S.
$85,478	Canada-Japan
$74,168	Canada-France
$22,019	Parliamentary Spouses
$181,000	7th Scientific and Parliamentary Conference

Overseeing the trips and budgets is a committee of MPs and senators that includes the chairmen of the parliamentary associations, whips of all parties in both houses and speakers and deputy speakers of both houses. Members must sign up with the various associations to qualify for travel. When a junket is posted, MPs apply to association chairmen who help pick the lucky winners. But the key players are party whips, the sergeant-majors of the various parties. Members who have been good get travel rewards. Those who miss votes or committee assignments, fail to follow party orders or commit other offences can leave their bags at home. They are going nowhere.

"Nobody can go without my signature," explains Hawkes. His job as Tory whip carries enormous influence. The eleven-year veteran does not take it lightly. "Your obligation is to compose a delegation who can get the job done. Sometimes it's more of a friendship job and sometimes it's very important," he says before cracking his whip. "If somebody won't attend committee meetings or be on time or go to the briefings or come to the committee report writing, they have not demonstrated the skills to be part of a delegation." The whips of the other parties use a similar carrot-and-stick approach to keep discipline in the ranks and decide who is ready to fly.

The selection of compatible fellow travellers is also considered. Aging and sometimes cranky Ontario Tory Stan Darling pestered one of Hawkes' predecessors so persistently that he finally won a flight abroad. Amazingly, he and his equally unilingual wife, Mona, found themselves touring for a week with a delegation whose members spoke only French.

The most exotic journeys to distant destinations are those lavishly arranged for speakers John Fraser of the Commons and Guy Charbonneau of the Senate. Next in line are House leaders, deputy speakers and party whips, few of whom enjoy any long Commons recess without at least a little tax-funded travel. The speakers usually lay a wreath at an unknown soldier's tomb or present a bit of Canadiana to their grateful hosts as they glide around the globe. During the visit of Mexican president Carlos Salinas de Gortari in April 1991, Fraser spoke about how trips south of the Rio Grande in the winter were of "very great importance" for understanding Mexico. He neglected to mention that few MPs spend much time in smog-clouded Mexico City, preferring instead the cleaner atmosphere of Bahia de Banderas.

Parliamentary business has recently taken Fraser to the Soviet Union, to Britain several times, to Malta and to Zimbabwe where Canadians were gratified to learn that he saw the "world-famous Victoria Falls." On a trip to Poland he reported that he and three aides, including chief of staff Stephen Ash, "did much to raise

Canada's profile," and that this is "likely to pay long-term dividends to Canada." In any case, taxpayers got to pay a second time, hosting a reciprocal delegation from Poland. Fraser took Ash and another faithful retainer, Clerk Bob Marleau, on an excursion to Hungary in April 1991. That just happened to be the week of a massive shake-up in the Commons administration. The speaker had arranged the shake-up, but left the announcement to be made by others. Press Gallery reporters foolishly felt that Fraser should have been in Ottawa, not Budapest, to explain what was going on.

Charbonneau, a Tory bagman, Mulroney buddy and former insurance executive who sits on key corporate boards in Quebec, is the most frequent traveller among today's parliamentarians. He and his wife, Yolande, have journeyed regularly to Europe, Asia, the Middle East, Japan and Australia. His travel reports are a sheer delight. A typical insight is this bit of travel guide trivia after a visit that included Plovdiv, Bulgaria, in June 1989: "We made a tour of the old city which features an old Roman amphitheatre and a network of narrow streets lined with houses dating back to the national renaissance in the 19th century."

In September 1990, Charbonneau led a five-member delegation to a conference in Singapore with a stopover in Hong Kong. They returned via Japan. The parliamentarians, except for Liberal senator John Stewart, who attended most conference sessions, spent much of their time away from the host city. While the ASEAN conference was taking place, Charbonneau and Tory MPs André Plourde and Gabriel Desjardins were on a "study mission" in nearby Malaysia. While there they boated down the Kedah Valley river to meet local fishermen, dined at the Komtar Palace in Penang and flew to Kuala Lumpur for further study. The day the conference ended they jetted back to Singapore for a farewell dinner. In his report to Parliament, Charbonneau concluded: "The complimentary visit to Malaysia was informative and useful, not only for Canadian parliamentarians, but for the local community as well, particularly in Penang where the last visit of Canadian Members of Parliament occurred in 1983."

Serious MPs do worthwhile work on some trips. Nearly everyone involved has evidence that the Canada-U.S. group, with one of the smallest budgets among the eight associations, does some constructive work. U.S. senators and congressmen debate contentious issues with their Canadian counterparts – such things as softwood lumber tariffs, free trade, extradition laws, acid rain and offshore oil drilling. "These are serious meetings," says New Democrat Jim Fulton, who has attended them all in his thirteen years as an MP. "The Americans always send senior members of the United States Senate and always twenty or so from the House of Representatives. We can deal with things that fail through diplomatic channels."

In May 1991 the association held its annual meeting just outside Calgary. Debate focused on the plan of President George Bush to allow offshore oil drilling along the coast of Alaska, a plan that has serious implications for British Columbia. "New Democrats, Liberals and Conservatives at these meetings stick together and hold together," explains Fulton. "We take a Canadian position, which I find uniquely helpful. We have been quite effective. We have managed to come to agreements that I don't think would have been found any other way." They also found time for some trail riding and, of course, elegant dining at the Banff Springs Hotel. Separate programs were arranged for spouses and sometimes children while the MPs went about their business.

Fulton said that the association did have "some flakes" who came on the trips because they "thought it was like the other parliamentary associations where it was just a perk." The do-nothings were weeded out when the association made it mandatory for MPs to attend intensive briefings before each conference. Even those who do their homework can barely keep pace with U.S. legislators, Fulton sheepishly confesses. "They are very well informed. They have incredibly highly qualified staff that travel with them. They travel with volumes of accessible computerized material with laptop computers. We are neither as technologically advanced nor as well-prepared informationally as the Americans."

Fulton has not joined other associations or taken foreign trips that he regards as "boondoggles where people go from a few days to a few weeks and basically just hang out in hotels and eat fancy meals and ride around on buses. . . they don't actually go and work." Few members speak out against the practice, though, because most have taken advantage of opportunities for a few free first-class holidays. Thus it is difficult to be precise about which trips are warranted and which are not, or who works and who does not. There would certainly be fewer flights if taxpayers had any say in how their money is spent. Obviously that's why parliamentarians keep such records confidential.

The Inter-Parliamentary Union brings members from around the world together several times a year. Canadian delegations include five to ten parliamentarians, plus four aides to take care of tickets, luggage, logistics and writing reports to Parliament. Some Canadians, including Liberal Sheila Finestone and Senator Joan Neiman, are regarded as serious delegates. They attend all seminars and draft committee reports on women's issues, technological change and human-rights abuses. For others the social, cultural, cocktail and epicurean aspects of the conferences are the top priority.

The Commonwealth group, with the largest budget and most members among the eight associations, has the most enchanting excursions. Its leisurely pace and exotic destinations have MPs and senators lining up to join. For years it was run by Lloyd Roseville Crouse, the dean of the Commons before he retired in 1988 after more than three decades as Conservative MP for the Nova Scotia riding of South Shore. Brian Mulroney rewarded him with the lieutenant-governorship of his home province, a prize Crouse has grumped about since. He wanted the Senate with its almost unlimited travel potential and no obligation ever to show up at the office. Crouse is said to have advised a rookie MP to be cautious about setting up a constituency office because people just keep coming in with problems.

He turned down an appointment as assistant deputy speaker, receiving instead the CPA chairmanship and world travel that goes with it. In his final two years as an MP Crouse took the floor of the Commons just nine times. Eight of them were to table reports about trips he had just completed. He was abroad when Joe Clark's government was narrowly beaten in the 1979 budget vote and absent too when fellow MPs paid him tribute on the thirtieth anniversary of his first election, June 10, 1957, in the first Diefenbaker victory. Only Robert Coates, a fellow Nova Scotian, and Alvin Hamilton from Saskatchewan, had lasted as long.

Another long-time Tory moved into the first-class seat Crouse had vacated after the 1988 election. Girve Fretz from Fort Erie, Ontario, has maintained such important traditions as "the Caribbean in winter, Britain in summer." While female MPs do not play a major part in association activities, parliamentary wives do. Fretz says spousal companionship is important and thus a legitimate cost for taxpayers. "It's justified by virtue of the fact that the work schedules members have can vary anywhere from I would say sixty-five hours a week to as high as eighty hours a week." Those who foot the bill could hardly object to Caribbean jaunts in winter because, Fretz explains, "that's the most enjoyable time to be there." Besides, they don't just go back to one favorite spot. Over three years delegations will shuffle around from Barbados and Dominica to the four Leeward Islands to the Bahamas.

Just what constitutes work on these long days is seldom recorded in detail. But a report Fretz presented after a seven-member, ten-day trip to Great Britain in November 1990 gives some idea. They talked to politicians and recovered from jet lag for a day in London before a flight took them to the Channel Islands of Jersey and Guernsey for some sight-seeing.

Fretz, Tory Len Gustafson and New Democrat Lyle Kristiansen visited two dairy farms while Liberal Joe Comuzzi lit out on his own to meet "Captain Cavey who is responsible for all ports in Jersey." On another part of the island Liberal Beryl Gaffney and Tory Fernand Jourdenais toured a "refuse incinerator power generation plant as well as the sold liquid waste treatment plant." In Guernsey, the MPs visited a museum and enjoyed a free lunch provided by the local bailiff, Sir Charles Frossard.

Most parliamentary travellers reveal too little detail for us to determine just how hard they work on their fact-finding missions. However, the schedule for Tory MP Pat Sobeski's 1990 trip to London, on which he was to learn about the mother of parliaments, provides some clues.

May 11
– Mr. John Sweetman [clerk assistant] gave address on "Parliamentary Scene at Westminster."
– Tour of the Commonwealth Institute, Kensington.
– Tour Grey Coat Hospital School, Westminster.
May 12
– Tour of London to include places of historical and contemporary interest.
May 13
– Prepared for and began tours to Durham, Tyneside, Lake District, Guernsey.
May 14
– Travelled to Swan Hunter Shipbuilders Limited, Welland.
– Visited Newcastle-upon-Tyne University.
May 15
– Travelled to the Lake District.
May 16
– Tour at the Cumbria Crystal Company, Ulverstone.
– Left Bowness by boat for cruise on Windermere.
– Boat arrived at Brochole Jetty. Walk to Lake District National Park Centre.
– Guests of South Lakeland District Council at Levens Hall.
May 17
– Travelled to Guernsey as guests of the Guernsey Branch, CPA.
May 18
– Discussed Constitution, Government and Administration on the Island of Guernsey. The procedure in the legislature, their method of election and the history of the Island of Guernsey were outlined.
May 19
– Returned to London.
May 20
– Free day.

Phew, and just in time too. Sobeski's constituents back home could hardly wait to see his slides.

The CPA has a francophone counterpart, which was established in 1967. The International Association of French-Speaking Parliamentarians operates in the same easy-going manner as the Commonwealth body. It just visits different places and speaks French while doing so. Winter favorites are Sénégal or the Riviera. Paris is favored over London in spring, summer and fall. There is also a Canada-France club to offer a few more chances at the fine wine, cheese and paté of different regions.

In 1990 the IASFP sponsored trips to Morocco, Tunisia, Egypt, Mauritius, the Seychelles, Madagascar, Switzerland and Sénégal, not a single one to Baie Comeau or Val d'Or. For years the association was run by Senator Martial Asselin, a Tory named to the upper house by Pierre Trudeau in 1972. At his last official function before installation as lieutenant-governor of Quebec, Asselin told a gathering in Tunisia how he would miss such international pampering – for example, he confided, on a recent trip to Mauritius he was "treated like a head of state. I was even invited to address the National Assembly. That gives you an idea of the way they welcomed me."

At the head of the 160-member NATO voyagers is Tory Bob Hicks and an all-male executive. The little school teacher in the tattered toupée is more of a transatlantic man than a House of Commons one. Since his first election in 1984, Hicks has joined more than a dozen tour groups, proudly listing them in his *Parliamentary Guide* biographical notes, which are otherwise bare of Ottawa accomplishments. The memberships are: Canadian Branch of the Commonwealth Parliamentary Association, Canada-Europe Parliamentary Group, Canada-U.S. Inter-Parliamentary Group, Canada-NATO Parliamentary Association, Canadian Parliamentarians for World Order, Canada-Arab Parliamentary Group and friendship groups linking Canadian MPs with Germany, Italy, Japan, Israel, Scandinavia, Greece, Korea and Taiwan.

All that travel left the energetic fifty-eight-year-old from Scarborough with barely enough time to rush into the Commons and table reports from eight trips between April 1989 and November, 1990.

He also took time to deny accusations by fellow Tory MP

Barbara Greene that his Canada-NATO group is "sexist" and a "private men's club" that does not give women an equal chance to play tourist. Hicks says the group reflects the percentage of women in Parliament. The last woman on the executive was Tory Louise Feltham from Wild Rose, Alberta, who was given the heave-ho in a 1990 vote for officers. "It was a democratic election and none were elected," he explains. "Everything Barbara Greene said in reference to the NATO Parliamentary Association was wrong," he fumes. "Traditionally women have not been strong supporters of NATO. I would welcome their participation in the future."

Spouses of members can go along for the ride when members attend annual meetings and major conferences. But the cost of first-class seats has taken such a big bite out of the association's budget that wives get only economy seats while the boys go first class. "We're cutting back drastically. The only circumstances that a wife can attend one of these two meetings is on an economy-class ticket and there are no other expenses paid for whatsoever. We're practically phasing out spouses because of budget restraint."

Hicks and fellow educator Terry Clifford from London-Middlesex, who heads the Canada-Europe group, are contenders for the Commons travel championship. Each has more than a dozen trips abroad to his credit. They include such critical assignments as the flight of a NATO delegation to San Diego and Phoenix to "lunch with NATO officials" in the winter of 1990. In the fall of 1989 Hicks went to Turkey where the delegation presented a "series of booklets prepared by the Department of External Affairs dealing with Canada's verification program." Obviously they could not trust the mail.

Hicks never seems to have trouble finding companions on his NATO junkets, including New Democrats who loudly oppose the organization itself. Derek Blackburn, the NDP veteran from Brantford who was a long-time defence critic for his party, is a world-class traveller. He partakes of many NATO freebies. The party's new defence critic, John Brewin, has lined up for a trip, and so has Bill Blaikie, a Manitoba preacher who advocates Canada's withdrawal from the defence pact. Hicks says the enthusiasm of New Democrats for NATO visits to European capitals is "hypocritical."

It reveals, he observed, "that their policy on NATO isn't really as rigid as they make it out to be."

Hicks cannot point to any specific benefit, such as helping Canadian business land defence contracts, that all the sky-hopping has accomplished for Canada, but he believes his presence at NATO meetings has made Canada a household name in the capitals of the world. "I can assure you that since I've been chairman and leading delegations to other countries, Canada's profile has risen very positively. Last November [1990] in London, England, I was elected vice-president of the North Atlantic Assembly, which I think is a tribute to Canada." The honor was little noted either at home or in the capitals of the world.

Canadian visitors seldom arrive empty-handed, nor is a box of Laura Secord's or a bottle of Bright's best considered sufficient to say thanks for the hospitality they enjoy. Just what gifts they hand their hosts are seldom revealed, but one troupe of travellers got front-page attention in the winter of 1989. The sole purpose of the thirteen-member visit was apparently to deliver a ceremonial chair to the Australian parliament. In his report, Tory Senator Heath Macquarrie informed the upper chamber that he got lost "in their Parliament buildings several times, but I can get lost in a telephone booth." He did, however, find time to down an ale in MacQuarrie's Pub.

MPs and senators cry foul when the media describe their frequent trips, particularly the winter ones to the sun-drenched Caribbean, as simply paid holidays. They insist that such travel improves their ability to oversee government policy, sharpens their judgement and broadens their outlook. One can only wonder why they do not tell the taxpayers more about a luxury learning program of such merit.

For parliamentarians, that is not the only way to fly. Companies, foundations, foreign governments and lobbyists are constantly bidding for their favor with freebies.

Nearly 150 MPs have accepted free trips from lobbyists, religious groups, airlines and foreign governments since 1989. Records reveal all-expense-paid junkets to Taiwan, South Korea, Africa, South Yemen, Turkey, Cyprus, Greece, Central America, Germany, Italy, New York City, Washington, D.C., and California. The tabs, including those for wining and dining spouses and girlfriends, were picked up by such diverse organizations as a West German bank, a Sicilian union, the East Timor Alert Network, the fundamentalist Christian Embassy and the Ahmadiyya Movement in Islam. No one knows how many such trips senators have taken because they keep no list.

MPs from all parties have accepted these junkets. Others frown on such practices. Most who take them wisely say little about them publicly, although they love to regale their pals with the fun-filled details. When asked by others about such freebies they describe them as fact-finding or trade missions. They may be, but the sponsoring organizations view them more as an effective vehicle for making influential friends right inside Canada's Parliament.

Many argue that this country's interests are better served when Canadian taxpayers rather than Taiwanese businessmen pay for our MPs' travel. "It is a corrupt kind of activity for parliamentarians to be involved in, to be accepting trips paid for by a foreign nation," says New Democrat Jim Fulton. "If it's important enough that you are undertaking activities on behalf of the Parliament of Canada then you should come to Parliament and get those funds and make them public and bring back a report as to who you saw and what you did and what the benefits are to Canada."

Even in such a murky moral environment, certain basic courtesies prevail. It is considered bad form to insult your hosts. Liberal Jim Karygiannis did exactly that in the spring of 1991 while a guest of the Social and Cultural Organization of Trinidad and Tobago. He accused the host government of human-rights abuses. The *faux pas* caused such a furore that his own colleagues threatened to expel him from caucus on his return. The member for Scarborough-Agincourt apologized to them, to the House, to the government of Canada and to the government of the Caribbean island nation. He concluded: "I shall henceforth not engage in activities outside my responsibilities." It was a wise decision if he ever hoped to enjoy future trips abroad at someone else's expense.

Despite concerns about the potential or perceived conflict of interest, Parliament has given its official blessing to a number of these travel clubs, inoffensively labelled "friendship societies." There are three official ones: Canada-Italy, Canada-Germany and Canada-Israel, and many more that are unofficial. Many of the latter are linked to repressive regimes or causes that do not have Canadian government approval. There are Canada-Taiwan, Canada-Korea, Canada-Turkey, Canada-Greece, Canada-Arab and Canada-Scandinavia friendship groups. All the groups are made up of MPs and senators who travel usually once or twice a year to the host country without paying a cent out of their own pockets.

The most controversial group is the Canada-Taiwan Friendship Association. It was formed by old-line Tory Robert Coates after Pierre Trudeau's recognition of Communist China in 1970. Diplomatic relations with Taiwan were broken off, and this led the Taiwanese to seek right-wing supporters in Parliament. Under the guise of the friendship society, Taiwan began to provide all-expense-paid trips for MPs and senators sympathetic to its interests. The free-enterprise nation of eighteen million people on mainland China's doorstep hoped the investment would pay dividends when a new government came to power here. Canada might, for instance, open an embassy on the island. The visits were also cited by the state-controlled Taiwanese press as proof that countries around the world supported the government's claim to be rightful rulers of China.

Some of the travellers in the association now sit in the Conservative cabinet, including revenue minister Otto Jelinek and Public works minister Elmer MacKay. Founder Coates is gone, a casualty of that brief encounter with Mickey O'Neil in the West German strip-club.

In the early years, the association dealt a lot in wine, women and sin. One Tory MP who was defeated in the 1988 election fondly reminisces about those bygone days of booze, parties and pretty Taiwanese companions. The girls lined up so MPs could pick their own hostesses. "She takes your shoes, she shows you what the customs are. She is an escort." Another MP recalls the pleasure of spending an evening with a young hostess. "I like to have my shoulders rubbed. She rubs your feet and shoulders when you are having dinner. If you don't want her to talk she doesn't talk. By the end of the day, you are in love with her."

Some of the trips have been paid for by the World Anti-Communist League, a controversial right-wing organization set up in 1966 by Taiwan and South Korea. Over the years it has been accused of anti-Semitism and racism by such groups as the League for Human Rights of B'nai B'rith. Its guests include Tory MPs Don Blenkarn, Felix Holtmann, Murray Cardiff and former party president Peter Elzinga, who is now Alberta's minister of economic development and trade. Blenkarn says he saw nothing wrong with such freebies. "Well, you know," he informed the *Toronto Star*, "somebody asks if you want to go to Taiwan, make a couple of speeches and that's all you have to do, well . . . you know."

Those trips were arranged by Patrick Chan, who ran the Taiwanese Chamber of Commerce office in Toronto until he was deported in 1986. Chan was believed to be a member of Taiwan's secret service. Canadian security service agents worried about his close links to federal politicians and finally got him thrown out. The expulsion caused a furore among right-wingers in the Tory caucus. They regarded Chan as a perfect friend, a nice guy, with the cash to pay for junkets to the Far East. Chan continued to meet Canadian politicians when they were in Taiwan up until 1990 when he was posted to Germany, according to Conservative MP Bill Attewell.

Frequent trips by MPs to Taiwan, South Korea and even South Africa so embarrassed the government that it set up an official registry in 1986 and required members to declare the free trips they accept from foreign governments or lobbyists. The registry did not clip their wings, but it at least identified the frequent high-fliers. Canadian law prohibits MPs and senators from acting as lobbyists for foreign governments, but allows parliamentarians to promote closer relations. It places no restrictions on free trips.

Jaunts to the steamy flesh-pots of Taiwan ended when Attewell, a Baptist accountant, took over the friendship group in 1988. He curbed the stag-party stuff but not the trips themselves. Taiwan, it seems, still likes Canadian parliamentarians. From 1989 to 1991 either its government and Chamber of Commerce or the World Anti-Communist League treated thirty MPs to visits. On one trip in March 1991 five MPs – Liberals Joe Volpe, Don Boudria, Jim

Karygiannis, Maurice Foster, and Tory Jean-Luc Joncas – took their wives for a week of what Volpe described as "intensive meetings."

One result of such free rides by opposition members is that it dulls their ability to attack the government on matters of ethics and conflict of interest. When rat-packer Boudria rises in Question Period to attack some minister for misuse of money or power, hooting Tories taunt him with reminders about his own questionable travel.

Attewell says his group, which includes eighty to a hundred MPs and senators, is trying to foster good relations between Canada and Taiwan and "specifically to expose some MPs and business people to trade and investment opportunities in both directions." He cannot point to any business or trade deals as a result of such visits, but the hope continues. The Taiwanese appear more forthright about their aims. It is not so much new Canadian business clients they are after. They want our politicians to help speed up the visa process and access to Canada. Attewell explains: "They would like to enjoy some airline opportunities here, you know, in terms of China Air being able to land in Toronto, in Vancouver. That hasn't happened yet."

He doesn't feel that the foreign freebies undermine his credibility. If parliamentarians did not accept such Asian junkets they might never get to visit at all. "I just think there aren't that many opportunities for some of us to see that part of the world and understand, frankly, what a success story they have been." They could, of course, pay like anyone else, out of their own pockets, but anyone who has talked about travel to an MP knows how ridiculous such a suggestion is.

Attewell has arranged for visiting Taiwanese officials and businessmen to meet with senior bureaucrats in Ottawa, but has not been able to set up any meetings with cabinet ministers. That is prohibited because Canada and Taiwan have not re-established diplomatic relations.

The largest of the friendly forces on the Hill is the Canada-Korea Parliamentary Association. More than one-quarter of our MPs and senators belong to it. The association was formed by the amazingly peripatetic Coates in 1979, when General Chun Doo-hwan seized power in a military coup and began a crackdown on dissidents and human-rights advocates. The former Tory party president travelled at least five times to Korea before he became defence minister in 1984, and several times more after losing that job. South Korean officials describe him as one of the country's closest friends. In 1985 he received an honorary doctor of law degree from Chung Ang University. He was awarded the Order of National Security Merit in 1987 for "distinguished service to the Republic of Korea" and for "keeping of friendly ties between our two countries and to safeguarding of national security of Korea."

Since Coates left the Commons in 1988 his place with the Korean group has been taken by another ardent right-winger, Bill Vankoughnet. The Tory member for Hastings-Frontenac-Lennox and Addington since 1979, Vankoughnet has also been a guest of the right-wing Turkish government. There is a Canada-Turkey Parliamentary Friendship Society, set up by Coates in 1986. His association with that country began during his short stint as defence minister when he master-minded a gift of twenty used CF-104 Starfighters to the Mediterranean nation.

Korea picks up the bills for four or five visits each year by parliamentary delegations. Delegates usually stay a week to ten days. The MPs who go insist that they are working to improve trade relations. They get help from scores of businessmen, senior civil servants and officials who belong to the Canada-South Korea group. Maj.-Gen. Gus Cloutier, the House of Commons sergeant-at-arms, sat on the board of one such society whose members included Gerry Shannon, ambassador for multilateral trade negotiations and a former ambassador to Seoul, and James Donnelly, former president of Atomic Energy of Canada Ltd.

Another big international lobby group is the Canada-Israel Committee, which regularly pays to fly parliamentary friends from Ottawa to Israel. Thirteen went between 1989 and 1991. The Israeli lobby will not reveal the cost of the trips, which include members from all three parties. Executive director Robert Ritter says the missions promote friendship by providing "opportunities to have a firsthand experience of the situation on site." He insists that MPs "get a broad exposure," including meetings with Palestinians.

That claim is disputed by some parliamentarians who have taken the trips. New Democrat Svend Robinson, who has also accepted freebies from Arab states, strongly disagrees with Ritter. "Certainly I was the person who set up contacts with Palestinian leaders during my visit to Israel. There was no attempt whatsoever to facilitate those kinds of contacts. Obviously, the objective of the trip was to promote an understanding from a perspective of the Israelis." Montreal Conservative MP Vincent Della Noce also found he got a one-sided view as a guest of Israel in the summer of 1986. The hand of hospitality carefully guided him away from Palestinians in refugee camps on the Israeli-occupied West Bank. "I just saw one side of the fence, and I was very disappointed that these guys tried to brainwash me and abuse the little intelligence that I have." Neither he nor Robinson has been invited back.

The success of the Israeli lobby in Parliament led to the creation of the Canada-Arab World Parliamentary Association, headed by New Brunswick Conservative MP Robert Corbett, who also happens to belong to the well-travelled Taiwan and Korean groups. The Palestine Liberation Organization used the society, which now numbers about sixty MPs and senators, as a pipeline into Parliament. Although the Arab lobby does not have the same clout as the pro-Israel lobby, it has laid a foundation that was virtually non-existent a decade ago. The Arab friendship group was set up in 1982 and has championed the Palestinian cause in Parliament and in all three political parties. In addition to Corbett, veteran Liberal Marcel Prud'homme, Independent Alex Kindy, Robinson and Derek Blackburn are high-profile members.

The Arab Information League, funded by Arab states, has been picking up the tab for free trips to the Middle East for MPs since 1982. On these visits to Tunis or Jordan the MPs often meet in secret with PLO chairman Yasser Arafat. But it is not all work and high-level briefings. Arabs have thrown lavish parties with cultural evenings to introduce some Canadian delegates to the intricacies of belly dancing. Corbett and former Liberal MP Ian Watson, head of the National Council on Canada-Arab Relations, have also set up a Middle-East Study Group, which often holds meetings on Parliament Hill. Members include scholar and former

Canadian diplomat Peyton Lyon and former Conservative leader Robert Stanfield.

The fact that participants say so little publicly about these activities gives them an aura of intrigue, whether or not there is truly reason for suspicion. Clearly the countries that jet Canadian parliamentarians around the world and entertain them in lavish surroundings believe they're getting some bang for their bucks. They also leave the distinct impression that Canadian politicians can be bought for the price of a luxury trip or two. Obviously, as Francis Bacon said: "Travel, in the younger sort, is part of education; in the elder, a part of experience." But it should be neither surreptitious nor paid for by others who want something in return. If parliamentarians believe in the value of such travel, they should justify the costs to Canadians, and have them foot the bills.

Sun-flights to the Caribbean, the Riviera, Australia and New Zealand by politicians who preach restraint only create public contempt. Those charged with serving Canadians in Parliament may wonder why they command so little respect. A look at their well-tanned faces in a winter mirror might give them a clue.

8
PATRONAGE HEAVEN

"The Senate can be boring too. But when it gets bad
I can go off and do other things . . . or
I can just go home."

SEN. PETER STOLLERY, 1984

SOME BANGED THEIR DESK TOPS UNTIL THE ANTIQUE HINGES broke loose. Others shouted, swore, blew whistles, shook fists and littered the splendid crimson carpet with books and debris. A few cowered in shock and embarrassment as ringleaders shoved helpless security guards aside, exhorting television crews to join the bedlam.

It was October 1990, and members of Canada's upper house were at work reviewing legislation. Under study was Bill C-62, better known as the Goods and Services Tax Act. So contentious was it that most of Canada's 112 senators, including 8 appointed especially to push that bill into law, temporarily forgot what the Senate is all about.

Very simply, it's the pot of gold at the end of the parliamentary rainbow – the top cash-for-life prize in our political lottery. Lucky winners get to sit – or not bother to sit, if they wish – in Parliament's regal chamber of "sober second thought." The phrase was coined by Sir John A. Macdonald when he began stuffing its plush seats with pals in 1867. To this day, their successors need only be thirty years old, own property worth $4,000 and win a spot on the prime-ministerial gift list. Senators scoop up a basic $75,000, part of which is tax free, and retire at age seventy-five on a handsome pension. Neither electors nor the government leader who rewarded them can undo the appointment. If they feel the urge they can attend every Senate sitting, an average of seventy-six days a year for two and half hours. Few do. They may be old, sick, tired or lazy. Or they may be attending to other jobs as lawyers, corporate directors, union bosses, authors, political hacks or adventurers. There's no limit to how many other pay cheques a senator can draw.

Depending on an appointee's age, elevation to the patronage palace is worth up to $5 million in salary and gold-plated pensions. The post includes an office, secretary, $55,000 for research and general office expenses, free rail and air travel and countless parliamentary perks. In exchange for the cash, a senator must show up in the red chamber only once every two consecutive sessions of Parliament. A senator can stay away for years without forfeiting his job or salary.

In the United States, senators such as Edward Kennedy, Robert Dole and Patrick Moynihan are rightly famous. Here, former premiers and federal cabinet ministers ring a fading memory bell. As Gordon Robertson, one of Canada's most astute parliamentary observers, once noted: "In the United States you have to win an election to get into the Senate. In Canada it is more effective to lose." Most members of Canada's red chamber remain anonymous or trigger a memory unrelated to political acumen. Thus Ed Lawson may be identified as a Teamster boss, or Anne Cools as the black activist who served four months in jail for her part in the 1969 sit-in and destruction at Sir George Williams University in Montreal (she was subsequently pardoned), or Michel Cogger as the Mulroney crony and campaign commander under lengthy police investigation for allegedly mixing Senate duties with private business.

Such accomplishments win them neither power nor prestige in their home country, but like Canadian artists, actors and athletes who enjoy stardom in the United States, our senators love to travel there. The title carries such prestige that it's a very rare senator from Ottawa who fails to proclaim it when travelling south of the forty-ninth parallel. Many Europeans are unaware that Canadian senators are not like their American namesakes. "You should see these guys puffing themselves up when they're overseas," marvels New Democrat MP Svend Robinson.

Since Confederation, many of our unelected parliamentarians have been content to take the cash and stay silent. One of them even gained a perverse fame by doing just that. George Casimir Dessaules occupied the Chamber of Sleepy Second Thought from 1907 to 1930 and spoke only twice. The first time was upon entering the house, when he denied that his appointment was the result of a corrupt bargain. The second was twenty-three years later to thank colleagues for a portrait on his hundredth birthday.

Senators can no longer stay around to savor their good fortune until they hit the century mark – with the exception of two remaining lifers. One is brewery tycoon Hartland Molson, born in Montreal in 1907 and named to the Senate by Louis St. Laurent in 1955. The other is Tory John Macdonald, a three-time election loser, who won the prize after a single term in the Nova Scotia legislature. Both earned their lifetime of comfort because their appointments preceded a 1965 change making retirement mandatory at age seventy-five. The average age today is just under sixty. Appointees who reach the Senate's hallowed halls by age fifty can expect a combination of pay, perks and pension that will reach $4 million or more before they shuffle from heaven on earth to the one beyond.

The Senate was not created just to reward the prime minister's buddies from the public treasure chest. It was meant to safeguard the less populated regions and to act as a "bulwark against the clamour and caprice of the mob," as Sir James Lougheed put it upon his appointment in 1889. Sir John A. had already hinted at its relationship with privileged Canadians when he said that the "rights of the minority must be protected, and the rich are always fewer in number than the poor."

The late Eugene Forsey, who served as a senator and knew more about parliament's beginnings than almost anyone, wrote: "The Fathers of Confederation distrusted democracy, mob rule. Against this danger, a Senate made up of mature men, with a substantial 'stake' in the country, with an absolute veto, would be an insurmountable barrier." The Senate was given formidable powers to act as a check on the will of the masses. Its powers are almost equal to those of the Commons, except that the red chamber cannot originate money bills. It can amend or toss out any bill as often as it sees fit. No bill can become law unless it is ratified in its final form in the Senate.

In practice these powers have been exercised only rarely through our first 120 years, as power in Canada, along with the rest of the democratic world, was increasingly given to elected bodies. The most famous head-to-head clash between our Commons and Senate occurred with Robert Borden's Naval Aid Bill in 1913. Ottawa wanted to spend $35 million for three battleships to be built in British shipyards and manned by British sailors. This caused a public uproar. The Senate blocked the bill, and the government, unsure of public support, backed down.

In 1926 the Senate blundered when it held up a bill to introduce old-age pensions. An election followed, and the government was returned with a substantial majority. The bill was then passed by both houses. Senate action at that time was highly unpopular, a circumstance that has been kept clearly in mind by strategists to this day. The upper house can effectively delay or scuttle legislation when it is on the side of the public and the government is not.

One of the best-remembered flare-ups was the Coyne Affair of 1961. James Coyne, then governor of the Bank of Canada, was ordered by the Conservative government to resign. Coyne, who had clashed with the Tories over economic policy, refused. John Diefenbaker countered by using his massive majority to pass a bill in the Commons to flip Coyne from office. The Senate balked, inviting Coyne to appear and defend himself. He did so, in some thirteen hours of testimony. Suitably vindicated in the Senate court, he then resigned with his head high.

In these cases the Senate simply performed as intended or, as Sir John A. declared: "It must be an independent house, calmly considering the legislation initiated by the popular branch and preventing any hasty or ill-considered legislation." In his authoritative text *The Modern Senate of Canada*, Frank Kunz says that the Commons has ceased to be a check on the cabinet and that "there is really no reason why the Senate could not play such a role." In our system of combat between political parties, the Senate has acted as a check only when one party dominates the upper house and another holds sway in the Commons. In this century of Liberal governments and a Grit-stacked Senate, the clash has occurred only when the Tories have briefly won power.

In the 1930s, when Tory R.B. Bennett reigned and Grits filled the Senate, a dozen bills passed the Commons but failed to get royal assent and become law. It happened to several more under Diefenbaker between 1957 and 1963. But in Liberal times the Senate quietly studied or snoozed, making only "technical" changes to bills before passing them into the statutes of Canada. The job, according to Forsey, became "to clarify simplify and tidy" bills from the Commons. Senators did a bit of useful work in committees on such subjects as mass media, poverty and science policy. They examined free trade, the fishery, national defence and the security service more quickly and cheaply than royal commissions would have. But the Senate never did what Sir John A. said it must not do, which was to set itself in opposition against the "deliberate and understood wishes of the people."

Its main role since 1867 has been as a "taskless thanks" for washed-up politicians, party bagmen, toadies, and flacks. The prospect of winning Canada's top patronage prize is what has kept many a party worker quietly toiling in the political trenches. On the other hand, almost every prime minister has moaned that awarding Senate seats is one of his toughest jobs. For each recipient delighted with the windfall, half a dozen grumble about being passed over. To appoint a political opponent or neutral senator is to provoke even greater anger in party ranks.

Every country has a patronage pay-off, and Canada is no exception. The upper chamber is on the level of the royal rewards in Britain or judgeships and ambassadorial posts distributed to party bagmen by U.S. presidents. Most of the 75 senators named by Sir John A. were Tories. All 81 gentlemen sent to Patronage Heaven by his successor, Sir Wilfrid Laurier, were Liberals. The prime minister who filled the most Senate seats in Canada's history was Mackenzie King. During his twenty-two years in power he named 103 senators – all Liberal. The trend towards solid party selections changed a tad with Pierre Trudeau who was a bit embarrassed by the Liberal tilt of the red chamber. Although most of the 81 senators he chose were Grits, he did name 7 Conservatives, 1 Social Crediter and 3 so-called independents. In the case of rival Tories, it was primarily to get them out of Commons seats that the Liberals would then have a chance of winning.

Probably Trudeau's most controversial appointment was that of his long-time confidant and aide Michael Pitfield in 1983. The brilliant but vapid former privy council clerk from upper-crust Westmount chose not to be labelled a Liberal. He sits today as an Independent. The furore was about greasing the lanky forty-three-year-old from the supposedly non-partisan public service to the juicy political sinecure. One veteran Liberal saw a bright side to the fuss. "Let's face it," observed then Senator George McIlraith. "The best thing that could happen is for more people to pay attention to us."

Attention was paid a few years earlier when oddball adventurer Peter Stollery was boosted from his downtown Toronto seat in the Commons to make way for an election bid by Trudeau schemer Jim Coutts. Coutts lost, but Stollery – former cab driver, film-maker, canoeist, explorer and collector of exotic objects – still enjoys the Senate plum he was given a decade ago at age forty-six. One objet d'art he proudly displays to office visitors is his two-foot petrified walrus penis, a handy conversation piece when Senate chat lags. Stollery, who found the Commons sometimes "great theatre," was becoming bored with it before he got the nod. "The Senate can be boring too," he told interviewer Brian D. Johnson a few years into his life of ease, "but when it gets bad I can go off and do other things, or I can just go home."

Then there is Jacques Hébert, the Quebec author and globe-trotting explorer of more than a hundred countries. His Senate seat was a gift for his 1968 book about travels with Trudeau in Red China. Hébert stretched out in the Senate foyer a few years back in a hunger strike to save a youth program, a move that prompted Tory senator Bill Doody to observe wryly, "It's a good idea. Too bad it's going to take so long." Hébert finally quit fasting and wrote a book about the whole thing, from which he pocketed the proceeds. The youth program remained unfunded.

Senator John Godfrey won his post for getting drunk at the 1968 Liberal convention and proudly displaying a Trudeau sign.

"The bar was full of people supporting Robert Winters or John Turner, so it sort of amused me to grab a Trudeau sign to show those buggers that at least one person was supporting Trudeau. My wife was absolutely horrified because she was for 'that nice John Turner.' She wouldn't even go into the bar with me when I was carrying the sign," he recounts. "I was the only person of any prominence in the business community who supported Trudeau at that time." He later turned out to be one of the few hard-working, outspoken and powerful Senate voices, until his retirement in 1987.

Not surprisingly, women were slow to pass through the ornate oak doors of Parliament's patronage paradise. They had the vote in 1918 and lobbied for a female appointee to the Senate after Agnes Macphail's breakthrough Commons victory in 1921. Recognizing the power of the female vote, Mackenzie King vowed to appoint a woman senator despite opposition from the Justice department, which argued that "women are not qualified." The Supreme Court of Canada got into the act in 1928, declaring that women were not "persons" and therefore were not entitled to Senate appointments. King appealed to the Privy Council in Great Britain, which ruled in 1930 that women were indeed "persons." That same year, King appointed Cairine Mackay Wilson, daughter of a deceased senator, to the upper house. Since then the Senate has often set the pace for the advancement of females in Parliament. It beat the Commons by ten years with the appointment of Muriel Ferguson as speaker in 1972, and it has been ahead in hiring female pages, clerks, senior messengers and a host of other employees.

Life in the red-plush haven has been generally happy and carefree. Senators would often nod off during debates, rousing early for dinner in the sumptuous Parliamentary Restaurant or to catch flights home. This pleasantly idle existence appeared ready, like the Mississippi, to flow on forever. Unfortunately, Canadians tired of the "natural" governing party and elected Brian Mulroney's Conservatives with a sweeping majority in September 1984.

Arrival of a Tory administration was an aberration the Liberal Senate had dealt with in the past. There was haughty, misguided R.B. Bennett in the Great Depression. His sad performance induced

Canadians to elect Liberal governments for the next two decades. Then Diefenbaker swept in on a populist wave only to prove such a woefully inept administrator that the people chose Liberal governments for nearly twenty-five years more, with the only interruption the Joe Clark blip in 1979. Most observers believed that Liberal senators would deal with Brian Mulroney in 1984 as they had with past Tory governments: raise a little fuss but not enough to disrupt an idyllic life. Things would get back on track with the return of the next Liberal regime.

Unfortunately for the Tories, Trudeau left behind a team of parliamentary guerrillas when he departed for his art deco mansion in Montreal. Trudeau, who despised the Senate but did little to improve it, had stuffed the place with sycophants and old parliamentary warhorses on the eve of his departure. One of those sent to his reward was Allan MacEachen, a cagey tactician who had served three prime ministers. The wily Cape Bretoner headed a cluster of former ministers, aides and Trudeau bureaucrats who were to act as protectors of their master's vision of the country.

It was MacEachen who plotted the defeat of Clark in 1979 and the resurrection of Trudeau for another four years as captain of the Liberal ship. Although Mulroney had won the most seats ever obtained by a single party, under MacEachen's sway the Senate treated the Tories as a gang of burglars who had broken into the Liberal Parliament while voters let their guard down. The democratic exercise that had somehow put the Tories in power must be nullified by the Trudeau appointees who owed allegiance only to the man who had put them in their cosy places.

For years MacEachen had regarded the Senate as a rubber stamp for the bills Liberals pushed through the Commons. Now the light dawned. Senators must play a powerful, partisan role in conducting the nation's business. "I do not believe that an invisible body has any place in a democratic society," MacEachen intoned in 1987. "Unless the Senate is capable of doing the things that we've been doing, then I think someone ought to put us out of our misery." Within months he confronted the government over a routine borrowing bill, tying Mulroney's hands for two months. He disregarded the tradition that the upper house would not use its power to hold up money bills. Though the Commons had moral and democratic principles on its side, MacEachen knew he could not be stopped, short of Senate reform or reversal of its Liberal majority. Mulroney swiftly retaliated by tabling a constitutional amendment to place a limit of thirty days on the hold-up of money bills and of forty-five-days on other Commons legislation. Then, although he had the backing of eight provinces, Mulroney seemed to lose enthusiasm for the idea. He let it die on the order paper, perhaps, because he was too busy plugging the place with his own friends and supporters.

The threat to clip senatorial wings and Mulroney's outraged denunciations of "Liberal rejects" and "political discards" simply fuelled MacEachen's own colossal partisanship. It was the devious "Celtic Sphinx" pitted against "Lyin' Brian" in the Battle of the Fattest. Parliament fans and odds-makers were in ecstasy as the politicians fired blistering charges and academics came down solidly on both sides. "It is not only desirable but necessary for the Senate to act as somewhat of a check on the government," MacEachen needled. "My title is not assistant director of a reading club. My title is Leader of the Opposition. And I get paid for that – not much, I admit, but I get paid to oppose the government." He somehow resisted quoting Cicero, whose thoughts on the subject are carved in the oak frieze of the Senate speaker's chamber: "It is the duty of the nobles to oppose the fickleness of the multitude." He was probably having too much fun to think of it.

In the next five years, MacEachen delayed or derailed no fewer than ten pieces of Conservative legislation. He forced an emergency one-day sitting in the summer of 1986 so that MPs could re-approve a parole bill the Senate had mischievously amended. There was a six-month show-down on a patent drug bill in 1987. MacEachen relented on that one only when Quebec Liberals convinced him of the huge price they would pay for losing its economic benefits. He forced the Commons to vote a second time on the Meech Lake Accord and bounced refugee and immigration bills back and forth so many times that most Canadians lost track of them completely.

With these clashes behind them, Liberal warriors took on bigger and bigger challenges, culminating in the stand-off that produced the free-trade election of 1988. Backed by John Turner, who was not always in tune with the Trudeau vanguard, Grit senators forced Mulroney to go to the polls in order to pass his Canada-U.S. free-trade bill. Election-proof senators could afford their fearless stand. MacEachen's troops took little notice of the rebuke voters delivered in returning Mulroney as the first Conservative with successive majorities in this century.

Undeterred by the election results, MacEachen set his sights on a fat new target – Mulroney's widely hated GST bill. The ensuing storm transformed even the most passive inhabitants of the sleepy chamber into raging zealots. Powered by polls showing massive opposition to the tax and support for anyone who would fight it, MacEachen and his Grit conspirators went to work. They had to convince sceptics that their stalling tactics and procedural tantrums were more than phony grandstanding. Thoughtful observers claimed that the Liberals were bluffing and would cave in at the last moment. Mulroney would get the blame when the bill passed, and a future Grit government would get its huge tax revenues.

MacEachen's job was to convince the public and the Tories that the Liberals were deadly serious. To do so Liberal senators shouted obscenities, blew kazoos, and read endlessly from any book that came to hand. Senator Philippe Gigantès, a widely ignored author who used to eat cigarettes in the chamber, took advantage of the filibuster to read one of his own volumes from cover to cover. He thereby obtained a complete translation in the verbatim Senate reports which apppear in both official languages. The Bible and phone books were both quoted extensively by senators who could find no new words with which to condemn the tax.

At the peak of the mayhem, new Liberal leader Jean Chrétien cheered his troops on from the Senate's public gallery. MacEachen even had the gall to say that the Senate had been too soft on past Liberal governments. "The Senate should not have tolerated Mr. Trudeau's attitude, or my attitude when I was in the House of Commons," he spluttered without blushing. "The Senate itself ought to have objected to the patronizing attitude that Liberal governments have taken towards it in the past."

Disliked as it was, the GST had not been a Mulroney secret sprung on the public only after an election. Other things, yes, but not the hated tax, which had been heralded for years. It was put forward in a white paper in Mulroney's first term and debated in the 1988 election, although it was almost totally overshadowed by the free-trade issue. Canadians who elected Mulroney got the tax in the package. They can undo the tax by throwing Mulroney out of office in the next election. What they can't do is touch MacEachen's happy band of unelected scrappers. Richard Lipsey, one of Canada's outstanding economists, warned that the system of government was in danger of being neutered by the tactics employed by MacEachen. "If the new practice becomes the norm, the government will have to face a major political battle [in the Senate] every time it tries to do something unpopular."

MacEachen's GST blockade so shook the government that Mulroney hit new heights of hyperbole in condemning it. His attacks on the "unelected Liberal hacks and rejects" were not even slowed by polls showing that Mulroney enjoyed the support of only 20 per cent of Canadians. Indeed, he went one giant step further, enlisting Governor General Ray Hnatyshyn, and even the Queen, in a plan to swamp the Senate with a collection of his own bedraggled political rejects. An archaic constitutional provision allowed him, with royal consent, to name eight extra senators and break the deadlock. The clause had never been successfully used before. When Alexander Mackenzie tried in 1873, Queen Victoria refused her assent.

Mulroney got the necessary approval and, with his own towering example of twisted logic, added more unelected hacks to Parliament in order to save democracy. "It is my duty to defend the rights of the House of Commons and its supremacy over the Senate," he declared in September 1990. Once again, Mulroney blinked first in the showdown with the Celtic Sphinx. He had not appealed to wavering Liberals or Independents to support a critical element of government economic policy. Instead he blew millions of additional taxpayers' dollars to install a new set of has-beens in senatorial splendor.

There was Mike Forrestall, who was already double-dipping after twenty-three unremarkable years in the Commons. Upon his defeat in 1988 he received a generous MP's pension and added to it when Mulroney gave him a post on the Veterans' Appeal Board. Ever loyal, he answered his summons to the Senate. So did Toronto millionaire lawyer Michael Meighen, grandson of a former prime minister, Arthur Meighen, who had once resigned from the Senate to run for the Commons. (He lost.) Michael, a former Conservative party president, would make no such mistake. He entered Parliament the easy way, by appointment, not election. Janis Johnson, former national director of the party and shopping mate of Mila, also answered the prime-ministerial call.

One name sticks out, more sadly dreadful than all the others. Dr. Wilbert Keon is an internationally renowned cardiac surgeon with no previous service on the political battlefield. His naive acceptance of a Senate seat tarnished his reputation, cost him friends, damaged the fund-raising causes he headed and made him wonder why he had not stuck with the simple business of replacing human hearts. His appointment epitomized a much-abused tactic of Mulroney's – that of placing one non-political name on a patronage list then claiming that the whole process is clean. It doesn't fool anyone, but it gives Mulroney the kind of glib excuse he loves.

Mulroney had already jammed fifteen GST-sympathetic Tories into the Senate before he pleaded with the Queen to add eight more. Among those lucky winners was the large, cheerless former trade minister Pat Carney from the west coast; defeated Nova Scotia MP Gérald Comeau; Toronto bagman Consiglio Di Nino; Quebec organizer Mario Beaulieu; and back-room boy Don Oliver, author of the cookbook *Men Can Cook Too*.

The truly outstanding names on that list were those of two Maritime premiers. Richard Hatfield had been at loose ends since becoming the most resoundingly rejected premier in Canadian history when he lost every one of New Brunswick's fifty-eight seats in the 1987 election. John Buchanan was the first premier to bolt from office to the Senate with the police in hot pursuit. He left Bluenose Tories in leaderless disarray, the allegations of kickbacks and corruption unresolved.

The shameless iniquity of Buchanan's rescue was greeted with shock and outrage across Canada. The dramatic "You had a choice, sir" television confrontation between Mulroney and John Turner in the 1984 election campaign instantly sprang to mind. These appointments made Mulroney's self-righteous condemnation of the Trudeau/Turner patronage list seem the ultimate in hypocrisy. His oft-quoted "there's no whore like an old whore" took on new meaning. The trough under Mulroney had not been cleaned up, just widened, deepened and filled with more rotting rewards.

The taxpayers' tab for Mulroney's generosity to his pals will be well over $30 million, depending on how long they luxuriate in the service of their country and how income swells as the years go by. Pat Carney will tally up a $2.3-million feed bill at the public trough before she's pensioned off in twenty years. Buchanan will add nearly $2 million to the handsome pension his provincial taxpayers already provide. The big winners are the youngest ones. Johnson and former New Brunswick cabinet minister Nancy Teed will collect $4.5 million or more apiece during their thirty-plus years of service.

What the orgy of patronage also ensured was final passage of Bill C-62 through the Senate on December 14, 1990. The government had won its battle against Liberal resistance that began in the Senate eight months earlier. MacEachen's merry band got one last laugh before the bill became law. It required royal assent, a traditional ceremony in which the gentleman usher of the black rod marches to the Commons and summons members to witness final Crown approval of legislation in the red chamber. The ritual was to take place on a Friday afternoon before the three o'clock Commons adjournment. MacEachen, his second-in-command, Royce Frith, and company gleefully delayed Senate proceedings until after that hour. Government House leader Harvie Andre threw a fit for delighted reporters outside the Senate doors. His flustered underlings, party whip Jim Hawkes and parliamentary secretary Albert Cooper, tried vainly to keep Commons business going until the ceremony could take place. In the end, cursing those dastardly Liberals one more time, they had to put it off until Monday.

With Mulroney's majority finally in control of the Senate such crowd-pleasing mischief will decline. The Senate's wealthy inhabitants can resume running the place like a dignified private club, rather than a circus. Since Confederation the patronage prize-winners have been left to handle their affairs without financial oversight on an "honor system." Considering their origins, such a code of conduct has always aroused some suspicion. To require honorable senators to open their books or provide receipts would, however, be vulgar. It's just not done.

The system produced the Hazen Argue scandal of 1988, one that continued to resonate three years later. A Saskatchewan farmer, Argue entered the Commons in 1945 as a member of the CCF (Co-operative Commonwealth Federation). Briefly its leader, he lost out to popular Tommy Douglas when the party was transformed into the NDP in 1961. He took his sullen genius to the Liberals but lost his seat in the 1963 election. Three years later Lester Pearson hoisted him from prairie stubble into the Senate. Trudeau later gave him a short turn in cabinet as wheat board minister when he found himself short of elected western Liberals.

Argue's reputation for eccentric behavior became legend. He and his wife, Jean, made frequent trips to faith healers in the Philippines. On a 1985 visit, a spiritual healer cured Jean's rheumatism and relieved the discomfort of a cyst on Hazen's neck by sticking two fingers up his nose. Argue recounted how the miracle-workers operated on patients without surgery: "We watched them operate behind a glass wall. They use their hands to open the body, blood flows and they take out the tissue and immediately they are finished. The wound closes, the blood is wiped off and the patient goes about his or her business." Argue's legislative initiatives include a call for federal guidelines governing the nutritional content of pet food. He once rose in the Senate to complain that the parliamentary tailor wouldn't press his rumpled brown suit. The tailor said it smelled too foul.

Things got much worse for Argue in June of 1988 when the *Ottawa Citizen* revealed that he had used Senate funds, resources and staff to help wife Jean in an unsuccessful bid for the Liberal nomination in the federal riding of Nepean, a city suburb. The allegations prompted confidential investigations by a Senate subcommittee. It found Argue guilty of misusing $5,607.40 worth of funds, staff and supplies. Taxi chits, phones and mailing privileges were among the items listed. The report also revealed that Argue had allowed a staff member to study French in a language course reserved for senators and their immediate families, at a cost of $3,570.

Argue insisted that he had not "knowingly abused my privileges as a senator," but agreed to repay the money. The Senate was content to sweep the matter under the red carpet. The committee concluded that he had acted in a way "that is not acceptable and which cannot be condoned." But it called for no further punishment. Some senators boasted that the incident somehow proved the honor system worked. In fact, if Argue had been more popular among his peers and the newspaper less persistent, the matter would probably have been overlooked completely in keeping with tradition.

The Senate had tried to keep its report secret and would have succeeded except for the seething anger of Mulroney and his Tories about the Liberal-dominated institution. In September 1988, a senior official of the Prime Minister's Office leaked the report to the *Toronto Sun*. The mud then flew, leaving few unsplattered.

The RCMP was not quite as willing as fellow senators to let the Argue matter fade quietly. They launched an investigation into misuse of Senate funds, including allegations that between 1980 and 1988 the senator in the filthy brown suit had filed false travel claims and inflated the cost of airplane trips. In 1989 Argue was charged with theft, fraud and breach of trust for using Senate resources on his wife's nomination campaign.

It was the first time in the 122-year history of the chamber that one of its members had been charged with misusing Senate funds. Senators who face charges are usually alleged to have committed their crimes outside Parliament. For instance, former Liberal senator Louis Giguère was charged with influence-peddling over the so-called Skyshops Affair, which had to do with airport duty-free stores. He was acquitted in 1979. Mulroney's little buddy Michel Cogger is still not through with the law. Argue, a victim of cancer, pleaded not guilty to all seven charges against him. The crown dropped the fraud charges in June 1991 for "humanitarian reasons" after reviewing medical reports of Argue's condition.

The uproar over this blatant misuse of public money and the obvious lack of sound accounting procedures led Auditor General Ken Dye to redouble demands for a look at the Senate books. His requests had been turned down since March 1988 by the Senate's Internal Economy Committee, the crew of in-house bosses who divvy up the bounty taxpayers provide. Along with other honorable senators, Tory Finlay MacDonald feared that Dye would go after all the "sexy stuff," such as free first-class travel and relatives on the payroll. The Senate decided to hire a private auditing firm whose report would remain secret. Dye launched a loud public denunciation of them for concealing the way they spent taxpayers' dollars, and the senators grudgingly reconsidered.

The chairman of the Internal Economy Committee was Roméo LeBlanc, another of those shameless appointments that accompanied Trudeau's hand-over of power to Turner in June 1984. LeBlanc agreed to let Dye look at the books, but only if he left attendance records and other clues to flagrant waste out of his study. "How often does the Senate sit? And is it cost effective, etc. That shouldn't be touched," insisted LeBlanc. It doesn't take the detective talents of Sherlock Holmes to figure out why. Here's the record of working days for the twenty-one years beginning with 1970: 91, 107, 50, 105, 77, 108, 95, 107, 97, 61, 74, 94, 96, 70, 69, 85, 74, 91, 90, 48, 107.

Individual attendance records for earlier years are almost impossible to unravel but have been meticulously kept since June 1990 when senators announced a plan to pay themselves a tax-free bonus of $153 for every day they showed up. Even with that incentive only nine made it to all seventy-two sittings in the fall. Despite whips who were rounding up members for each day's critical face-off, seven senators got to fewer than half the GST sittings. The absentee rate for the period was about 20 per cent. Without the GST and the hoped-for cash bonus for attendance fewer than half the members bother to drop in regularly.

Senators are supposed to lose $120 for each day's absence over twenty-one during a parliamentary session. They are excused for illness or if they are absent on Senate business. Every absentee claims to be either sick or doing Senate work elsewhere. There is one exception. Independent-minded Doug Everett, appointed by Pearson twenty-five years ago, refuses pay when he doesn't show up. A 1989 report on parliamentary salaries recommended that absences of over seven days should cost senators $600 for each missed sitting, $500 from salary and $100 from their tax-free allowance. The report gathers dust in the Library of Parliament.

Salaries and working hours aside, Dye found plenty of room for improvement in the way the Senate does business. His report was based on the 1989-90 budget when there were 89 senators, before Mulroney added 15 to fill vacancies and another 8 to push the GST into law. Dye pointed first to a serious lack of controls and accountability on its annual spending of $42 million. The Senate enjoys other services valued at $11.5 million that do not show in its budget. These come out of some other federal pocket, such as Canada Post, Public Works, Secretary of State, Treasury Board, the RCMP and the Library of Parliament. All of that brings the per-senator cost to well over half a million dollars.

It's no wonder. They spent $6 million flying themselves around the country, phoning free anywhere (a privilege extended to family and staff) and churning out printed matter with no regard for efficiencies. The Senate's forty-four messengers pick up and deliver mail hourly. They also handle 40,000 "urgent" messages a year at a cost of $8 apiece. Many of these messages travel a few feet, a distance, Dye says, that secretaries could easily cover. Messengers also run errands, including delivering laundry, parcels, bank deposits, and other "personal items between Parliament Hill and hotels, apartments, airports and transportation terminals." The tab for all that running around was a mere $1 million last year. While there is virtually no limit on where parcels can be sent, there is one on how big a load messengers can carry: 5.4 kilograms. Anything more requires a wheeled vehicle.

The Senate's forty-nine cleaners, waxers and polishers ring in at slightly more – $1.2 million. Dye noted that they do a good job. But though most of the time there is no one around to dirty the place,

Senate cleaners shine only 800 to 1,000 square feet an hour, while commercial office cleaners do 3,000 square feet.

A total of sixty-seven security guards keep the place safe for sleeping and, so far, free of murderers and kidnappers. However, Dye noted, "it's not clear who is in charge." He suggested a considerable tightening up of security practices and lines of authority.

The personal secretaries of senators are nearly all at the top of a generous scale. They have enjoyed pay hikes at a compounded rate of 8.6 per cent since 1987. This is nearly twice the increase most of the 437 other employees have received. The advent of the GST senators will boost the number of workers to 455 and add some $2 million to the annual bill.

The auditor general's report points out that not only is there roughly one messenger and one cleaner for every pair of senators but that members of the red chamber enjoy substantially more than half a security guard apiece. The difference in pay between their personal staff and that of other employees can be partly explained by the fact that family, friends and faithful retainers usually work in the former capacity. Dye spotted a number of relatives on senators' payrolls and termed the practice "inconsistent with the spirit of the Parliament of Canada Act which states a senator cannot have a direct or indirect interest in a contract funded with public money." Nearly all personal secretaries, already at the maximum salary level, also get $800 bilingual bonuses. Overall, Dye concluded that "there are few incentives to manage office expenditures with due regard for economy and efficiency. At the same time a policy should be established so that conflict-of-interest situations are avoided."

Possibly senators cannot keep an eye on red-chamber spending because they travel so much, racking up an average annual bill of almost $20,000 each. The top traveller in 1990 was Calgary Liberal Earl Hastings at $55,037. Nobody checks on whether trips have anything to do with Senate business. Families fly free too. They don't have to be with the senator or even winging in the same direction. In answer to a questionnaire, senators told Dye that most do not favor public disclosure of dates, destinations, costs or names of people taking the free trips. Dye recommended limits, disclosure, return of frequent-flier points for general Senate use and employment of a travel agency to cut costs.

He also considered phone bills a tad high. With no control on who is calling whom, where, why or for long, senators' telephone accounts averaged about $10,000 each a year. Seven senators topped $2,000 a month, many of them calling from their winter homes in Florida and Arizona to say "Hi" to colleagues stuck in Ottawa's horrid winter. A few previously little-known perks were uncovered by Dye's detectives, including a philatelic service that issues "first-day covers" to Senate stamp collectors. This little treat cost taxpayers $300 per stamp transaction. Along with that service, Dye noted, cut-rate haircuts in the Senate barber-shop, meals and free exercise facilities are used much more by staff than senators themselves. Salaried reporters and transcribers who record Senate debates are paid as full-time employees but work fewer than 150 days a year, often fewer than 100.

Just how the Senate gets its story out to the public puzzled the auditor general. The Information Services' office is a tiny one headed by ex-newspaperman Gord Lovelace, whose principal tools are scissors for his clipping service, a portable "shoe phone" and a bar tab at the National Press Club. While Lovelace's budget is a mere $388,000, Dye noted, it pays for "an activity which can have an impact on how the Senate is perceived."

In all spending areas, Dye said, scrutiny should be tightened up and public disclosure practised. In forty-six pages he made twenty-seven detailed recommendations. To it all Senator LeBlanc responded: "We welcome the report," adding that the upper house would study its suggestions.

The Internal Economy Committee that runs the place is a fifteen-person clique. At this writing, in addition to LeBlanc and Tory vice-chairman Bill Doody, the powerful players on the subcommittees are Trudeau appointees Colin Kenny and Tom Lefebvre and former Tory party president Nathan Nurgitz. Their discussions on how to divvy up the loot are secret.

It was the Internal Economy Committee that dreamed up the tax-free treat of $153 a day for simply showing up for work. The upper chamber quietly passed the motion in June 1990. Oddly, it came while the first ministers were debating Senate reform as way of breaking the Meech Lake deadlock. Millionaire senator Pietro Rizzuto said that the bonus was justifed to pay for the $1,000-a-month apartments senators rent when in town. Many, of course, alrcady live in the capital. Deputy Liberal leader Royce Frith said that the bonus was needed to keep cash rewards in line with the $20,600 tax-free (now $27,300) allowance of MPs. Before voting against the measure, Tory senator Duff Roblin declared: "I'm afraid the public reaction to this will not be good, and it certainly won't do the image of the Senate much good."

In late March 1991, their brand-new bonanza was whisked away just before it could be locked in with final approval of Parliament's spending estimates. When those came before the Commons, Tory back-bencher René Soetens protested. He insisted that the Senate grab was an illegal device granting a back-door raise that should only be provided through legislation. Speaker John Fraser agreed, thereby eliminating a $1.2-million annual cost, delighting MPs and infuriating scnators.

"The whole concept of what they were proposing was wrong. The dollar amount was wrong, the process was wrong, the legalities were wrong," barked Soetens. "The process of paying someone extra money to show up to do a job that they are paid to show up and do is wrong, whether it's in legislation or it's not in legislation. They're paid $64,400 to do a job. Do it."

It was not the first scam senators have tried in an effort to slop up a little more gravy. Back in 1987, Kenny proposed additional goodies that would have hiked the Senate budget by a full 25 per cent. These included full pension payments after fifteen years rather than twenty-five; salary increases for those with special positions such as whip and committee chairman; doubling of the tax-free allowance to about $20,000; and tripling of the budgets for hiring staff to $100,000.

The proposal was described by most MPs and some senators as "insane," and was rejected. Kenny and the Internal Economy crew have had more success with padding other perks. They quietly expanded their free-flight plan. Free flights were previously limited to trips between home and Ottawa; but senators can now jet first class anywhere in Canada. Even more secretly they extended that perk to cover travel outside the country; it is supplemented, of course, by the extra trips they win with their frequent-flier freebies. None of this has anything to do with the many, many junkets senators and their spouses take around the world as members of "inter-parliamentary delegations."

Senate flack Gord Lovelace explained that the frequent-flier bonuses offering all-expense-paid holidays abroad are an example of Senate efficiency. If they were to be returned and used for future Senate travel, he said, an employee would have to be hired to do the paperwork. The auditor general thought it would be well worth the expense – since it is already done by the Commons at a declared saving of $1.25 million annually – even though many MPs skirt the rules and still pile up their taxpayer-funded credits for holiday trips.

Kenny said that the travel policy needed to be revised to include foreign trips because many senators had important business outside the country and were being forced to pay the fare themselves. Besides, he did not believe that the new rules would be abused. "The people on the Internal Economy Committee are responsible people and they will not squander public monies," he reassured those who asked.

Certainly Kenny would never think of squandering taxpayers' hard-earned dollars. One of the last flunkies Trudeau slipped into an upper-house easy chair in 1984, Kenny has devotedly made life easier for senators and harder for staff. A veteran of bureaucratic infighting, he's a graduate of the Amos Tuck School of Business Administration in Hanover, New Hampshire, and of years in the trenches for Trudeau. Executive director of the Liberal party in 1968 when Trudeaumania infected the country, he became special assistant to the prime minister two years later and then director of operations. It was in the latter role that the press gallery nicknamed the short, bald back-room boy "Colonel Klink" in reference to the bumbling commandant in the TV series "Hogan's Heroes." "He looks at the Senate as if it's his personal little empire," grumbled one senior senate official. He gets involved in the $153 a day right down to such minor things as who should park at the Victoria Building.

As chairman of Internal Economy's subcommittee on accommodation and facilities, Kenny flooded Senate staff with memos on "stuff like the quality of soap in the dispensers and the quality of toilet paper in the washrooms," says one staffer. His record has been one both of preserving senatorial privileges and of enhancing the staff, supplies and services that grow with them. Although most of his 1987 package of goodies was discarded, Kenny managed to salvage one treat, a new $50,000 allowance for unspecified research and office expenses. It has now risen to $55,000.

One of the best examples of his concern for pinching public pennies came in a $20,000 report he commissioned in 1989 on renovations to Senate space in the historic East Block. It was conducted by consultants Pierre Marquis and Frank Currie, who happened to work for LeBlanc when he was in the Trudeau cabinet. A high-ranking Senate official says that those two, along with former LeBlanc trouble-shooter Andy Perrier, now have cushy jobs overseeing Senate space. "They are in control and we are even supplying them with a secretary."

The report called for sound-proof senatorial offices with three-piece bathrooms, private dressing rooms and three-quarter-length mirrors. The renovation list included an exercise room with sauna, fitness equipment and beds fancier than those in the suntan parlor Kenny runs as an outside business. The beds, of course, would be used after a gruelling workout. Also recommended were a private dining room – the exclusive Parliamentary Restaurant wasn't good enough – and a lounge for female senators, complete with a kitchenette. None of the senators felt that the expense was too much. "We're just asking that the space we have be used more efficiently," huffed Liberal senator Dalia Wood, who was Trudeau's riding secretary before she ascended to patronage heaven. "If we want to redistribute the space we have what does it matter? We're not out to spend a lot of money."

A firestorm of protest over the luxurious and costly renovations sent the senators running for cover when the secret report was leaked to the *Ottawa Citizen*. But the outcry did not kill Kenny's grandiose plans. The Internal Economy Committee sneaked the renovations through the back door using the eight extra GST senators as cover for the remodelling work. The Senate spent nearly $2 million for new offices and committee rooms in 1991. Eleven executive offices were built in the Victoria Building on Wellington Street. Each has a private bathroom and separate offices for secretaries and their researchers. During the renovations the secretary of Liberal senator Michael Kirby had workmen raise the floor in her office three inches so she could gaze out the front window. "Then she was pissed off," an official said. "She was complaining about pigeon shit on the ledge."

In March 1991, the committee also approved a secret expenditure of $29,200 for a "fitness centre" on the second floor of the Victoria Building. Kenny is a fitness freak who can often be spotted jogging along the canal with his wife, Petra. The private spa for senators and staff is in addition to three free gyms already on Parliament Hill – one for staff, another for parliamentarians, and one for female MPs and senators. Rarely do senators, or MPs for that matter, flex their muscles there.

The Senate also built a women's lounge in the Centre Block, which it disguised in official budget documents as a "women's cloakroom," and constructed a separate "workroom" in which members could watch television. There is already a reading room off the Senate chamber where fruit, soup and sandwiches are provided while senators unwind. "That's too common for them," said one Senate staffer. The "workroom" was added as a place for senators to doze and contemplate their good fortune.

Kenny's way of running the upper chamber led René Gutknecht to resign abruptly in May 1990 as gentleman usher of the black rod. The Canadian *Parliamentary Handbook* describes the gentleman usher as "responsible for the security service and certain maintenance services," and for serving as personal attendant to the representative of Her Majesty in the Senate. Gutknecht, a retired army lieutenant-general, had been barely a year on the job when he quit. He complained that Kenny had repeatedly thwarted administrative changes and did not contribute "to the modern management of the Senate." Kenny claimed that Gutknecht had tried to sidestep the chain of command. "Senators run the Senate, not the Black Rod." He insisted that he had implemented several reforms in the wake of the Argue investigation. "You can't even get a ballpoint pen now unless you sign a chit."

Kenny and his Senate mates may have difficulty finding a ballpoint pen, but they haven't had any trouble finding public money to splurge on travel and research. Figures in the Public Accounts show that Kenny, who lives in Ottawa, spent $24,957 on travel and $44,875 on research in 1990. The year before he spent $29,512 on travel alone. Ahead of Kenny, however, was Argue, who somehow managed to spent $31,354 on travel and $44,150 on research while disabled all year with cancer.

Just what Senate researchers do is a mystery, although at least one does it mostly at the Press Club bar on behalf of a female Maritime senator. But Kenny found useful work for his researcher. He hired a university student to prepare a document listing Internal Economy decisions. Kenny then got the Senate to spend $8,000 to hire the same student for a quarterly update on the booklet titled *Selected Legislation, Rules, Committee Reports and Other Reports Pertaining to Senators.* "It's something we can do here with the staff," a senior administration official remarked. "All you have to do is write down the decisions and put it in the binder."

Among the perks Kenny and the Internal Economy Committee have approved in recent years are free food in the reading room near the Senate chamber, cellular phones, faxes for their homes, personal laptop computers, stereos and even video cassette recorders and cameras. The video cameras were justified on the grounds that senators use them in speech training. Those who ask are told they set the cameras up at home, deliver speeches to them and then analyse their performance.

Kenny even proposed, on March 7, 1991, that senators have "duress alarms installed in their offices and those of their secretaries" at a cost of $185,658. The silent alarms will be put under the desks of all senators and those of their assistants. A senator choking on a chocolate could alert security guards by pressing a button. The proposal did not meet with unanimous approval. Tory senator E.W. Barootes objected, fearing that Parliament Hill could become an "armed bastion" much like Capitol Hill in the States. The silent alarms are expected not only to summon help to subdue possible "deadly" intruders but also to alert outside help should a senator suffer a heart attack.

The committee also set aside $20,000 to rent a second grey minibus to carry senators the half block from the Victoria Building to the front door of the Senate. The Commons already has nine shuttle buses circling the same route, but the senators shun their use.

Nothing is too small for Kenny's committee to consider. They agreed in 1991 that the bronze plaques on senators' doors "can be taken by the Senator when he or she retires or resigns." But Kenny did save the taxpayers a few dollars in 1991 by changing the policy under which grandparents, grandchildren and their spouses could fly free. The new definition of "immediate family" is the "spouse of the Senator, children and any person residing with the Senator on a permanent basis."

Senators are quick to look for savings that will not impair their own comfort. They ordered all employees, except their own, to use accumulated leave by the end of 1992. Employees must submit a pink slip for any absences and a blue form at the end of the month confirming their attendance. The same rigorous policy does not apply to personal staff. Up to ten secretaries rarely appear for work, according to one insider. Because some senators, such as Grit Andy Thompson or millionaire Liberal fund-raiser Leo Kolber, rarely turn up for sittings, their secretaries stay at home with office phones on call forwarding.

The new policy for Senate staff has already led to a 50 per cent cut in accumulated leave. "The same sort of success has not been achieved with Senators' personal office staff," Senate clerk Gordon Barnhart wrote in a briefing note to Kenny's committee in November 1990. "Staff of office holders are expected to increase their accumulated leave by 25 per cent at the end of this fiscal year [March 31, 1991]." Even though the Senate sits only about two and half months a year, it secretly agreed to pay off senatorial secretaries. Instead of asking them to take time off, senators approved a plan to buy out all stored-up holiday time, a total of 493 days. Pearl Hunter, Allan MacEachen's long-time secretary, banked 136 days from her service with him while he was deputy prime minister. Hunter's holidays will cost taxpayers $21,620.34. Kenny's secretary, Donna Routliffe, had more than 54 days, worth $7,461.99 according to Senate documents. Others with valuable time owed are Claire Bourdon, secretary to Hartland Molson, at $19,305.35 and Senator Jim Balfour's secretary, Jean Bye, at $9,584.

The Senate story is one of an institution gone badly astray. It is guilty of either inactivity or hyperactivity. Agreement with government is viewed as a mere rubber stamp. Resistance to government is seen as obstruction. The Senate has long since given up its mandate to speak for the regions. It speaks only for the parties and for the self-interest of its members. Short of a major overhaul, Canadians might at least hope for reforms to curb its extravagance.

9
THE PLUM TREE

*"Remember that every dollar you pay to the end of your
days will go to pay for the golden retirement of tired Liberals.
It's a deceit and a sham. It has to be corrected by dramatic
gestures, and I propose to do that."*

BRIAN MULRONEY, JULY 1984

M R. JUSTICE BUD CULLEN RECLINED IN A SOFT LEATHER
chair as the faithful Commons factotum buffed his
black oxfords. It was years since Cullen had trod
the polished marble halls as a cabinet prince in the
court of King Pierre. His hair had thinned and his waist thickened
since he had escaped from the incoming tide of Tories to the high
ground of the Federal Court in 1984. But, like most former parliamentarians, he could never put the glory years on the Hill completely
behind him. He had ridden into Ottawa on the Trudeaumania wave
in 1968. Effort, charm and luck had made the cheerful little lawyer
from Sarnia a popular MP and later a minister with the pay and prestige top rank accords. The combination of judge's pay and parliamentary pension today has rewarded him even better, with an income
package of $200,000 a year. Not only that, the $1 shoeshine and
bargain buffet in the majestic parliamentary dining room, among the
best deals in town, are still available to Cullen as an "old boy" in the
parliamentary club. The restaurant would always be a place of fond
memories, of battles won or lost but never forgotten by those who
fought them. Much of the restaurant's daily business is with former
political gladiators who return to bask in the glow of recognition and
the balm of nostalgia – recalling past events in anecdotes that improve
with time and repetition. Political enemies often become friends in the
warm bath of post-parliamentary remembrances.

Cullen may return to the Centre Block to get his shoes shined, but
he need never feel lonely on the bench. There are plenty of his former

Commons comrades right there with him for company. Of the twenty-seven justices of the Federal Court of Canada, five are former cabinet ministers named by Trudeau. The associate chief justice of that court is Jim Jerome, a former Liberal MP and Commons speaker from 1974 to 1980. He took a slightly trickier route to the prestige and power of the bench as a reward for political service. Joe Clark sent him there in 1980, the price Jerome extracted for remaining in the speaker's chair during the 1979 minority months. By getting a Liberal to take the chair, Clark kept his own ranks at full strength and reduced the opposition by one critical member. Jerome, who enjoyed the perks of a job he did well, knew that his decision to help out a Conservative prime minister would preclude any future rewards from his own party. Thus the deal with Clark.

Elevation to the bench is even better than a summons to the Senate. Although both senators and federal judges are somehow felt competent to work ten years longer than the rest of us before mandatory retirement at age seventy-five, the courts pay far more handsomely. Judges have to work, of course. But the job bestows some prestige and power without such odious labels as hack and bagman.

Most Canadians choose to believe that judges cast off their political prejudices with their street clothes when they don the robes of office. Certainly they are supposed to be free of political taint. Public faith in the judicial system can be dangerously undermined if they are perceived as partisan. Even Sir John A. Macdonald, every bit as proficient in the patronage arts as Trudeau and Brian Mulroney, believed that the courts should be relatively free of partisan prize-winners. "My rule is to consider fitness as the first prerequisite for judicial appointments and that political consideration should have little or no influence," Macdonald said. "I have always felt that the judicial officers stand on a quite different footing from all others, that fitness with respect to the bench must be the first consideration and that no political exigency however great would warrant the government in appointing an unfit judge."

One way or another, lots of them made it to the bench in the years that followed. The appointments are made by the justice minister, but the senior ones are initiated or at least approved by the prime minister. Ray Hnatyshyn recalls that when he was justice minister, the country's most ardent Conservative, Erik Nielsen, inquired about a top court appointment when it came time to leave the House and cabinet. Such an appointment for parliament's top partisan was too much even for the man who went on to become governor general and no stranger to the patronage trough himself. Nielsen had to rustle around in the government loot bag for another prize.

Hnatyshyn and other justice ministers confide that there is a steady stream of senior Canadian lawyers trying to wheedle their way onto the bench, despite the apparent sacrifice that pay of only $150,000 or so would mean. So political appointees do not get there because of a shortage of other suitable, less partisan candidates.

In addition to Cullen, the other ministers Trudeau squeezed onto the bench of the Federal Court (Canada's second highest after the Supreme Court), were Mark MacGuigan, Yvon Pinard, Patrick Mahoney and J.E. Dubé. All are still there. He also popped a couple of lesser ministers into lower courts just before election disaster overtook his Liberals. That was the last orgy of "jobs for the boys" under the Trudeau/Turner deal that so incensed Mulroney. In the batch of patronage appointments, seventeen sitting MPs were sent to what Mulroney called "Grit heaven." Oddly, for a man so committed to an immaculate judicial process, Trudeau was unable to find a single Conservative fit for elevation to the bench.

His use of political pay-offs still troubles legal authorities, especially the final bounty that produced the famous "You had a choice, sir" television encounter between Turner and Mulroney. Of the judicial appointments, the Canadian Bar Association was equally critical: "This court is perceived, rightly or wrongly, as a government-oriented court because so many former politicians and federal officials have been appointed to it." As late as February 1990 the legal prizes were still raising serious concerns. "The mythology of an apolitical judiciary is crumbling," claimed Robert Martin, an expert in constitutional law at the University of Western Ontario. As he told the magazine *Alberta Report*: "Justices have abandoned their traditional reluctance to become openly political. The fact that some well-known cabinet ministers have been appointed to the Federal Court of

Canada in the last decade may have something to do with the expanded role the court has been playing recently. These are people who aren't accustomed to obscurity."

The flock of Liberal MPs who scooped up lucrative federal jobs just ahead of the 1984 Tory tide became a key campaign target for Mulroney. Armed with polls showing that Canadians were fed up with politicians "cutting up the cash," Mulroney hammered away relentlessly and effectively. "There's not a Grit left in town; they're all gone to Grit heaven," Mulroney trumpeted throughout the campaign. "I undertake today that all political appointments will be of the highest unimpeachable quality. I am going to send out a dramatic signal of renewal in this area of Canadian life."

In fact, Mulroney has been careful not to name many high-profile Tories to the bench. Two-term Conservative MP Chris Speyer, former Ontario attorney general Roy McMurtry and ex–Manitoba premier Sterling Lyon were given judicial posts. But less conspicuous party connections were an undoubted factor in many other judgeships.

A study by two University of Toronto professors – Jacob Ziegle and noted constitutional expert Peter Russell – found that nearly half the 224 judges approved by Mulroney since 1984 were Tories, many of them party workers. Patronage was particularly rife among appointees to senior courts, such as provincial courts of appeal and superior courts. "We see no reason why Canadians should acquiesce in a system that seems bound every year to produce a few really bad appointments to the higher courts of this country," the professors wrote in their report issued in June 1989. They concluded that Mulroney's vow to end the system of judicial patronage was hollow. It would not be the first time, or the last, that Canadians found some discrepancy between pre-vote talk and post-vote action.

There is also a big difference between the selfless sacrifice of personal careers that MPs describe and the rich rewards they enjoy in Parliament and afterwards. There is undeniable stress, strain and job insecurity for MPs, just as there is for other Canadians. Hardly anyone enjoys long-term employment guarantees at a time of economic upheaval and technological change. But few enjoy such a generous pay package while working and almost none makes such a soft landing upon leaving as do the 295 men and women we choose to represent us in Parliament.

Yet it is those career uncertainties, interruptions of home life, long hours and frequent travel that they cite as reasons for the lavish pay and pension package they have awarded themselves. Those who retire or get fired by the voters get up to $7,500 to hire professional career consultants to help them readjust. There is also an Association of Former Members of Parliament. It was set up by former Trudeau minister John Reid as a career and social clearing house for idle ex-members. It meets sporadically.

The average time in office of an MP is about six years, just the time it takes to qualify for immediate pension. Although they embrace the principle that voters hire and fire them, they argue that pay for public service should be enough to reduce temptation towards bribery and graft. Most claim that better pay attracts better candidates. Since Stanley Knowles' departure, few have argued that the rewards for public service are not to be found in a pay cheque. Many also claim that they could do better financially in careers outside the House, although statistics show that the average for teachers, accountants, broadcasters/journalists, business operators, consultants and farmers all fall well below the Commons pay and perks package. Only doctors and top lawyers make more.

Until Louis St. Laurent introduced a pension plan in 1952 there was no program to assist ex-members when they walked away from Parliament Hill. The first pensions were paid only to those who had served for at least sixteen years and did not draw any other government payment. In the early 1970s, with inflation heating up, MPs sweetened the mix to make it the most generous pension plan in North America.

Now, after just six years in the Commons, any member who leaves gets at least $23,390 a year. Payment begins immediately whether the ex-member is twenty-five or fifty-five. The amount increases by 5 per cent for each year of service up to fifteen years, at which point the recipient gets an annual pay-off equal to 75 per cent. The base figure on which the percentage is calculated is the average income of the member's best-paid six years. For ex-ministers and others who get premium pay in Parliament, the dividends are substantial for the rest of their lives. And that includes a lot of members. At any time nearly a hundred of them are collecting premiums as ministers, parliamentary secretaries, whips, deputy speakers and so on, all of which sweetens the pension take when their public service ends. For instance, if Joe Clark quit today he would collect $62,000 annually for life or $2.6 million assuming he lives to age seventy-five. Mulroney became eligible after only four years for two-thirds of his salary, or $100,000 for life once he leaves 24 Sussex. That compares quite favorably with the Canada Pension Plan. In April 1991, it was announced that the CPP will jump 2.1 per cent to keep pace with inflation, an increase of $8.45 a month to $362.37.

But there is still more of a cushion for the former parliamentarians to rest on after leaving politics. At age sixty, they begin to enjoy automatic inflation indexing, a catch-up for all the earlier years and a protection until death against the price hikes that ravage others. Special treatment goes even beyond the grave. When a former MP dies, his or her surviving spouse continues to collect the total pension, unlike most Canadian plans that cut widows and widowers to 60 per cent.

On September 4, 1990, the sixth anniversary of the 1984 election, seventy-five members of Parliament grasped the gold ring of lifelong income after the merry-go-round of politics. That security is a big reason so few members resign. Bloc Québécois members choose to fight Canada in Parliament where they can draw every possible buck from the system even after they eventually leave. Even for the few who get disgusted enough to leave before the voters throw them out, departures invariably come when the pension qualification period has been passed. Until then most just hang on to their seats, while coming less and less often to the House to sit in them.

A study by the National Citizens' Coalition (NCC) found in March 1990 that 168 of today's 295 MPs are eligible for pensions. Of those, 93 could expect to receive more than $1 million in payments if they quit now and lived to age seventy-five, assuming an annual inflation rate of 5 per cent a year. New Democrat Lorne Nystrom, with twenty-three years in the Commons, would receive

$46,000 annually. Perrin Beatty, the forty-one-year-old communications minister who has been in the House for nineteen years, would get $67,000 a year. By the age of seventy-five, Beatty will have scooped up $5.2 million. Liberal Lloyd Axworthy, with twelve years under his belt, would begin collecting $40,000. When Jean Chrétien vacated his uncomfortable opposition seat beside John Turner after the 1984 election, he received more in annual pension than he would have in basic salary by staying in the House. His pension, of course, was based on long, well-paid years as a Trudeau minister.

MPs contribute 11 per cent of their basic $64,400 salary to the pension treasure chest, 10 per cent for the pension and 1 per cent for inflation. That comes nowhere close to funding the golden years of post-parliamentary life. In 1989 taxpayers chipped in more than $7 million to cover payments to 315 former MPs. Recipients may like the scheme, but they do not enjoy talking about it. A report by G.W. Poznanski, chief actuary at the Office of the Superintendent of Financial Institutions, concluded that taxpayers face a $144 million tab to bail out the pension-for-life scheme.

"These people [MPs] are filling their pockets with our money – and then coming back for more," fumed David Somerville, president of the NCC. "You try and find any deal like that in the private sector. It's an absolute scam." Somerville has argued for years that the Commons plan should be brought into line with those in the outside world. No MP has yet come forward to lead the fight.

Few MPs seem troubled by Somerville's concerns. "I don't feel any embarrassment about it," says Murray Dorin, the Conservative member for Edmonton Northwest, who hit pension age at thirty-six. He explained how taxpayers could avoid paying the huge pension bill: "Don't forget, you don't get your pension until you leave. If people want to prevent people from collecting their pensions then just keep re-electing them." Tory Don Blenkarn, a powerful preacher of restraint, believes that MPs should be proud of their achievement when they gain entry to the lucrative club. He congratulated his newer colleagues when they joined the winner's circle in 1990. "Obviously the boys who have now been here six years have a right to be a bit relieved," he told reporters. "They now qualify as being on the team. They've now made the cut. They should rejoice." A millionaire Mississauga businessman, Blenkarn served from 1972 to 1974 and again from 1979 until now. That means he will be a fifteen-year, grand-prize-for-life winner before the next election.

New Democrat Howard McCurdy, who represents the blue-collar voters of Windsor-Lake St. Clair, exploded with indignation when *Windsor Star* columnist Gord Henderson raised the issue with him in June 1990. McCurdy reeled off the familiar argument about MPs being special cases. "Most of us come to resent the notion that a parliamentarian should be here on a volunteer basis with no support staff, no pensions and earning no more than somebody working in McDonald's." According to Henderson, McCurdy described the NCC as an organization "opposed to every civilized aspect of this country."

The idea that MPs should get fair compensation for public service is one that few Canadians quarrel with. It is necessary to attract capable people who do not have independent means of support while performing public duties. Many feel that the rewards have now become so rich, however, that the job is drawing candidates who are interested more in the pay and perks than in public service.

Some former MPs have more reason to rejoice than others. They are the lucky "double-dippers" who get two scoops from the trough of tax-paid treats. Double-dipping allows a former MP sitting on a federal court, board or agency to collect both pension and full salary from his or her appointed post. Senators, limited to one parliamentary payment, cannot double-dip, although they can hold any number of outside jobs or directorships. That is one reason former MPs sometimes prefer non-Senate plums. Former Liberal cabinet veteran Bryce Mackasey turned down a Senate offer from Trudeau in 1984. Over drinks in the National Press Club, Mackasey told reporters he had asked for the ambassadorship to Portugal so he could collect his MP's pension plus a foreign-service salary while living almost free as a diplomat. It was a sound financial plan that went awry. Mackasey should have taken the Senate sinecure, which cannot be revoked. He lost the Lisbon posting in one of Mulroney's first anti-patronage acts after winning power. The same thing happened to Eugene Whelan, who chose not to doze in the Senate when Trudeau offered him a chance. Instead he won an ambassadorship to the Food and Agriculture Organization in Rome, only to have it withdrawn by the new prime minister three months later. Whelan, who lost his long-time post as agriculture minister when John Turner briefly took power, brags that he was fired by two prime ministers in three months. "I'm the only person I know ever to have received such an honor," he says in his autobiography, *The Man in the Green Stetson.*

Five years earlier Mackasey came out on top in a similar government turnover. Trudeau had given him a rich and comfortable spot as chairman of Air Canada just before Joe Clark won power in 1979. The terms of the appointment meant it could not simply be revoked by the new government. The Tories paid Mackasey a quarter of a million dollars to leave. The pay-off left a sour taste in the mouths of many Tory MPs. They felt that Clark was quick to get rid of Mackasey but slow to reward the party faithful before the 1980 election.

In 1984, another Trudeau appointee put up such a fuss about having his sinecure withdrawn that he won a pay-off. After fourteen years in the Commons, Maurice Dupras had been sent to luxurious rest as Canada's consul general to Bordeaux in the heart of France's wine country. The salary was $69,000, which, combined with a $40,000 Commons pension, would have allowed the sixty-three-year-old Dupras to glide comfortably into his golden years. Claiming that his dismissal was "discriminatory, arbitrary, capricious, malicious and of bad faith," Dupras had Mulroney subpoenaed for a Federal Court hearing before an unrevealed out-of-court payment finally pacified him.

The Conservatives chose to live unhappily with another former Trudeau minister in a top patronage post for a full seven years. Pierre Juneau was named communications minister in August 1975 without having been elected. He then accomplished the seemingly impossible feat of losing a by-election in a safe Montreal seat. After that he resigned from cabinet. Trudeau gave his old friend a number of other jobs before naming him president of the CBC in 1982, a secure seven-year appointment. The Conservatives had a choice of buying him out or living with him as hated head of a key Crown agency. Possibly mindful of public disgust at the Mackasey buy-out earlier, they left Juneau in place, happily kicking the corporation around for his full term.

While Mulroney had some trouble with Trudeau's patronage appointments and double-dippers, he was happy to reward his own loyalists. In 1985, a commission recommended that pensions be deferred to age fifty-five in favor of improved severance pay. The idea was rejected. A year later a Commons committee suggested that MPs who later take federal jobs should not collect full pensions at the same time. Nothing came of that idea either. Former Tory minister Jack Murta, for instance, enjoys a $45,000 annual pension plus a salary of $91,700 as a grain commissioner.

Liberal (former Conservative) MP David Kilgour has been a rare voice of pension protest in the House. In March 1991, he put two private members' bills forward on the subject. One would have deferred payment to age sixty. The other would have prevented double-dipping. That one got support from rookie Liberal MPs Ron Duhamel, Dr. Rey Pagtakhan, Beryl Gaffney and Reform Party MP Deborah Grey.

"Why don't we just go one step farther and defer pensions for Members of Parliament to age sixty whether they're working in the private or public sector?" Grey asked the Commons. "I think that would bring us much more in line and that we would not be held in such contempt by the Canadian public." Neither Grey's nor Kilgour's proposals had a chance. An all-party committee that could have allowed extended debate on one Kilgour bill instead permitted just one hour. It was "talked out" without a vote. The other bill was subject to a random draw and was not chosen for any debate at all.

MPs may find their pensions comfortable, but talking about them is not. When forced to, they usually fall back awkwardly on the argument about a tough readjustment to the work-force after years of public service. Few concede that their job prospects are greatly enhanced because of knowledge and contacts they acquire during their stay on the Hill. Liberal Doug Frith is an example. A pharmacist from Sudbury, he parlayed two terms as an MP into a nice pension and a top job with a senior Ottawa firm of lobbyists/consultants, Public Affairs International. Others secure a return to their jobs before they leave for Ottawa. Two top Tories who argue strenuously for top pay and perks because of the uncertainties of political life are Harvie Andre, first elected in 1972 and colleague Jim Hawkes, elected in 1979. Both professors at the University of Calgary, they have insisted that they retain the right to return to their academic posts whenever they leave Ottawa with their fat pension packages in hand. Andre, as a long-time minister, and Hawkes, as party whip, will enjoy extra sweet retirement benefits when they return to their jobs.

Nevertheless, another professor of another political stripe from another university says it is not that easy. "For someone who's fifty or fifty-five, they're out in the labor market without any easy capacity to get back into what they were part of," says forty-four-year-old New Democrat Steven Langdon. It may be difficult for New Democrats to find work, but it hasn't been for former Conservative MPs in the last few years.

Virtually all those who did not return to Parliament after the 1988 election have been handed well-paid government jobs. Forty of them today enjoy rewards ranging from Senate seats to diplomatic posts, to top jobs with Crown corporations, federal agencies, boards and commissions. Even spouses board the gravy train. For instance Kate Schellenberg, whose husband, Ted, lost his B.C. seat after one term, landed a job as a Citizenship Court judge at $60,300 annually.

Most of the 3,500 patronage jobs that Mulroney and his cabinet have to hand out are filled by faithful party friends. Appointments are listed in the *Canada Gazette* when Orders in Council (cabinet orders) are passed approving them. In the weeks following the 1988 election the names of Tory losers and key campaign players were sprinkled through its pages. When Liberals held patronage power, their officers and foot-soldiers were similarly placed.

Most politicians argue that some patronage is needed to make the system work. It provides an incentive to party volunteers and keeps members in line. To stray from the party is also to abandon the goodies that await. In his autobiography, Whelan says a third of all such appointments should be political ones, both to establish the primacy of elected politicians who control the process of appointment and to give workers a hope of reward. Others maintain that such a process simply perpetuates a bad party system, attracts political players for motives of greed rather than public service and gives all politicians a bad reputation. What it boils down to is that those inside the party system believe in patronage as an essential element of politics, while those outside do not. The system, and the argument, have been here since at least the time of Sir John A. The practice grows more entrenched yearly as the list of government jobs and partisans to fill them increases.

The most luscious plum on the patronage tree is a five-year appointment to Government House. The governor general gets the usual perks of high office – a limousine and chauffeur, bodyguards, use of government jets, oodles of staff and so on. There is also the sumptuous Rideau Hall estate, across the street from the prime minister's home at 24 Sussex but far larger. It has a tennis court, a cricket pitch, magnificent gardens and greenhouses and a rink, toboggan run and ski trails. There is a second residence for the Queen's representative, in Quebec City. Known as "the Citadel," it is a former fortress, now a luxurious château, on the Plains of Abraham.

For generations members of the British nobility filled the post of Queen's representative, with the monarch playing a part in the selection in London. That changed in 1952 when Vincent Massey was finally rewarded by Louis St. Laurent, after years of lobbying and political contributions, with appointment as the first Canadian governor general. Massey came from Canada's own aristocracy, the legendary farm-equipment manufacturing family. He was succeeded by widely admired Georges Vanier, a dignified French-Canadian general. Former Commons speaker Roland Michener was next, having first been "depoliticized" by a four-year term as high commissioner to India. Michener, a former Conservative MP, was appointed by a Liberal prime minister, Lester Pearson. Next came the refined and respected ex-diplomat Jules Léger. His wife, Gabrielle, took on many of the viceroy's duties when he was partly incapacitated by a stroke early in his five-year term. All four appointees were powerful national symbols who were seen to be non-political.

Pierre Trudeau began the nomination of less-than-eminent politicians who wore their partisan colors right up to the gates of Rideau Hall. He astounded many Canadians by awarding the viceregal post to the former NDP premier of Manitoba, Ed Schreyer. Fluently dull in four languages, Schreyer, his wife, Lily, and their four children stripped much of the pomp and grandeur from Government House. Teenage rock and a youthful atmosphere permeated the old estate, as high-school friends visited poster-covered family rooms and old pals like author Farley Mowat wandered the halls and grounds, glass in hand.

Following the Schreyers, Trudeau lifted Speaker Jeanne Sauvé directly from the Commons cauldron into the governor-generalship. Her appointment was announced two days before Christmas 1983. She resigned from the House when members returned in the New Year, on January 14. The comfortable distance between the viceregal office and the mean arena of daily politics disappeared. With it the symbol of historical dignity had clearly been reduced to a shabby political pay-off.

Sauvé restored the air of elegance to Rideau Hall but at a cost that drew fire from close range. A stone and steel fence surrounding the eighty-eight-acre property became a symbolic barricade against the neighbors who had wandered the grounds through its history. The gates were kept closed and the fence was upgraded, at a cost of $700,000, officially as a security measure initiated by the RCMP, unofficially to keep neighborhood dogs, Rockcliffe riff-raff and indiscreet lovers off the grounds.

Restoring the 1836 mansion to symbolic grandeur did not come cheap. The cost of running the 185 room residence soared from $4.8 million when Sauvé moved in to $10.6 million today. The governor general's tax-free pay almost doubled from $48,000 when Sauvé arrived to $88,000 today. For the Sauvés it was stacked on top of two hefty parliamentary pensions, hers as former speaker and cabinet minister at premium pay and that of her husband, Maurice, as a former Pearson minister. That was still not enough to meet all their personal needs. Taxpayers paid $8,000 for them to attend their son's 1989 wedding in Paris, including the cost of getting the viceregal couple over there and of providing a chauffeured limousine and overtime pay for support staff.

The old home itself slurped up still more for such essential improvements as an $18,000 air-conditioning unit in the wine cellar, repainting throughout, reupholstering and some fancy work on the cornice of at least one salon. The governor general complained that "just to save a few dollars" the renovators had used gold paint rather than gold leaf. The bemused reporter whom she told about the shoddy job had not previously noticed the wretched results of state penny-pinching.

One thing Ray Hnatyshyn did when Mulroney awarded him the job in 1990 was to reopen the imperial gates to allow neighbors and lovers access once again. "If the Berlin Wall can come down, the gates can be open," a beaming Hnatyshyn said of the gesture. Not only is the public allowed on the grounds much of the time, but Ray and Gerda Hnatyshyn have invited the neighbors in for tea on occasion. The gesture has been rewarded with much goodwill.

If public relations is Hnatyshyn's forte, he is also no slouch at dispensing taxpayers' money. It cost more than $3.2 million in the 1990-91 fiscal year to operate and maintain Rideau Hall. In a six-month period in 1990, he managed to spend $485,384 on flights aboard the government's Challenger jets. His annual travel budget is $800,000, costs that are never questioned. He recently approved a $700,000 plan to renovate the service wing, where up to eighty waiters and waitresses polish the silver, iron the napkins and prepare the food for guests. But Hnatyshyn did save a few pennies the night of the May 1991 opening of Parliament. He threw a black-tie party for 800 of Ottawa's elite but, instead of a sit-down dinner, guests had finger food to chew on. He also opted for an Air Force quintet rather than the usual orchestra that performs for such events.

Losing his Saskatchewan seat in the 1988 election may have been one of the best things that ever happened to the cheerful viceroy. He naturally got pensioned from Parliament on the basis of his cabinet salary, then was awarded the country's top prize as consolation for his loss. Hnatyshyn's political partisanship had not even been tempered by a term in the "neutral" role of speaker, as had Sauvé's. He remains an ebullient member of Mulroney's inner circle of friends, a group that is indistinguishable from his circle of political cronies. A few such old comrades-in-arms get together for small, intimate occasions such as New Year's Eve at the Prime Minister's Harrington Lake retreat.

When he was sworn in, Hnatyshyn, of proud Ukrainian heritage, declared: "The governor general belongs to the people of Canada – not to any one linguistic, cultural or economic group – but to all Canadians." He could have added that, as never before, it now belongs to the party in power for use as a blatant tool of political patronage. Instead he told an interviewer for his hometown newspaper, the *Star-Phoenix*, "My dad would be so proud." There is no doubt his father, John, who died in 1967, would be both proud and wise about the process by which his fifty-six-year-old offspring achieved top spot on Canada's protocol list. John Hnatyshyn had been awarded a Senate seat by John Diefenbaker thirty-one years earlier.

Dad would probably have liked the newly tailored military uniform Ray dons for ceremonial occasions, a throwback to his university days in the Reserve Officers Training Program and later the RCAF auxiliary. He would also appreciate the new family coat of arms that heraldic experts designed for his prominent progeny. It's a pretty busy work of art, featuring Ukrainian and Danish symbols (for the viceregal couple's ancestry), trees, wheat, water and sky (for Saskatchewan)and the royal crest with lions and the scales of justice (to represent the governor general's legal background; his final cabinet post was as justice minister).

Hnatyshyn's is not the only viceregal payment Mulroney has awarded for past political services. He has scattered Conservative lieutenant-governors across the country too. The office comes with prestige and a residence and little work. The lucky winners of those political trophies get royal-sized perks – limousines, splendid entertainment facilities, top billing at public events and so on, along with

$88,000. They too get their own flag and coat of arms and a comfortable, expense-paid five-year term. The office was described by Jeffrey Simpson in his book *Spoils of Power* as a "convenient nesting place for politicians whose pasts are more glorious than their futures." Sir John A. explained that he never reappointed lieutenant-governors for a second term because, "If I reappoint one lieutenant-governor the others who are all political friends would feel slighted if the same favor were not granted them." Such are the continuing burdens of power.

Mulroney has sent five former Tory MPs through these portals to paradise, ignoring Sir John A.'s counsel by naming one of them, Ontario lieutenant-governor Lincoln Alexander, to a second term. Party bagmen, provincial politicians and other Conservative loyalists have also become royal representatives in provincial capitals. The rationale varies with each appointment. It can be a simple reward for long, loyal service, a device for defusing potential trouble-makers or a way to persuade an old war-horse to vacate his seat for a rising star. Alexander was not only a much-loved veteran but also the first black to achieve the lofty roost, thus giving Mulroney a credit on the "visible minority" account.

Jim McGrath, an accomplished but volatile Newfoundlander, won his prize place for a combination of reasons. He was potential trouble in Ottawa, where he brooded about Mulroney's choice of John Crosbie as the top representative from the island province. McGrath had backed Mulroney in the 1976 Conservative leadership race but stayed with Clark through the 1983 brawl that eventually chose the present leader. Mulroney also wanted to open a St. John's seat for former adviser and whiz-kid Ross Reid. Today McGrath reflects on his thirty years in Parliament in the distant governor's mansion in the Newfoundland capital.

Lloyd Crouse was another aging survivor of the Commons class of '57 who went to his reward back home. His Nova Scotia seat has passed to young, ambitious Peter McCreath, and Crouse thinks about life, if he thinks at all, in viceregal surroundings in Halifax. Never considered bright enough for a cabinet job, Crouse had become one of the Commons' most renowned world travellers. On the basis of long study in both Halifax and Ottawa, respected Canadian Press journalist Gerry McNeil has observed: "his brain has been dead for twenty years."

The monarch's newest representative in Canada is Gordon Towers. During his long, unremarkable career as the MP for Red Deer, Towers made one significant contribution to public life. He opened his office to Mulroney's henchmen in the dirty battle to unseat Clark. One of the key strategists in the campaign of mean jokes, vicious rumor and other lethal political weapons was Pat MacAdam. On the public pay-roll as an aide to Towers, Mulroney's old school chum MacAdam now lists his 1979-83 employment in a registry of Ottawa lobbyists as Ottawa consultant for Iron Ore of Canada – the company Mulroney ran while MacAdam was helping to oust Clark.

The seventy-one-year-old Towers claims to be led by divine guidance. In an interview with the *Edmonton Journal* in March 1991, he said that he had predicted the OPEC oil crisis a year before the cartel drove up prices. "What caused me to say that?" the Zion Presbyterian Church elder wondered. "There was nothing happening then that could cause me to say that." Now settled in as lieutenant-governor, Towers says his priorities are to promote family values and garbage composting.

Martial Asselin is a multiple prize-winner in the game of politics. A Diefenbaker MP, he was named to the Senate in 1972, then became Quebec's lieutenant-governor in 1990. After a long apprenticeship in the field of perks, upon arriving in Quebec City he ordered up a $38,000 Chrysler Imperial as one of his top priorities. The limousine was twice the cost of the Chevrolet Caprice that had sufficed for his predecessors.

The diplomatic service is a burgeoning dumping ground for political left-overs, although Mulroney is certainly not the first prime minister to unload partisans into ambassadorial posts. Canada House in London has long been a reward for distinguished political service. Its occupants have included Paul Martin, Sr., Roy McMurtry, and Donald Macdonald.

Mulroney has used the foreign service more than any of his predecessors to pay off political pals. Since 1984 he has made thirty-five senior appointments from outside the ranks of professional diplomats at External Affairs. Trudeau named seventeen non-diplomats to foreign posts during sixteen years in office. Mackenzie King made eighteen such appointments in twenty-two years. Some of those Mulroney sent abroad include Lucien Bouchard as ambassador to Paris, MacAdam to an information position at Canada House in London and party strategist Jean-Carol Pelletier to the number-two job in Zaire. Pelletier's pay of around $100,000 is more than that of his boss, Ambassador Claude Laverdure.

Several former MPs also owe their hitch in that elite corps to Mulroney's thoughtfulness. Doug Roche became Canada's disarmament envoy at the United Nations after his long term as an Edmonton MP. He was replaced by Margaret Mason, previously policy adviser to Clark. Former environment minister Tom McMillan, defeated in the 1988 election, was sent to Boston as consul general. He replaced long-time Mulroney friend Pierrette Lucas. McMillan gets $125,900 as consul general. His $45,000 parliamentary pension is extra.

Age is no barrier to the diplomatic trough nor is lack of a suitable opening. A new one can simply be created, as in the case of George Hees, who today collects $138,500 as an ambassador-at-large. His job is to see that Canada's foreign-aid funds are not wasted. The eighty-year-old folk hero who helped to plot Clark's downfall remains a valued Mulroney friend. In the latter's first term, the former Diefenbaker minister was a popular head of the Veteran's Affairs department. His thirty-two years in Parliament today provide an indexed pension of more than $60,000. The ambassadorial job not only adds a bit extra for groceries, but provides a car and driver.

One of the more ingenious uses of the External Affairs budget was to buy a tropical plum for long-time Winnipeg MP, the late Dan McKenzie. In 1989 he was given a $50,000 contract to stroll the beaches of the Turks and Caicos Islands in search of trade opportunities. He performed his $2,000-a-day task while Canadians hunched deep in their parkas. When Southam News correspondent Les Whittington caught up with him, he found McKenzie had been sun-burned "blood vessel red from a boat ride earlier that day."

From what Whittington could determine, McKenzie had investigated the trade possibilities of Caribbean food and tropical booze among the waves and palms. Questions were raised about the assignment, a logical follow-up to McKenzie's sixteen-year effort as an MP to annex the sunny islands.

He had won earlier headlines for a different tour in the sun. Back in 1982 McKenzie returned from a trip to South Africa paid for by the government of Cape Town. With new-found wisdom he concluded that blacks were too primitive and too afflicted with alcohol and moral problems to be trusted with political power. He did concede that they made good mechanics and suggested that Canada could learn from South Africa how best to deal with troublesome natives.

One of the disarming tricks of those who serve up the pork is to provide a few choice pieces for political rivals. During his years in power, Trudeau occasionally bestowed a goodie on a Commons opponent, usually to give Liberals a chance at the resulting vacancy. Senators Jack Marshall and Robert Muir entered the red chamber that way. Mulroney has refined the tactic even further to include key people and jobs well beyond Parliament. Several New Democrats have benefited. They vow not to sit in the upper house, but have fewer qualms about accepting other treats. Since NDP ranks are short of lawyers, judgeships are also out, although at least one former MP, Stu Leggatt from B.C., is on the bench. Their pious commitment to social services, labor and the underprivileged makes New Democrats perfect appointees to "humanitarian" posts.

Thus we have Ed Broadbent accepting a rich Mulroney offer to become president of the International Centre for Human Rights and Democratic Development. When his handsome pension of more than $45,000 is combined with his salary of $138,300 a year, the Oshawa auto-worker's son today fares better than most of his fellow socialists.

Stephen Lewis accepted Mulroney's offer to become Canadian ambassador to the United Nations. He combined the salary for that job with substantial pension benefits from his stint as NDP leader in the Ontario legislature to produce a comfortable pay package without compromising his cherished socialist principles. What Mulroney gets from it is a chance to crow about non-partisan appointments. It is meant to disarm critics, just as he deflated New Democrats who stormed about cabinet perks by giving Broadbent a car and driver when he was NDP leader.

While Lewis and Broadbent merely double-dip for two public incomes, their colleague Ian Deans is a triple-dipping patronage all-star. He combines $151,300 as chairman of the Public Service Staff Relations Board with pensions from both the Ontario legislature and the House of Commons. Not bad for a former Hamilton fireman.

Deans prides himself on being a man of principle. An outstanding speaker on the subject of public morality, he quit politics in 1986 because of a lack of integrity in the Tory government, which "has reached the point of obscenity. . . . I just don't think these people [Tories] deserve to be in government. . . . They just don't know or understand the necessity of forthrightness and being up front with the Canadian people."

Deans made those remarks a month before he accepted the Tory plum, having determined first that the Liberals would not rescind it if they should happen to win the next election. His outrage over the evils of Conservative government fortunately peaked with his dramatic resignation just after he passed the six-year threshold for an MP's pension. What Deans proved, with a helping hand from Mulroney, is that pious social democrats are just like members of the other two parties when it comes to elbowing their way to the trough.

One of the hazards of patronage orgies is the guest who gorges himself then fails to say thanks. When Lewis completed his term at the United Nations he let the public know that he had serious objections to much of Mulroney's international policy. Almost enough to make him quit before the money ran out, it seems, but not quite.

Former Mulroney hatchet-man and deputy prime minister Erik Nielsen had hardly wiped the gravy off his chin when his tell-all memoirs appeared. Fortunately for Nielsen, he was securely seated on his $150,000 throne as czar of the National Transportation Agency when he lobbed the literary bomb into his former Tory caucus. They would have to buy him out or wait him out to the end of a seven-year term before they could publicly counter-attack. Mulroney awarded Nielsen the sinecure in 1987. It has been one of the most comfortable jobs around since Jack Pickersgill invented it and then moved in after a long life as a key Liberal minister. He was followed by Edgar Benson, another Liberal prize-winner, and then by Jean Marchand, one more. Next in line was Transport's first Tory, Yukon Erik.

Nielsen opened his Velcro lips to tell a stunned nation that Mulroney was deficient in matters of ethics. He had, he wrote, been overjoyed when Mulroney slugged John Turner on the patronage issue during that famous televised election debate. The cringing, " I had no choice" image of the Liberal prime minister remains vivid for Canadians today.

"I suppose it is inevitable that a certain amount of patronage will remain, but the last flicker of my idealism was entirely snuffed out when it became clear that we were to behave in a way that was little better than the conduct followed by the Liberals before us, and which we had pledged to reform," Neilsen wrote in his book *The House Is Not a Home*. "I had thought that we were going to clean up politics once and for all, but for some people, it was clear that the intent was simply to clean up."

Missing from Nielsen's revisionist history was the role he played in setting up the patronage machine in 1984. Friends of Mulroney's were happy to oblige in providing these details to reporters, only hours after his cutthroat book hit the stands. Some reporters were given access to a confidential letter Nielsen had sent to party officials on patronage. The letter explaining how the patronage system would be created clashed with this statement from his book: "Anyone who takes the trouble to follow my activities will discover that the rage I felt three decades and more ago has never faded; I have spent my career condemning patronage, political favoritism, and influence-peddling whenever I found them." Friends of Mulroney helped to explain Nielsen's "activities." A former aide phoned *Sun* reporter Tim Naumetz to say, "I've got some numbers on Nielsen." While Nielsen's transportation agency salary would normally be confidential, the former henchman had "happened to see" a file that showed the figure to be $149,000. There was further information provided about perks and Nielsen's parliamentary pension.

The key revelation, however, was that Nielsen had lobbied hard for an appointment as chief justice of Yukon despite opposition from the Canadian Bar Association. "Nielsen was angry at Prime Minister Mulroney's refusal to override the bar's objections and proceed with the judicial appointment anyway," says Bill Fox, former PMO communications director. In the end, Nielsen took the job as top man at the National Transportation Agency. His memoirs infuriated his party and drew attention to the hypocrisy of the author, who felt he was ideally suited for the patronage plum while others were not. As Christopher Dafoe wrote in the *Winnipeg Free Press*: "The vanity of many men in political life is so colossal that even as they stand at the public trough with the gravy running down their chins they cannot agree that they are getting anything more than their due."

The vast majority of retired or defeated government MPs regard it as a right to dip into the federal job jar. Most of their prizes escape public notice. The high-profile plums are usually reserved for cabinet ministers or close associates of the prime minister. But there is a rich motherlode of postings to federal agencies, boards and commissions, about one-quarter of them full-time.

In some cases, Mulroney used the prizes to lure Liberals out of seats he felt the Tories had a chance of winning. Liberal Keith Penner accepted a $100,600-a-year seat on the National Transportation Agency, while Prince Edward Island colleague George Henderson jumped at a chance to sit on the Canadian Pension Commission for a salary of $83,900. Both also had their parliamentary pensions, of course. It was a costly gamble for Mulroney. The Tories lost both seats.

In other cases Mulroney plunked an MP on a board to make way for a rising star. Quebec Tory Charles Hamelin vacated his Charlevoix riding to open up a seat for Lucien Bouchard in 1987. His reward was a $91,700 position on the National Parole Board. After the election, Hamelin was joined by three defeated colleagues and Mulroney's former riding watch-dog, Keith Morgan. The pay-off to Hamelin was costly not only to taxpayers but also to Mulroney, when Bouchard bolted the cabinet to form the Bloc Québécois.

As noted earlier most Conservative MPs who did not return to Parliament have passed into Tory heaven, some more comfortably than others. It can be a tiny plum, like a part-time job on the Farm Credit Corp. or the Farm Debt Review Board. New Brunswicker Fred McCain won't get rich on his $3,000 salary plus $300 per diem as a member of the Farm Credit lending institution. But it is decent pocket change coupled with his $40,000-plus Commons pension.

The most sought-after postings are to the National Parole Board, Immigration and Refugee Board, International Joint Commission, Canadian Grain Commission, Civil Aviation Tribunal, Canadian Labour Relations Board, Canadian International Trade Tribunal, Fisheries Prices Support Board, harbour commissions and the Canadian Human Rights tribunal. Full-time appointments to most of them pay in excess of $70,000.

B.C. Tory Robert Brisco is enjoying life on the Immigration and Refugee Board at a salary of $83,900 after losing his seat in the 1988 election. There are four other MPs on the board. One-term MP Morrissey Johnson landed a cushy $91,700 a year job on the Fisheries Prices Support Board, while colleague Sid Fraleigh is making do with $100,600 at the Canadian International Trade Tribunal. Over at the International Joint Commission sits one-term MP Claude Lanthier at a salary of $96,500.

Citizenship judgeships are also a hot ticket. Tory Bill Lesick was appointed to the bench after losing his Edmonton East seat to New Democrat Ross Harvey in the last election. Lesick was a one-term member who will have to make do with a salary of $60,300, about $30,000 less than he earned as an MP. The Veterans Appeal Board is another cosy home of former MPs. Mel Gass and Robert Howie sit there at $83,900 annually. Mike Forrestall, the former Dartmouth MP, landed on the board but gladly jumped again when called to the Senate.

The steady stream of partisan appointments to these boards and commissions undermines their independence and leads to a loss of confidence in them, according to the Canadian Bar Association. In a task force report issued in September 1990, the association urged the prime minister to stop using the boards as a pay-off for politicians the voters have rejected.

"If appointments are made only from amongst supporters of the government in power, there may be a perception that the tribunal is neither independent nor indifferent when it is called to adjudicate cases in which the government appears as a party," it concluded. "When an appointment is made solely or indeed largely as a reward, there may be a perception on the part of the person receiving the appointment that he or she is not under any obligation to work hard."

The association called for public advertising of these federal jobs and above-board screening of applicants by an independent commission. Anyone hired by cabinet should also face review by Commons committees, which could force the government to withdraw unsuitable candidates. The government showed no inclination to adopt the recommendations.

Mulroney's promise to clean out the patronage system and appoint people of the highest merit was a farce. The operating principles remain exactly as before: condemn the practice while in opposition and grab the goodies when you get into government. Of course, not all the blame lies with Mulroney. The hypocrisy extends to MPs from all parties. And the message the rich pensions and lucrative patronage jobs send to voters is one of blatant excess and unblushing hyprocrisy. The words, "you had a choice, sir" are as true today as they were when Mulroney slapped John Turner with them in that 1984 campaign debate. But the prime minister seems to have forgotten them.

10
SEXISM AND THE SLAVE TRADE

"This is a male institution. This is a male culture. This is a system of government that has been developed by men for men."
DAWN BLACK, MP, MARCH 1991
"I don't think workers on Parliament Hill should lose their [labor] rights. I don't think MPs are above the law. They should set an example."
DEBRA BROAD, COMMONS EMPLOYEE, MARCH 1991

S LIGHT, BEWHISKERED JOHN WHITE WAS THE MP FOR EAST Hastings, Ontario, from 1871 to 1887. His unremarkable political career was comfortably forgotten for most of this century until a Queen's University historian dug up a single, interesting fact. John White was really a woman named Eliza McCormack White.

Scholar Don Akenson has revealed details in his fascinating account, *At Face Value*. In the book he explains that Eliza came to Canada and assumed her brother's identity after he died back home in Ireland. Small-breasted and broad-backed, Eliza was the right shape, but she had to glue on whiskers, practise male mannerisms and even marry another woman to complete the deception. "Certainly the whole thing sounds out of whack," says Akenson, an expert on Irish history. "Yet when you look at it from a historical perspective, it makes sense. During that time, women could only really assume power in two ways. One was to be part of the monarchy. The other was to be a man."

The claim makes John/Eliza Canada's first female parliamentarian, fully half a century ahead of the woman to whom history has always accorded that honor, a thirty-one-year-old school teacher, Agnes Macphail. She was elected by Ontario farmers as a Progressive in 1921 and held her Grey South East (then Bruce-Grey) seat until 1940. A small brass plaque outside room 629 in the Centre Block notes that the office was used by Canada's first female MP.

The earlier sex-switch story is not as bizarre as it first appears.

Sylvia Van Kirk, a teacher of women's history at the University of Toronto, says that the practice was actually quite common. There are other well-documented examples. Dr. James Barry, inspector general of hospitals for British garrisons serving in Montreal in the late 1850s, was found, upon death, to be a woman. In fact the charwoman who laid out the corpse described the late doctor as a "perfect woman." In 1807 John Fubister worked for the Hudson's Bay Company until he blew his cover, simultaneously revealing himself to be Isabelle Gunn and becoming the first woman to give birth in the West.

While being a female remains a distinct advantage in child bearing, being a man is a far better start towards a career in Parliament. Just forty of today's 295 MPs are female, the highest number ever and four times the number only eight years earlier. As recently as 1968 there was just one, New Democrat Grace MacInnes. The first female cabinet minister, Ellen Fairclough, was chosen in 1957, the first female Commons speaker, Jeanne Sauvé, in 1980 and the first of her sex to serve as a national party leader, Audrey McLaughlin, in 1990. All House of Commons rule books were revised just a decade ago, replacing dozens of references to "Mr. Speaker" with "The Speaker." The Senate led the elected House by almost ten years in that respect. Both Maureen Ferguson, from 1972 to 1974, and Renaude LaPointe, from 1974 to 1979, had served as presiding officer in the upper house before the Commons breakthrough. In each case, Pierre Trudeau made the appointment.

More impressive than the raw statistics is a tour of Parliament's Gothic-revival corridors, which are adorned with the portraits, some of them strikingly awful, of Canada's political leaders through the years. Women are 2 for 23 among speakers of the Senate; 0 for 25 among government leaders in the upper chamber. In the gallery of prime ministers outside the sixth-floor Parliamentary Restaurant, women are 0 for 18. A little farther along the hall, you'll find Margaret Thatcher, the sole female, at the end of a line of 49 British prime ministers. Down in the Commons' speaker's corridor on the second floor there is an impressive row of huge portraits in ornate gold frames: 28 men and Jeanne Sauvé. John Bosley and John Fraser are not yet framed and hung.

For those who conclude that the male-female ratio is similar the world over, it is worth noting that 33 per cent of legislators in the Soviet Union in the late 1980s were female. A United Nations survey of 160 countries in 1991 found that Canada was the second-best place in the world to live, after Japan, but that we also had a high degree of sexual discrimination in our political system. One out of nine members of Parliament were women, well below the world average of one out of seven, the report said.

Absolute male dominance of our parliamentary system is gradually weakening in favor of the 51 per cent of Canadians who are female. But any objective assessment would conclude that the process is slow and somewhat reluctant, since women gained the right to vote in 1918. Important symbols remain masculine, including the mace, which is simply a club dressed up with fancy gold doodads. It is the key to Parliament's authority and is paraded in a formal military-style ceremony into the Commons chamber each day to permit business to begin.

If the portrait collection is about as masculine as that in the Hockey Hall of Fame so is much of the atmosphere. During baseball's World Series and hockey's Stanley Cup play-offs, if the house is sitting, lobby TVs will get far more attention than any debate in the chamber. Most of the booze and poker action disappeared when regular night sittings ended a decade ago. During an "emergency" night sitting in the late 1980s, however, the Conservative whip had to advise some of the good old boys to shift their high-stakes poker game from the lobby, where reporters might see it, to an office where they wouldn't.

Closure debates that keep MPs around for a late-night vote still precipitate table-stakes action in at least one Centre Block office. With a minimum bet of $5 and no limit on raises, each hand produces a pot of $50 to $500. The office TV monitor remains at low volume to ensure that players won't miss an early adjournment or a chance to taunt the video image of an opponent.

The lobbies themselves took on a more modern look in the mid-1980s. The heavy, dark leather couches and chairs that shouted "private men's club" were removed. Pastels and brocades have replaced them. The forty-two university students who pick up

$10,000 a year as pages, answering phones and delivering notes and water to members, are evenly split between male and female. There's a comely woman deputy sergeant-at-arms, Marie-Paule Charbonneau, to stand symbolic guard over proceedings and to bear the mace in and out on occasion.

A woman, Mary Anne Griffith, holds the second-highest officer's position in the Commons' elaborate hierarchy, sitting each day at the clerk's table in the centre of the action. And, of course, high-profile woman ministers, such as Barbara McDougall (External Affairs) and Kim Campbell (Justice), along with NDP leader McLaughlin, deputy Liberal leader Sheila Copps and other prominent legislators on both sides, represent the leading edge of the female wave.

At the rate that wave is rolling, gender equality could be accomplished in Parliament within half a century. A lot of people think that is not good enough. The protests of feminists are becoming louder and more frequent as the country's leaders appear to lag farther and farther behind the pace of changes elsewhere. Despite endless lip-service to the cause of sex equity, those who run the political machinery ensure that women are kept well away from the controls. There is only one woman holding a senior post in the office of Prime Minister Brian Mulroney and one in that of Liberal leader Jean Chrétien. Marjorie LeBreton, a long-time Tory strategist, is Mulroney's deputy principal secretary. Chaviva Hosek, the former Ontario housing minister, heads up the research team in Chrétien's office.

Male political leaders eagerly point to the rapidly increasing number of women candidates in each successive federal election. In the 1988 federal election, 302 women ran – 19 per cent of the total number of candidates – but only 152 women ran for the three major parties. The number of women candidates is not as important as the number of female winners, however. Women are often nominated as little more than political cannon-fodder in hopeless seats. Without money, organization and heavyweight party support in such ridings, women are sacrificial lambs with as much chance as Saddam Hussein's front-line troops in Kuwait. Like those soldiers, they represent impressive numbers and temporary propaganda value – until the shooting breaks out.

The ones who do win seats in Parliament often find themselves somewhat uncomfortable. Like the female sports reporters who have recently been admitted to men's locker rooms to do their job, it's less of a treat than a lot of people imagine. Just ten years ago, male MPs guffawed for more than a minute when B.C. New Democrat Margaret Mitchell raised her voice to protest the fact that one in ten women in Canada is battered by a husband or boyfriend. "I don't beat my wife. Do you beat yours?" shouted one male cut-up, in a misguided bid for laughs. Such sexist cracks are far from eliminated today, although most members have learned not to make them too loudly in public.

Newfoundland's biggest gift to buffoonery, John Crosbie, still hasn't caught on. The bombastic minister of fisheries made an indelible mark in the records of sexist stupidity when he said to Sheila Copps, "Quiet down, baby," during a 1985 Commons clash. Ever eager to take advantage of a political opportunity, Copps squawked loudly about the label, then penned an autobiography entitled *Nobody's Baby*.

Crosbie, with a legendary talent for lighting fires then dousing them with gasoline, followed up this scrimmage with another stupid jibe during the 1990 Liberal leadership race. He joked to a delighted Conservative crowd that the candidacy of the brash Hamilton MP reminded him of an old song: "Pass the tequila, Sheila, and lie down and love me again." Copps may not have loved him, but the new minister responsible for the status of women did. Just six days into her sensitive post, Mary Collins gushed that Crosbie was "absolutely marvellous, as always," when she thanked him for the speech that included the offensive jest. John Crosbie is a treasure who can, Collins added, "explain what we're doing in such down-to-earth, common-sense terms that I don't think anyone could disagree." Plenty did, drawing attention to the sexism and insensitivity that permeate Parliament.

Some women MPs and senators complain that it remains almost as much of a male enclave as it was when Eliza White had to glue whiskers on to get in. "This is a male institution. This is a male culture. This is a system of government that has been developed by men for men," complains B.C. New Democrat Dawn Black, who levels charges of rampant sexism at every opportunity. Such views earned her the label "fishwife" from Conservative Bill Kempling during a debate on women's issues.

When she arrived as a rookie MP in 1988, Black immediately concluded that women were not really welcome in Parliament, partly because she was given a valuable but thick-backed identification pin designed for a man's suit. Her husband was handed a brooch. "That may seem like a small example, but the unspoken message is that you don't belong here. This is a place for men. If they expect women to be elected they would have some pins for women."

In fact, the advent of several dozen female MPs has made a variety of adjustments necessary to the traditional parliamentary structures. The long-standing Parliamentary Wives' Association has become the Parliamentary Spouses' Association. Its active members in the 1980s included Copps' husband, Rick, from whom she is now separated, and Charles Lynch, the famous journalist husband of ex–Conservative MP Claudy Mailly. The legendary Lynch is one of the most ribald raconteurs on the Hill, with a treasury of stories and satirical songs dating back to the days of Mackenzie King. He's also a committed "women's libber," having been instrumental in prying the doors of the National Men's Press Club open for women in a celebrated battle twenty years ago. He became an active Hill spouse and relished the role and attention, which he unfortunately lost when Mailly was defeated in 1988.

Such enlightened views are not universal among Hill old-timers. Sexism is considered such a problem that female MPs and senators from all three parties have created their own Women's Parliamentary Association, headed by Quebec Tory Pierrette Venne. They are pressing for improvements to the working hours for women MPs with children and for safer conditions for those who stay late. They say such simple things as better lighting in the parking lots used at night by MPs and staff are important. Several assaults on Parliament Hill's darkened east side, including one against Conservative MP Barbara Greene, in the spring of 1990, emphasized the point. The speaker promised improved lighting and better security.

Greene, a single mother and MP for Toronto's Don Valley North, is even tougher than Black in her assessment of Parliament as a male enclave. "Systematic sexual discrimination and harassment are rampant," she told the Commons in March 1991. She cites detailed instances, without revealing names, of male MPs trying to "feel up" female aides in Commons cafeterias. "There's one member – they call him 'hands,'" she says of one Alberta lout. "It's really shocking."

Legendary tales of sexual adventure inside Parliament's hallowed stone walls abound, although today's changing social standards, the termination of regular night sittings, reduced alcohol consumption and fear of exposure have curbed the most outrageous behavior. The famous Senate twins, whose double delights included some office work, are no longer. Nor are "Wonderful Wednesdays," the wild office bashes that members used to host on the one week-night the Commons did not sit until 10:30 p.m. Ministerial and members' staff competed to throw the best party. Hill "groupies" abounded. Even into the 1980s, one handsome Alberta MP vied for the top party-man title far from his home and family, where he practised pious parenting.

There is also a long list of greying graduates who shed wife and family when they discovered the non-domestic pleasures of public service in Canada's capital. You see many of them still clinging to their post-political appointments and the plumply aging former secretaries who are now their mates. One less fortunate office worker still receives compensation from the injuries she suffered two decades ago when dropped during a game of catch between two big, fun-loving Conservative MPs.

Women just won't put up with this stuff anymore. New Democrat Joy Langan broke down the barricades at the all-male MPs' gym in the Confederation Building in the spring of 1991 by simply walking in and starting to work out on the exercise equipment. "Fitness is a co-education activity," she huffed about the facility, which is far better outfitted than the female health room one floor up. As her Manitoba colleague Rod Murphy pointed out, "Sometimes you just have to take direct action, and that's what she did."

External relations minister Monique Landry told a Montreal

conference marking International Women's Day that she is sick and tired of being treated like a "little girl" by some of her colleagues. She said that, despite some inroads by women, politics remains a man's world. "The chauvinism, I'd say, is a question of individual men. A lot of colleagues consider me an equal, but others tend to think of me as a girl, a little lady," observed the attractive fifty-three-year old. "It drives me crazy, facing a colleague over a certain dossier, trying to discuss things with dignity but not being allowed to do so." On the other hand she described Joe Clark as a "fantastic" man to work with.

Women members are forced to take on extra duties to ensure that their sex is represented on up to thirty standing, special and legislative Commons committees. They hold few of the key positions, however. Only one of the twenty standing committees – bodies that correspond roughly to government departments – is chaired by a woman. Women constitute 14 per cent of Commons membership. They make up 21 per cent of committee membership on "soft social issues," but just 7 per cent on "hard issues." The special subcommittee that studied violence against women drew no male members. It issued a report *The War Against Women* that failed to win endorsement of the Health Committee or concurrence of the House.

Sexual discrimination does not target female MPs and assistants only. The homosexual NDP MP from Burnaby, B.C., Svend Robinson, has often been ridiculed by other members while protesting federal policies that discriminate against gays and lesbians. The day actor Rock Hudson was being buried after he died of AIDS, Robinson was interrupted in the House by a Manitoba Conservative, the late Dan McKenzie, who hollered across the aisle: "Why aren't you at Rock Hudson's funeral?"

While Robinson has been undeterred by such harassment, some of it within his own NDP caucus, many Hill employees are afraid to go public with their complaints. The price could be embarrassment or loss of their jobs. And, of course, it is difficult to establish the precise point at which off-color remarks or lascivious looks become harassment. Despite lots of stories, in only a few verifiable cases have MPs been openly accused of sexual harassment.

In 1981, Robinson horrified MPs when he charged that employees of the Commons "were being hired and fired at will and harassed, sometimes sexually, without any appeal mechanism whatsoever." The reference to sexual harassment provoked an angry outburst from other MPs and threats of retaliation against Robinson.

In 1982, a Commons page was sexually assaulted by a Liberal cabinet minister on a government Jetstar en route to Halifax. The young woman, who was from Newfoundland, had been offered a ride part-way home. She later told two Liberal MPs that the minister "put his arm around me and kissed me on the mouth. That old man with his wrinkly lips kissed me. It was repulsive. What could I do? I just froze." The incident was hushed up when one of the MPs spoke to the minister and the girl, now married with two children, asked that it be forgotten.

In 1984, Liberal MP Al McBain was accused of sexual harassment by his former executive assistant, Kristina Potapczyk. She complained to the Canadian Human Rights Commission, alleging that McBain had leered at her and used sexual innuendo. The commission upheld her complaint and appointed a tribunal to assess damages. McBain, parliamentary secretary to justice minister Mark MacGuigan, was found guilty and ordered to pay Potapczyk $1,500. A year later, however, the Federal Court of Appeal – while not overturning the commission's verdict against McBain – reduced the damages to zero because of a flawed process.

In 1984, Robinson threatened to reveal the name of a Toronto Liberal MP if he did not leave his female staff alone. Several female aides had quit because the MP kept trying to bed them down. Robinson even approached Pierre Trudeau to make sure that the harassment would end. The MP did not run in the 1988 election.

In 1985, Tory defence minister Robert Coates was accused of sexual harassment by his appointments secretary before his resignation from cabinet. Cecile Hébert, a thirty-two-year-old divorced mother of an eleven-year old son, alleged that he had made improper advances to her in his apartment. The Human Rights Commission investigated the complaint and cleared Coates of any wrongdoing. By then he had resigned from cabinet for visiting a strip club while representing Canadian taxpayers on a trip to West Germany. The dalliance may or may not have created a security risk. What it did demonstrate was abysmal judgement.

Such incidents posed enough problems to prompt, in December 1988, a letter from speaker Fraser to all Hill employees, informing them of their "right to employment free of sexual harassment." Fraser has since named three Commons employees as designated complaints officers to handle sexual-harassment cases. The complaints officers are not allowed to handle complaints raised by staff of MPs, however. Problems must be raised individually with the party whips, who are hardly likely to divulge the name of an MP found guilty of sexual harassment. Revealing the name of an MP would harm his or her re-election chances, thus dampening the enthusiasm for public disclosure.

The current human rights commissioner, Maxwell Yalden, says that the commission has dealt with a number of cases "from persons working in Parliament" in addition to those involving McBain and Coates. Most incidents never become public because they are either dismissed or settled in private. In March 1991, the commission was investigating a "couple or three complaints" from people on the Hill, according to Yalden.

That parliamentarians have failed to achieve an impeccable record in dealing with matters of sexual discrimination and harassment is understandable. While expected to set a leadership example, they are sadly and obviously human, at least as guilty of lust and misbehavior as those who elect them. But one area where Canadians have a right to expect them to set high standards is that of employment practices. In fact the Hill continues to do just the opposite, maintaining unbelievably unfair labor practices for those who serve political masters.

The 3,000 employees who fall under House of Commons authority are denied the basic rights that are routine for other Canadians because the ancient tradition of parliamentary privilege exempts the institution from federal and provincial labor laws. A decade ago, *Windsor Star* journalist Gord Henderson described labor relations on the Hill as "worthy of a tear-stained Charles Dickens novel." His exaggeration made the point that the welfare of Hill workers depends almost entirely on the goodwill of their bosses, not on collective rights.

A distinction must be made between those employed by the House of Commons – about 1,700 workers – and those 1,300 who toil for individual members. The former have some group rights achieved through a bargaining process, although they do not have the right to strike. The latter, MPs' staff, have only the whim of their bosses for job security.

The right of Commons workers to form any kind of union was hard won in 1986. Their uphill battle during the twenty previous years saw a succession of speakers pass the jurisdictional buck to prime ministers who passed it back without results. Aggrieved employees took their troubles to individual MPs, including the dogged and revered dean of the House, Stanley Knowles, in the hope of getting help. Reports of scandalous waste, mismanagement, theft and corruption erupted in a full-scale investigation in that period. It led to some firings and a major clean-up by Jeanne Sauvé. But little was done about the problems of favoritism, nepotism, sexual harassment and arbitrary management decisions.

Labor unrest was growing. The first public indication of it came in 1982 when Commons messenger Jacques Audette led fellow workers in a march beneath the Peace Tower. The result was a slash of $4,000 to their already skimpy salaries, a cut the administration effected through job "reclassification." Instead of wilting in response to the clear message, other Hill workers stepped up salary and job-security demands in keeping with the Sauvé administration reforms.

The Public Service Alliance of Canada joined the battle. It went to the Canada Labour Relations Board to argue that "employees of Parliament were being denied collective bargaining rights guaranteed to every Canadian by the freedom of association provision of the Charter of Rights."

The CLRB ruled in April 1984 that it had jurisdiction over Parliament. It allowed the certification of Commons unions with the same bargaining rights as private-sector workers. However, the House of Commons appealed to the Federal Court of Appeal, which upheld Parliament's privilege. Hill employees were back to square one.

Finally, in 1986, after intensive lobbying by public-service unions, the Conservative government grudgingly passed legislation to grant limited union rights. The unions and NDP MPs accomplished that partly by using Brian Mulroney's own words to paint him into a corner. As a high-priced Montreal labor lawyer, Mulroney had been an outspoken advocate of unions and collective bargaining.

Even so, the law that was adopted denied workers the right to strike. Further, the personal staff of MPs and senators were exempted from the provisions. Parliament remains the only federal institution in which unionized employees are prohibited from striking. Disputes are to be settled by mandatory arbitration. MPs insisted that work stoppages could disrupt their critical parliamentary function and even interrupt their meal schedule. "Quite frankly, I could almost question whether I could do without lunch," said Conservative Doug Lewis in response to the possibility of a Commons strike. "Suppose there's something happening between twelve and one [o'clock] or we're in an emergency debate? Who is going to provide lunch? Do you want us all running out to Friendly's or Christopher's, for crying out loud?" Lewis's discerning views have won him advancement to the position of government House leader, minister of justice, minister of transport and now solicitor general.

The government House leader of the day, Ray Hnatyshyn, termed the Parliamentary Employment and Staff Relations Act "progressive and enlightened." It did not come close to meeting the standards that Canadians expect of employers. First, it did not include those who toiled directly for individual parliamentarians. The rest – personnel such as messengers, librarians, cafeteria staff, cleaners and so on – were granted the right to form unions, but the government failed to proclaim two sections of the legislation. As a result such minimum labour standards as the right to overtime pay and guarantees of health and safety are not covered.

The last issue is a key one for Hill workers, as it is for employees everywhere. Since the summer of 1989, the five unions on the Hill have been raising fears that workers are being exposed to cancer-causing asbestos. The fibrous material was regularly used for fireproofing and insulation in the 1970s, before its link to occupational diseases was established. During the 1960s asbestos insulation was sprayed on beams and pipes in the Wellington Building and West Block, home to 67 MPs and their staffs, another 200 or so workers.

Many of them had complained about headaches and unexplained respiratory illnesses, which they attributed to poor air quality and poor ventilation. The unions feared that fibres from damaged asbestos in some attics and basements were circulating through the air-recycling systems. For reasons as yet unexplained, senior Commons officers took no action until a leak by Greenpeace in late 1990 of a two-year-old study commissioned by Public Works. Fraser and members of the powerful all-party BOIE claim that they had never seen the report. Its main conclusion? "There could quite conceivably be an emergency situation" in the West Block, which, the study said, is contaminated with floating asbestos in several places.

While workers clamored for action on the asbestos hazard, Speaker Fraser proudly boasted about his environmental crusade on the Hill as an example to the nation. The "green campaign" he launched recycles tons of parliamentary paper and glass. It encourages workers to use china cups rather than styrofoam. It's a big deal, according to Fraser's press secretary, Jim Watson: "We want to set an example for the rest of the government and the country to ensure we are leading by example." Meanwhile Fraser had dispatched MP David MacDonald, the red Tory from the ultra-rich Toronto riding of Rosedale, as an emissary to end the public spat with the unions. But the coalition never heard back from him when they insisted that the health and safety law be put into effect.

With the release of the asbestos report, Fraser acted with uncharacteristic speed to order an independent inquiry into levels of airborne asbestos in all Hill buildings. By now MPs were howling indignantly about the fibrous threat, demanding to be moved to other offices until they got answers. The second study tested air samples, a method many experts consider inadequate in detecting long-term asbestos dangers. It concluded that there was no danger as long as the asbestos in the buildings went undisturbed. The union rejected the findings. Fraser then promised to reactivate an asbestos-clearance program to wipe the buildings clean.

The tempest highlighted the problem of workers with no clear-cut rights. "If we had that [part three of the bill, which was not proclaimed] we'd have the right to refuse dangerous work," says Debra Broad, a union representative who also led the fight to gain collective bargaining. "MPs see that as affecting their ability to function, that people would walk off the job. In reality all it means is that they would have to relocate us to some other place to work." A calm, sensitive library technician, Broad bristles at the fact that she does not have the same rights as other Canadians, who can refuse to work in an environment that is considered unsafe. "I don't see why workers on Parliament Hill should lose their rights. I don't think MPs are above the law. They should set an example."

At least Commons employees have unions to speak for them and to bargain for better pay and working conditions. The same cannot be said for those who work directly for MPs and senators. Our lawmakers can fire them without cause, change their pay on a whim and demand whatever work from them they choose. Jobs in an MP's office come without security, overtime provisions or assured levels of pay. Older office employees can, and are, simply let go when younger, quicker, cheaper, more energetic or better-connected ones come along.

Hill staffers can be fired for the most trivial excuses. Something as minor as lack of knowledge of a new piece of office equipment can be a reason for dismissal. So can having the "wrong" friends. Cynthia Moore, a youthful and fervent Tory from a well-to-do Calgary oil family, was fired by Michael Wilson in 1983 because she was dating an aide to Liberal cabinet minister John Roberts. Erik Nielsen, the House leader who was to become deputy prime minister a year later when the Tories swept to power, had summoned Wilson to his office and he ordered Wilson to "get rid" of Moore if he wanted to remain in Mulroney's shadow cabinet. Nielsen was certain Moore's boyfriend would pry Tory secrets from her over a candlelit dinner.

Other aides complain about being subjected to the peccadilloes of their employers, which is certainly not part of the job description. Jennifer Sloan, who worked briefly for Liberal David Berger, recounted how the son of the owner of the defunct Montreal Alouettes football club would call her into his office, sit her in a chair in front of him, and read his interminably boring speeches or books to her.

Barbara Mitchell, a twenty-seven-year-old aide to Tory Barbara Greene, says that MPs demand up-to-date expertise of their staff in the computer age, but there is "no support system to give these people new skills." Many are terrified of losing their jobs as the Commons changes over from Micom computers to WordPerfect. "That's one of the biggest problems, because there is no recourse. Members of Parliament have an awful lot of power over individuals."

The power to set salaries and working conditions has been jealously guarded by MPs from the time they were first given budgets for part-time assistants in 1913. It has produced wide disparities in salary and work-load. Some MPs pay extremely low wages and work employees long hours, while others may be unrealistically generous. Much of it has to do with how hard members work. "I remember the old days when cheap ministers would pay an assistant $14,000 and the minister across the hall would pay his $32,000," says Gus Cloutier, sergeant-at-arms in the Commons. "It's still the same way today. MPs want the latitude to do what they please."

Each of them has an operating budget of $165,000, which can be somewhat higher for many with larger geographical ridings. From that they pay salaries and office expenses, for computers, fax machines, copiers, televisions, VCRs and other equipment. Constituency work-loads, which include dealing with such things as constituents' unemployment-insurance problems and immigration questions, can be heavy, so that MPs usually have to hire up to three staffers in Ottawa and one in the constituency. All staffers do political work, which is necessary to meet every MP's first priority, getting re-elected. Although the funds don't allow for handsome salaries, a bigger complaint is the basic unfairness of the system.

Some MPs pay their female aides $18,577 a year, while a few male legislative aides make as much as $56,106. Some MPs may hire just two well-paid aides to handle a large work-load, while across the hall there are eight staffers working at minimum wage. "The House of Commons needs a pay structure for members' offices," says Mitchell. "They should definitely be given strictures as to the number of staff they can hire out of their budget, and there should be a salary range for the various jobs."

The only ones who enjoy any security are aides to NDP MPs who belong to the Parliamentary Association of Support Staff (PASS). The association was formed in 1976 by workers who wanted a minimum base salary, regular vacation periods and reduced office hours when the House was not in session. They signed a voluntary collective agreement with caucus covering those working conditions that are controlled by individual MPs. The agreement covers grievance procedures, technological change, education and other basic rights that most workers in the private sector take for granted.

David Pepper, president of PASS and an aide to Svend Robinson, says that all NDP MPs must have a minimum of four full-time employees and may have a maximum of four full-time and one part-time. The union has also implemented a salary base of $27,545. Most staffers earn about $32,500 a year. "We have a leg up over Tory and Liberal aides. We can't be fired, dismissed or reprimanded arbitrarily in our caucus."

But life is not a bed of roses for NDP staffers. There are NDP MPs who are just as adamant about their archaic rights to set salaries, working hours and vacation guarantees without any input from employees. Four NDP MPs from British Columbia – Bob Skelly, Sid Parker, Lyle MacWilliam and Lyle Kristiansen – refused to sign the collective agreement. Skelly, the former B.C. party leader, did not want to pay per diems to his staff, while the others objected to the staff numbers under the contract. Kristiansen, who is a member of the International Woodworkers Union, says he supports collective bargaining as long it doesn't apply to him. "MPs' staff are in a position of trust. I don't think MPs' personal staff should [have] a union. It's a management-rights issue."

But most New Democrats support the association and argue that the agreement created few problems. Dawn Black, the Vancouver-area member who as a constituency aide to former MP Pauline Jewett helped form the union, says that the majority of MPs could not care less about human rights when it affects them. "I don't think employees of the House of Commons should be excluded from rights that are given to employees of any sector of our society. You can't take away people's basic human rights that are afforded to other Canadians."

The existence of a double standard – one rule for MPs' own employees versus progressive labor laws for the rest of the country – was brought home in the 1989 ban on smoking. The government banned smoking on Parliament Hill but gave special rights to MPs. They could still light up in their offices, as could reporters in the Parliamentary Press Gallery. The exception struck Hill employees as fundamentally undemocratic. "When I became a Canadian citizen ten years ago, the judge said everyone in Canada is equal," said Franco Britti, a worker in the refinishing shop who emigrated from Italy only to learn that here some are more equal than others. (The ban on smoking was later extended to include MPs' offices.)

And then there are the hiring procedures. Those with the best chance at work on the Hill are not necessarily the best and brightest; sometimes they are simply the best-connected. Without any screening system, standards or selection process beyond a parliamentarian's personal preference, the field is wide open for patronage and nepotism.

The practice of putting relatives or girlfriends on the payroll was so widespread that a regulation prohibiting the hiring of spouses and children by MPs was passed in the 1980s. Ontario MPs Terry Clifford and Bob Hicks got around it by putting each other's daughters on the pay-roll. When the scheme became public and they were investigated, they insisted that they had committed no offence. The matter was dropped.

Not only does the example raise questions about ethics, it presents an interesting legal conundrum too. Does a prohibition against the hiring of family members violate the Canadian Charter of Rights and Freedoms? The former chairman of the Commons Committee on Privileges and Elections, Vancouver Tory Chuck Cook, believes it does. He says an MP's spouse, parents, children or any close relative should have the same opportunity to work for the member as anyone else. Cook adds that he doesn't expect to see any MP test the rule in the near future. His committee's Liberal deputy chairman, Peter Milliken, chimes in with one good reason not to do it: "It's difficult to fire a member of your family."

That may be the problem of a number of members who somehow find themselves with siblings on their staff payroll. The rule on relatives doesn't prevent that. Liberals Joe McGuire from Prince Edward Island and Brian Tobin from Newfoundland have helped relieve the chronic unemployment pressures back home by putting their brothers on the Ottawa office payroll. Tory Ricardo Lopez employs his daughter-in-law back in the riding office in Châteauguay, Quebec. The live-in companion of Bloc Québécois MP Gilles Rocheleau works alongside her lover in the Ottawa office.

The son and daughter-in-law of Conservative whip Jim Hawkes were lucky enough to find work as ministerial assistants, he for Michael Wilson, she for Joe Clark. A while later even Hawkes' little brother, Reg, somehow stumbled onto work back home on the west coast, where he helps Charles Mayer, the minister for western economic diversification. Multiculturalism minister Gerry Weiner's son was also fortunate during the recession to find a job with consumer affairs minister Pierre Blais.

These comings and goings are now being tracked down and listed in a saucy new weekly called the *Hill Times*. A feature column titled "Hill Climbers" is a must-read for all staffers looking for work, tracking careers or seeking contacts. The publication provides both hard news and great gossip about Canada's biggest political playground.

For instance, there is John Crosbie's cousin, William, magically beating out the competition to land a job right in the minister's office as executive assistant. And then there's the daughter of Deputy Speaker Steve Paproski. She found work with another Tory MP, Brian O'Kurley, almost at the same time that justice minister Kim Campbell found an opening in her office for the son of Treasury Board president Gilles Loiselle. Or Liberal Ethel Blondin's son, Troy, who briefly landed work in the office of Dartmouth MP Ronald MacDonald. The music goes on and on.

In his "Bureaucrats" column in the Ottawa *Citizen*, Frank

Howard notes that many ministerial appointees find a safety net by transferring into the non-political public service. They get priority for such transfers, without competition, after three years. New Democrat Neil Young from Toronto's Beaches-Woodbine riding, has proposed a bill that would allow MPs' staff members the same privilege. With large numbers of ministerial appointees switching to secure public-service jobs before elections, and the prospect of MPs' political underlings doing the same, Howard suggests that the public service may well become thoroughly politicized. Public-service managers are resisting on the perfectly proper grounds that they prefer to hire the best people, not necessarily those with the best political connections.

For those who don't get rescued in some such fashion, MPs' staff jobs become particularly uncomfortable at election time. If the member who employs them is defeated, the staffers are immediately thrown out of work. Incoming MPs can hire them, but they're under no obligation to do so. Most resist the hiring of workers who have loyally served a member of another party.

The people we have chosen to lead have created in Parliament a magnificent model – of sexism, favoritism, waste and unfair labor practices. They have demonstrated that politics is indeed the art of the possible. They have created two classes of Canadians on Parliament Hill while publicly proclaiming that they are treating everyone, the powerful and the weak, in exactly the same way. Our Parliament is founded on traditional values. The most important of them is clearly embodied in the maxim: "It's not what you know, but whom you know that counts."

11
SPREADING THE WORD

"Show us as we really are. If we are asleep, chatting, etc.,
that's what the people should see. And if we don't like it,
then we should smarten up."

DEREK BLACKBURN, MP, 1977

THE AGITATED SENIOR CITIZEN FROM PARRY SOUND BRAN-
dished a crushed box and bellowed to fellow parliamentarians that the cake inside had suffered even greater
ravages at the hands of brutal postal workers. Veteran
Tory Stan Darling had just made a winning move in the new game
called "Commons Television."

Six anti-metric Conservatives hefted the world's biggest petition
to their shoulders, then onto the floor of the chamber and into the
record books. As they trundled the monster document, pasted
together and rolled onto a long pole, towards the centre aisle, Peterborough MP Bill Domm read its vital statistics – 3.5 miles (5.6 kilo-
metres) long, weighing 247 pounds (112 kilograms), and bearing
135,000 names. It was a 1982 show-stopper that provoked a thirty-
minute parliamentary uproar.

In the years that followed, MPs waved stuffed birds to protest the
death of the "Crow rate" for shipping western grain, plopped a two-
foot salmon on the prime minister's desk in the cause of environmental protection and displayed the housing minister's phone
number in foot-high letters so that hard-pressed mortgagees would
know whom to complain to.

Some keen-eyed viewers may have caught John Fraser's disap-
pearing act one pre-Christmas morning as the clerk, sergeant-at-
arms and a couple of MPs met for quick royal assent to some year-
end bills. All other members had already headed home after a festive
farewell in the speaker's suite the previous evening. Fraser stumbled

stepping down from the speaker's dais, fell out of camera view for a moment behind the clerk's table, then regained his feet, donned the traditional tricorn hat and carried on.

The hat also gave stand-in Speaker Charles DeBlois a few problems when he took his initial turn at leading the parade from the Commons to the Senate for royal assent. He puzzled over whether to wear it with a flat side or one of the three corners at the front. With some on-camera assistance and some fumbling he got it right and proceeded with the task at hand.

Those tiny incidents have nothing whatever to do with the conduct of the nation's business. But they demonstrate the humor, drama, embarrassments and mugging that began when our most important democratic chamber became a live TV studio in 1977. The *Windsor Star* even gave the show a name. It titled a column on Commons TV by Gord Henderson "The Daze of Their Lives."

It is a show that has run for fourteen years, to mixed reviews, but with no prospect of cancellation. And it is one over which the producers – MPs themselves – do not always seem to have control. Thoughtful members warned that this could happen if they were not careful with their own scripts and performances. One of the most prescient during the debate on whether to let cameras in was senior Conservative rules expert Ged Baldwin, then the MP for Peace River. "This House should reform its proceedings," he advised members on all sides, "so that when we do come to broadcast the proceedings the public can see a Parliament that is functional, operative, active, with powers and responsibilities equivalent to its duties. If that is not the case, then we will be accelerating the demise of the system of democracy under which we function."

His colleague, the late Walter Baker, warned: "We should resist any changes that confuse relevancy with entertainment." Social Crediter André Fortin added: "We have been elected to represent the people, not to entertain them."

Many members heeded those admonitions and do so to this day. But the late political scientist Norman Ward came close to the unfortunate truth when he told a committee studying parliamentary TV: "Television can lie more spectacularly than any unaided human being . . . and the members will want to help it along."

They have done it, with the eager assistance of the media, for whom flair, conflict, the quick thrust and the glib phrase are the stuff of news. Thoughtful, persuasive argument does not make it in the era of the ten-second clip. As consultant Tom Van Dusen, a recently retired senior Mulroney adviser, cautioned those planning for the advent of television: "You can't let it walk in and take over. There is tremendous power in this medium."

Indeed there is. It has become the principal way Canadians learn how the country is run and what part Parliament plays in that process. It is so pervasive that few even recall what they knew of Parliament before TV and how they learned it.

Television's transformation of that process came in two stages. Before the 1950s, print journalists sat in the row of gallery seats above the speaker and took notes on the debate, rounding them out with interviews and background files in order to tell the country what its Parliament was doing. It was not until the late 1950s that the first radio reporters were admitted to the gallery. Their newspaper rivals sometimes used hand "clickers" to sabotage the interviews of the upstart broadcasters. Prominent print journalists such as Blair Fraser and Charles Lynch (still an active Press Gallery member) were the real reporters. When television began, the CBC news service hired those people for some parliamentary coverage, and for the remainder simply rewrote wire copy for announcers to read.

Norman DePoe changed that. He dominated screens across the country at news time with his daily CBC report, from Ottawa or wherever political events took him. There was no CTV then, nor was there last-minute footage of events because of the time required to process and edit film. DePoe might be stumbling one minute as he made his way from the Sparks Street Press Club to the Château Laurier studio, only to deliver incredibly authoritative, lucid reports seconds later.

The DePoe legend grew, and the list of first-rank journalists began to include the names of broadcasters as well as print reporters. Many made the switch as it became clear that both the public impact and the "ego hit" of television could be far greater than that of newspapers. Tom Earle, John Drewery, Ken Mason, Ron Collister, Tom Gould, Tom Leach, and Bruce Phillips entered Canada's living rooms direct from Ottawa. The new medium, with its "stars," immediacy and "pictures-don't-lie" deceptiveness, fed a news-hungry public.

With no cameras in the Commons chamber to show what was actually happening, broadcast accounts were dressed up with interviews and re-enactments. The participants repeated for the camera outside the House what they had just said inside. Sort of. What happened in the replays, performed in a basement room in the Centre Block, was often remarkably different from what had taken place in the chamber moments before. What purported to be "parliamentary coverage" was, in fact, a phony version revised and improved for TV. Goaded by the media and the public to show the "real thing," MPs agreed in 1977 – over some strenuous objections — to let the cameras in.

Very few people, inside the House or out, are happy with the results. Dress has improved and some aspects of behavior are also better. MPs no longer slam their antique desk tops up and down to show approval. Instead they applaud. Speeches have been shortened, as have votes and other procedures. An electronic *Hansard* shows, for posterity, exactly what was said and how. (Tory Allan Lawrence, who mimicked Jean Chrétien's speech and crooked mouth, for example, was forced to apologize for something no printed record could show.) Live TV coverage and a taped video record became such an important part of the Commons process that adjournment of the House was moved when a technician spilled coffee into the control console, knocking out six of the seven House cameras.

While everyone realized that the prying eye of the camera was in to stay, no one knew how many Canadians would really be interested in the dull goings-on of Parliament. In a "name-the-show" session for a weekly package of highlights, one wag in the Ottawa bureau of CBC News suggested "See Your Member Erect," on the grounds that a hint of sex never hurt ratings. It became "This Week in Parliament" and drew up to 800,000 viewers on particularly lively weeks.

What they saw was far from the whole picture. The Commons maintains restrictions on what the cameras can show, so what Canadians get is a sadly distorted picture. In fact, shots were much "wider" at the outset than they are today. Essentially we see the head and shoulders of the MP with the floor. There is a fuller view, of the speaker, maybe including the clerk's table in the foreground, at all other times. There are no cover shots showing big sections of the House, no pans, zooms, split-screens or over-the-shoulder views that would give perspective and life to the proceedings, showing, for instance, the reaction of the subject while he or she is asked a question. Just how ridiculous the guidelines are is brought home when a vote is called. Viewers cannot see the five or more members who must rise to demand a recorded division. Not only can they not tell who "forced a vote," they cannot see how many members are in the chamber when a "quorum count" is called. Business cannot start unless 20 or more of the 295 MPs are present, nor can it continue with fewer members if one of them insists on a count. In reality, however, debate often proceeds with as few as half a dozen in the chamber. Certain items can proceed unless 25 members rise to object. We never see them.

Behind those restrictions is the MPs' fear that the public will realize how few are actually there most of the time. If there are only five or six on one side they will gather behind the speaker, "doughnutting" to give the impression of a crowd in rapt attention. Early in the TV days, Edmonton old-timer Steve Paproski became famous for the "Commons shuffle"; he appeared behind just about every Conservative who spoke. Paproski became puzzled about the frequency with which pages summoned him to lobby phones, only to find no one at the other end. Then he realized that Liberals were calling him out of the House each time he appeared on Commons TV monitors. But others watched too. A dentist once contacted Bill Kempling, who enjoyed a prominent place as whip behind leader Joe Clark, to tell him that chewing ice was bad for his teeth. Kempling did that occasionally in the House. Hundreds of viewers complained when members such as former Liberal defence minister Jim Richardson "crossed the floor." His dramatic switch from government to opposition did not appear on TV because of the rule that gives coverage only to the recognized speaker. Nor have any other defections been covered.

Members, including former NDP leader Ed Broadbent, sometimes deliberately used unparliamentary language such as "liar" in order to get themselves thrown out in a dramatic television protest scene. Rather than create such media heroes, Speaker Fraser began refusing to recognize such members for further contributions until they apologized. No one has been "named" and thrown out for more than four years.

TV has done more than anything else to empty the House of members and reporters. They can monitor proceedings from their offices while working on something else. Members do run the risk, however, of being accused of sloth if they are not seen in the House. In fact, they do most of their work outside, in their offices or in committees. Nevertheless they regularly hear complaints from constituents who "never see them on TV."

The contest to catch the cameras and later newscasts has made Question Period almost the sole focus of parliamentary attention. Cunning showmen such as Liberal Brian Tobin can get on national newscasts with a perfect made-for-TV phrase, while the longer, more thoughtful contributions of veteran colleagues may be totally ignored. That is what happened when Tobin dubbed Michael Wilson's 1991 presentation "the mother of all budgets" at a time when Saddam Hussein's Iraqi aggression had made "the mother of all battles" a household phrase. The more meaningful responses of finance critics Herb Gray and Ottawa Liberal John Manley were not the kind of "quick hits" TV reporters use.

Because Question Period allows the opposition free rein for offence and shows ministers in often-uncomfortable defence, governments do not like Commons TV. Until Mulroney's free-trade election victory in 1988, the myth was growing that no party could ever again win back-to-back majorities. The current government has done two things to combat the negative image. It has cut the number of sitting days and thus the number of Question Periods. But it has also approved long-demanded broadcast coverage of committees, where most back-benchers claim to do their best work. It was the fear that opposition members would hijack on-camera committee meetings that prevented such coverage for years. The government now hopes its new spirit of "consensus," plus strong chairmen, will keep opponents in line and that wild "rat-pack" attacks will be condemned by the public. While performances by Liberals Brian Tobin, Sheila Copps, Don Boudria and John Nunziata drew plenty of media attention after the 1984 election, it is generally agreed that public respect for the institution went down as a result. In fact one Toronto school superintendent refused to expose classes to the unruly behavior of Question Period.

Probably the most flagrant misbehavior ever on Commons TV occurred the night the Tories "charged the chair" when a closure vote cut off debate on Trudeau's constitutional plan. Shouting "we demand to be heard," fist-waving opponents advanced on Speaker Lloyd Francis.

With only tiny snippets of drama extracted and packaged in news reports from a full day of Commons activity, there can be no question that the public gets a distorted view of Parliament. Deliberate scene-stealers and the television medium's need for conflict, brevity and visuals make matters worse. But the biggest single problem may be that Parliament itself has allowed its primary function to all but disappear. The Question Period "accountability session" gets the attention it does partly because Parliament no longer does its main business effectively. Its purpose is to act as a curb on government legislation and spending. The first real step in restoring public respect might be not to limit what TV sees but to give Parliament worthwhile work to do and remove the party straitjackets from MPs.

The up to a million viewers a week who tune in to the House of Commons channel or other more extensive broadcast coverage see more than the tiny "clips" chosen by news reporters for inclusion in their items. Thousands of these watchers have written letters of thanks to John Warren, former network host and co-author of this book, for his explanations of parliamentary proceedings and for the unedited daily broadcasts he introduced. While the CBC continues satellite delivery of full Commons coverage across Canada, Warren and French-language host Gilles de Lalonde were eliminated from the service in June 1991 – a curious cost-cutting gesture at a time when government House leader Harvie Andre, Speaker Fraser and others were appealing for more explanation and public understanding of the parliamentary process. Just how the Commons channel will be dealt with in the future is under study by a committee that is expected to report in the spring of 1992.

Some parliamentarians see full television coverage of committees as an essential ingredient of parliamentary renewal. But public respect can be restored only if the work of those committees affects the course of the nation. No government can expect peak performance from MPs unless it is willing to accept their contributions as a key element of policy making. U.S. congressional committees are widely followed and respected because they do serious work with serious results. If committees did the same here, the public might thrive on nutritious parliamentary fare rather than the fast food the media serves up today. Two C-Span (Cable Satellite Public Affairs Network) channels in the U.S. have 60-million in paid-up subscribers. They get round-the-clock coverage of the House of Representatives, the Senate, Congressional committees, panels, public hearings, speeches and news conferences – a far more substantial political menu than Canadian TV offers.

Most of the news Canadians get about Parliament originates with the 360 reporters, editors, camera and sound persons, columnists, clerks and photographers who belong to the Parliamentary Press Gallery. They represent 80 radio and television networks and stations, wire services, newspapers and chains, magazines and international correspondents. For old-timers, the Gallery was a "hot room" of typewriters, phones, telegraph dispatchers, noise and clutter. From it the Commons chamber could be reached in about 20 seconds, at full gallop. The fireplace mantel in the Gallery lounge bears the inscription: "But words are things and a small drop of ink, falling, like dew upon a thought, produces that which makes thousands, perhaps millions, think." A nearby Second World War photo shows 44 newsmen – no women in those days, of course – who worked and drank and fought and played there.

But the Gallery today is more a memory than an entity. Most media members use that room as a mail drop and occasional stopover on the way to a "scrum" or interview. Their real work is done over cameras, television monitors, editing suites and computers in offices scattered through half a dozen buildings off Parliament Hill. The ragtag few with no other downtown work space include Ottawa correspondents for the *London Free Press*, *Windsor Star*, Halifax *Chronicle-Herald*, United Press International, *Alberta Report* and several free-lancers, such as columnist Claire Hoy. Their use of the publicly funded facilities saves them each about $18,000 a year in office rent.

The men and women (in about the same nine-to-one ratio as Parliament itself) who process each day's news use Gallery membership as a credential. It gets them into government buildings, news conferences and other secure areas. But the length of the Gallery list and the variety of jobs it represents mean that the ID card is no longer a ticket to a close-knit social-professional club.

The contemporary reporter is better equipped and educated than his or her predecessors, who kept the beer machine and "blind pig" humming. The liquor cabinet is now gone, photocopiers and fax machines having taken its place in the late 1970s and '80s. The hot-room doors are now locked at an hour when the rowdyism of former night sittings was just beginning. When he retired in 1988 after forty-seven years on the Hill, Gallery clerk Archie Langill said it had been ages since he had found phones stuffed with blue cheese or the ear-pieces covered with indelible ink following a late-night revel. Fun-loving newsmen no longer competed for the longest corridor-kick of a metal waste-basket, he noted, "and I haven't seen a snowball or beer fight in here for quite a while."

While some claim that there is still a long way to go, reporters today are far less partisan than those who practised the trade up to the Diefenbaker-Pearson era. In the nineteenth century, political bias was part of the job on newspapers, which were all closely allied with one or other of the main political parties. Arthur R. Ford recalls an example in his book, *As the World Wags On*. Ford joined the Gallery in 1907, working for the Winnipeg *Telegram* and later the Fredericton *Gleaner*. One day in 1913 when the contentious Naval Aid Bill was under debate, he listened to a good speech by Sir Wilfrid Laurier and a poor one by Tory minister Douglas Hazen, who was a friend of the *Gleaner*'s publisher.

"I wired the *Gleaner* to this effect: 'Sir Wilfrid Laurier has spoken on the naval question,'" Ford recounts. "'How much do you want?' Then as an afterthought I added, 'Hazen spoke this afternoon. Do you want anything of his speech?' Back came the wire: 'Ignore Laurier entirely. Send Hazen verbatim.'"

The great reporters of the first half of the century were clearly partisan. Bruce Hutchison of the *Winnipeg Free Press*, *Victoria Daily Times* and the *Vancouver Sun* and Grant Dexter of the *Winnipeg Free Press* were Liberal friends of Mackenzie King, about whom Hutchison wrote his book *The Unknown Canadian*. Grattan O'Leary of the *Ottawa Journal* was on the other side, a friend of Arthur Meighen and named to the Senate by Diefenbaker in 1962. Growth of the nonpartisan Canadian Press wire service, which provides coverage for papers of widely differing views, helped to subdue the tone of Ottawa reports. So did the Second World War. At the time, because the government had to appeal to everyone for support regardless of political bias, it treated the news less as a patronage prize to hand out to favored journalists. Newspapers also toned down their partisanship as they began to compete for mass readership.

While newspapers may lean towards one political party or another, few are as rabid as their ancestors of just a few decades ago. Many run columns and editorials that represent conflicting viewpoints. All journalists are used to being accused by each political party of favoring the others. The phenomenon is most striking as elections approach. People whose careers depend on the success of a particular party cast themselves as judges of media objectivity. They accuse journalists who fail to agree with them of lacking integrity.

Most media organizations try to draw a distinction between straight news and opinion. The latter is supposed to remain the clearly identified domain of columnists and editorial writers. Their views frequently favor a party's stand on one issue and oppose it on others. But writers who show a whiff of sympathy for the government viewpoint often receive special briefings or easier access to sources. Michel Gratton wondered in a *Sun* column "where all this Meisel stuff is coming from" in the damaging campaign over the integrity of CBC-TV news chief Elly Alboim, when the report that triggered it had not even been published. The columnists who had "stumbled" on it had all written several favorable columns about Mulroney at a time when he was under general attack and at 14 per cent in the polls.

The low esteem in which many reporters hold politicians is returned in kind, although each needs the other to survive. In his autobiography Jack Horner described the press as "by and large, a pretty shallow lot." Referring in a speech to those in the Press Gallery seats above him, he pronounced: "The vultures sit up there waiting to see if a member is going to be in a dangerous position and then they flock in to feast upon the bones."

While reporters have no difficulty in spotting ethical lapses in politicians, they often fail to apply the same strict standards to themselves. Members of the Press Gallery seem as content as MPs to dine at the public trough, while saving themselves the trouble of getting elected to qualify. For a $50 membership fee (paid by employers) most Gallery reporters have access to free parking worth $1,300 a year, office space and a desk in the Centre Block, the services of nine clerks and two messengers, telephone answering service, the use of fax and photo-copying machines, free letterhead, pens and pencils, free long-distance phone privileges, library research privileges, individual mail-boxes into which news releases and personal mail are delivered half a dozen times day, access to the taxpayer-subsidized restaurant, cafeterias, barber-shop and shoeshine parlor. Salaries for the staff who service the Gallery come to more than $300,000 annually.

A suggestion that the hot room be converted to a committee room or badly needed offices was met with furious resistance by the Gallery executive in 1990. Government whip Jim Hawkes argued that taxpayers should not provide the proudly independent media with prime accommodation. In its campaign to save their precious quarters, the Gallery executive appealed to Speaker Fraser. They claimed that they were protecting not a privilege but a tradition. The speaker allowed the issue to die rather than further incur the wrath of the pampered media.

The government destroyed a far more significant tradition when it converted the historic reading room, one floor below the Gallery, into committee space that doubles as the Tory caucus room. Huge murals glorifying the "Spirit of the Printed Word" still fill the upper walls, while magnificent bookcases, newspaper racks, carved wooden tables and leather couches and chairs were removed from the popular haven for politicians and Hill staff. Nearly 600 small-town weeklies were eliminated, leaving only 31 dailies to tell readers what was happening in Canada's "grass roots." A few long-time journalists, including Doug Fisher and Charles Lynch, mourned the loss publicly, but there was nary a peep from the "tradition-conscious" Gallery executive.

Just a few months later the former reading room was the site of a revealing display of today's media reality. PMO lackeys scurried in to arrange the flags, sound system and other trappings of an event of heart-stopping importance. U.S. President George Bush and our very own Prime Minister Mulroney were to hold a joint news conference. As reporters filed in, aides took charge of the seating. "That row is for the stars," staffer Kim Cross told reporters Dan Dugas of *Broadcast News* and Ross Howard of the *Globe and Mail* as he directed the print and radio reporters away from the spots up front. In the very room where a torch at one end and printing press at the other honor the power of print, TV personalities David Halton, Mike Duffy, John Burke, Bill Rodgers, and Craig Oliver, along with their U.S. broadcast counterparts, were ushered to the prized places.

Reporters' work takes them around the world with the political stars. It also provides a huge harvest of frequent-flier points. While MPs and bureaucrats are not supposed to use these for holidays and other personal benefits, some do. Many who follow the rules do so partly for fear of the media criticism that would result from breaking them. But news crews themselves – including those of the CBC, whose travel is paid from the public purse – seldom hesitate to grab the freebies. Of course, those are "taxable benefits," which they would never fail to declare.

The Press Gallery seems to be at least as inept as the politicians in dealing with ethical issues of its own. In the 1970s, some Gallery members embarked on long, loud and fruitless arguments in an attempt to get news agencies to pay for the hot-room space and other benefits they receive at public expense. And the battle still rages over whether the annual Press Gallery Dinner should remain "off the record." That is the huge event that brings journalists, politicians and top bureaucrats together for a boozy exchange of speeches and bawdy entertainment. Much of the humor is tasteless and risqué, to say the least, but details are supposed to remain confidential. Many believe that it is scandalous hypocrisy for the media to make a colossal effort to kick at the closed doors of government while also hosting a secret event of its own. Journalists like Allan Fotheringham who breach the Gallery's own code of silence have sometimes been refused tickets to the next year's dinner.

The Gallery has also wrestled unsuccessfully with the task of codifying standards of conduct in its own membership rules. Journalism – like politics, but unlike truck driving or hair dressing – requires no formal training or tests for entry. Since reporting began, its practitioners have supplemented their once-meagre pay by moonlighting. Salaries are much better today, but so are the rewards for stars who accept fees as conference speakers, panelists and report writers. If such moonlighting is for government agencies or interest groups that the reporter is also supposed to examine and explain to the public, a conflict can easily result. One Gallery old-timer who earned thousands of dollars as a translator spent weeks rendering a secret copy of the original urea-formaldehyde (UFFI) report from English to French without ever divulging its contents. Once details became public about the dangerous insulation, headlines, court cases and lawsuits continued for years.

In March 1990, the Gallery suspended a member for three months because his name had appeared on a government-paid study of business reaction to the Canada-U.S. free-trade deal. A clause in the Gallery constitution that prohibits Gallery members from receiving benefits from the government as a result of their membership was invoked to do it. Steve Hall is the editor of an electronic newsletter on Parliament called *Publinet*. He had made a few calls to contribute to the work of the consulting firm, Informetrica, that owns *Publinet*. His "offence" came to light when he was thanked in the report. The resulting loss of privileges was the first such expulsion in the Gallery's 150-year history.

That prompted *Ottawa Citizen* columnist Frank Howard to begin a hunt for journalists who might have compromised themselves with outside work. He announced that he intended to use the access-to-information process to find those who had cashed government cheques for services rendered.

Globe and Mail reporter Hugh Winsor then confessed to having been paid $350 for a speech on media relations to senior mandarins. He insisted that he had done no wrong and attacked Howard's witch-hunt. "I didn't realize that the mills of the gods grind so finely at the *Citizen*," he said. Howard then discovered that *Globe and Mail* columnist Jeffrey Simpson had received $500 to speak on media relations to the federal Centre for Management Development He also received $1,500 in 1988 for talking to officials in the Finance Department and in 1991 pocketed more than $7,000 for chairing a seminar on occupational health sponsored by the Department of Labour. Simpson, too, felt that he had done nothing wrong. "If the Gallery is going to judge that speaking to a non-partisan group and getting paid is unethical, it is beyond my comprehension," he told Howard.

Michel Vastel, columnist for a chain of French-language papers and regular free-lancer for CBC and Radio Canada, wrote to Howard to say that he had been paid $400 to talk to government officials about the media. Others soon followed. Manion Corneillier, a member of the Gallery executive that had given Steve Hall the boot, confessed that she had written several articles for the Canadian International Development Agency and accepted a free trip overseas.

And W.A. Wilson, a free-lancer, revealed in a letter to Howard that he had raked in $3,000 to write speeches for Simon Reisman on the free-trade deal in 1988. Wilson, an aristocratic former columnist for the defunct *Montreal Star*, declared that he had done nothing unethical: "I hope I am not being self serving, but I can see no grounds at all on which it can be considered unethical for a columnist to support, through other work, a viewpoint he has been expressing in his column over a period of years. The idea that support for your ideas in secondary ways is improper strikes me as preposterous."

Faced with these embarrassing developments, the executive set up a study by "eminent persons" under journalism professor Stuart Adams, who got $1,300 for his task. The study was as bland as dishwater and, needless to say, did not recommend any action against senior journalists of the type used to discipline Hall. In February 1991 the Gallery scrapped all reference to ethical behavior in its constitution, so that no member can be suspended or expelled from the Gallery for that reason. Most members agreed that they had no business judging the ethics of fellow members, although they rejected efforts to give Wilson a lifetime membership, a slap on the wrist for playing both sides of the fence. Charles Lynch, the veteran columnist, who had put Wilson's name forward, was furious. "I just couldn't believe they'd be that vindictive," he told the *Hill Times*. "I thought it was an honor [to make him a lifetime member]. He's a very well-known and respected journalist and we let in all kinds now who don't do any writing. I simply don't think a lifetime in the business should be cancelled because of one thing. At seventy-three years old, it's a little late to punish people."

The Tories didn't need to hire a print reporter to write speeches for them. They did better than that. Far ahead of the other parties in both budgets and propaganda techniques through the 1980s, they took a still greater leap forward in 1988. They were reeling from a series of scandals, criminal charges and resignations as an election approached, and were convinced that they could not get their honest story told by the "biased" Ottawa press corps. So they set up their own Tory TV network.

The party hired right-wing broadcaster Ken Lawrence to do "non-partisan" interviews with ministers and Tory MPs so that the "true story" could be delivered to the people. Lawrence meets each morning with the whip, key caucus members and the House leader's staff to discuss the day's expected events and how they can best convey the Tory version of objective news coverage. As reports are released and parliamentary exchanges identify items of interest through the day, Lawrence's crew waits just outside the chamber doors to get the reaction of Tories whom the mainline media neglect. The resulting news clips are beamed by satellite to TV and radio stations across the country, and are available free to any editor who wants to use them. Lee Clark from Brandon, Manitoba, or Doug Fee from Red Deer, Alberta, may not have stood in the House that day, but their instant reaction to the issue of the day will be delivered big as life for viewers back home.

Tory TV costs more than half a million dollars a year. That is a bargain price for getting the party's message sent to hundreds of thousands of viewers each night. It is an ideal vehicle for getting MPs on home-town newscasts, showing them holding forth right there in the Commons lobby surrounded by media and political bigwigs just as if they had delivered a speech in the chamber itself. To help cover the cost, a special fund-raising letter was sent to party members in 1989 by then Conservative party president Bill Jarvis. He asked them to donate $41.50 each to support the "non-partisan" Parliamentary News Service, a title that has a nice, legitimate ring to it. "We make sure the material is factual and newsworthy," Jarvis wrote. "Government policies and programs are reported straight up." He did concede that the purpose is to "ensure that the Prime Minister's and our government's message of progress, success and accomplishments is carried to all parts of Canada."

Critics felt that some news editors would reject material from such a source. They were wrong. Small stations with limited budgets were delighted with the "freebies." They could get their local MP on the air regularly from Ottawa, even when the Press Gallery was concentrating on bigger game. Most small stations run the clips without identifying their source. Said one Timmins, Ontario, news director: "We don't really care who shoves microphones in a person's face as long as we get the clip."

Lawrence tried to retain his membership in the Press Gallery after taking on the lucrative contract, but it was rescinded by the executive. Liberals and New Democrats were predictably critical of the Tories for skirting the media to deliver their message. "In the Soviet Union, Gorbachev has begun the end of the propaganda society," squawked Liberal Brian Tobin. "In Canada, Prime Minister Brian Mulroney is just beginning to build a great propaganda machine he hopes will turn us into a regime of non-thinking idiots." Most observers felt that the pious whining of Grits and New Democrats was prompted chiefly by jealousy. The party brass admitted that Tory TV was a brilliant idea and that they would emulate it if they could afford to.

Lawrence's service is sometimes confused with those the taxpayers provide to help members of all parties polish up their image via television. In the late 1980s a state-of-the-art television studio was built in the South Block at a cost of about one million dollars. Staffed by House of Commons Broadcast Branch employees, it was used mostly to record MPs' "vanity videos" for use on cable stations back home. These were often interviews of up to half an hour in which a member's views on various subjects were delivered in response to "softball" questions lobbed by an aide or colleague. The tapes were then run as "Parliamentary Reports" along with the drum-majorette contests and giant zucchini displays on community television. From 1987 on, Rogers Cable complemented the daytime taping service with an evening one conducted in a nearby studio rented from Global TV.

After a staff cut shut down the Commons service, Phil Lind of Rogers Cable, wrote to Dr. Ash, the fixer in the speaker's office. He proposed to rent the splendid Commons studio to produce all video householders. That was in January 1990. Within months Rogers and the Board of Internal Economy had worked out a deal for studio rental at the figure Lind had suggested – $5,000 a month.

Parliament's broadcasting possibilities are growing rapidly, but so too is the rest of the Commons' information domain, headed by Susan Wright. The wife of a former aide to Hawkes, she was hired by the speaker's office in 1988 to draft a proposal that became the blueprint for a Public Information Office. The Commons, which normally enforces its strict bilingual requirement when hiring, then engaged the unilingual consultant to direct the PIO. So effectively is Wright plugged in to the Commons brass that she often sits in on top-level meetings that are off limits to her immediate boss, Bob Desramaux, director general of support and information systems.

Since Wright did her study, the PIO has grown to command a budget of $1 million a year and a staff of 20. The office responds to letters and calls for Commons information, produces hand-outs for MPs and prepares education kits for schools about Parliament and how it is supposed to work. The 40 Broadcast Branch employees and their $1.6 million budget have now been folded under Wright's wing, providing the potential for new video-information projects. The tour guides, pages and Visitors and Education Services staff added about 60 more employees. In total Wright, herself a contract employee, supervises about 120 Commons staff members.

All this amounts to a pretty hefty tab for getting information to Canadians about their Parliament. But more is apparently needed. The speaker constantly emphasizes the importance of better public relations to help citizens understand Canada's principal democratic institution. And Harvie Andre complained in a letter to the editor of the *Ottawa Citizen* in April 1991 that "Canadians simply do not get enough direct experience and hard information on Parliament and how it works."

One thing that has fouled lines of communication is the all-pervasive public-opinion poll. It has virtually eliminated the influence MPs had over leaders and policy as the source of "grass roots" opinion from across the country. And it has become the tool of news agencies, which call on anonymous pollsters to do "scientifically" what reporters used to do with pens, pads and shoe leather. The media wizards no longer quiz MPs to learn how their constituents feel. They read the latest poll results, then pursue politicians for a reaction to what the polls say. The rise of polls is far more significant than a mere triumph of technology. It is part of a revolution in political behavior that makes the parliamentary process more irrelevant every day.

Patrick Boyer, a writer, public-policy expert, lawyer and Conservative MP for Etobicoke-Lakeshore, is incensed by the way authorities spend taxpayers' money on polls to bypass the democratic process. To Bill Gillespie of CBC radio's "The House" he commented: "There is no question the volume and extent of opinion polling in Canada has had a transforming effect on the roles of political parties and elected members by bypassing those of us who are sent here by the people to speak for them." He explained that when government turns to "what purports to be a scientific sampling and gets some numbers from that, they're going to follow, much more probably, the results of that sample of opinion than the views expressed by those of us who are actually out there dealing with the men and women in our constituencies."

Boyer calls the pollsters "Rasputins." He is working on a private member's bill that would force government to release all public opinion polls paid for by taxpayers. "The dollars are so significant, the issues are so important, that it ought to be in the public realm," he told "The House." "If it's being done it is because somebody thought it was worth doing. If it was worth doing, let's share it with all Canadians."

The matter of polling secrecy is one that the bureau chief of the Canadian Press in Ottawa, Kirk Lapointe, understands well. He has made a determined effort to find out what polls have been commissioned by Ottawa agencies and to pry the results loose. Lapointe estimates that taxpayers foot an annual bill of $25 million for government polls, not counting those conducted for the PMO and PCO. Giant contracts for such work are awarded constantly to such firms as Angus Reid and Associates, Decima Research and Environics. Mulroney and his top advisers know every day how the previous day's pitch played. Angus Reid explained to Gillespie that the "rolling wave technique" of continual overnight polling provides a daily update on the public's mood and perception of events. The government can thus tailor its message each day to respond to its constant public pulse-taking.

But the public does not have the benefit of that information. Polls funded by political parties and by the taxpayers remain closely guarded secrets in the hands of a few prime-ministerial intimates. As Lapointe explains, the process of learning that government polls have been done, asking for them and then filing formal access-to-information requests is a lengthy one. Often, results are released, if at all, six months later.

Journalist, author and Press Gallery curmudgeon Claire Hoy has written a book on the subject. He says that all three parties, by relying on polls to guide them, have "abandoned their responsibility to provide leadership." Hoy believes that Conservatives, Liberals and New Democrats used to have distinct ideologies and philosophies. But now, "everybody comes to the sort of mushy middle where nobody stands for anything." Parties shy away from any stand if the polls show the people will not like it, regardless of the principle involved, says Hoy.

When Canadians now tune in to the news, Peter Mansbridge and Lloyd Robertson come armed with multicolored charts and graphs to tell them how they feel about Parliament and politicians. "Not keen" is the answer. That is, in fact, the most flattering interpretation that can be put on the opinions logged, computerized and regularly released with as much fanfare as if they were real news. We almost forget that our heads, our guts and our conversations have already told us much more about ourselves than the networks and technicians can.

Canadians hardly need pollsters to tell them they're mad as hell at the way their Parliament works and they should not take it anymore.

12
SAVING THE SYSTEM

"I do not think the public is going to give any integrity to the system unless we change the system. We are the servants of the people. We are not the masters."

RON MACDONALD, MP, MAY 1991

I T WAS THE "MOST EXHILARATING, PROUDEST" EVENT OF RON MacDonald's life. The energetic little Liberal had just wiped out the 14,000-vote margin Mike Forrestall had racked up four years earlier, beating the aging Dartmouth Tory by 2,000 ballots. It was November 21, 1988, and the thirty-five-year-old Nova Scotian had just realized a dream. He was on his way to the House of Commons. A lifelong politician, MacDonald had been an aide to Atlantic legend Allan MacEachen and had served as executive director of the provincial Liberals before knocking Forrestall from the perch he had occupied for twenty-three years. "You come up here and you are out to change the world and you think you can," says MacDonald of the day he took his back-row seat in the Commons as his wife beamed from the visitor's gallery above.

The surge of euphoria did not last long. It was quickly replaced by disappointment, resentment and then anger. "You come up here and you find all the cards are stacked against you, every single one," laments MacDonald, still shaking his head at his enthusiastic idealism of two years ago. Stringent party discipline, useless debates in which speeches are written by bureaucrats for MPs to mouth and a strangled committee system left him profoundly disillusioned. MacDonald assumed that Parliament represented the hope of the people; he discovered that it was the source of their discontent. It hurt to return to the riding to hear his constituents complain that MPs were out of step with their joys, heartbreaks, hopes and hard work. "There are times when I'm embarrassed to say I'm a member of Parliament."

251

Bob Horner, who arrived in 1984, is equally chagrined. The veterinarian and former Mountie is a member of the famous political clan that had sent three cousins from the prairies into the Commons before him. None of them was able to explain just what frustration he would face. The problems he has encountered when trying to present his constituents' views on issues like the Official Languages Act or carrying out his work as Tory chairman of the Justice Committee have left him as disillusioned as MacDonald.

One thing that enrages them both is seeing earnest Canadians take heartfelt, meticulously prepared briefs into committee meetings in the mistaken belief that they can somehow make a difference to what the government does. What those witnesses, and freshmen MPs, fail to realize is that most committee meetings are make-work projects for members whose reports will gather dust. "We get paid to waste our time, so I quess we can't complain," MacDonald grumbles. "But there are a hell of a lot of good witnesses who take time to put presentations together . . . and you just wonder if they'll ever go through the process again when they watch what happens." Committee meetings are often cancelled when half a dozen members can not be rounded up for a quorum or when partisan bickering makes it impossible to proceed with business.

Proceedings in the Commons chamber, the mythical cut and thrust of debate in the highest court in the land, are even more of a set-piece farce. MPs may know on the government side that legislation is flawed, or on the opposition side that it is sound, but they will vote, without exception, the way their party whips direct. Government supporters stand for the bill, opposition members against it – no matter what it contains. Often they don't know anything about the bill they are passing into law. The team with the most players wins. Serious debate takes place "behind the curtains" among MPs from all parties. Away from their whips, they discuss the pros and cons of legislation they are not allowed to change. And they lament the fact that Parliament has been neutered. "All the debate that takes place is moot, and it's redundant," admits MacDonald. "We should get half our salaries and show up once a year to nod our heads like sheep in favor [of] or against legislation.

Surely to goodness there has to be a better way to work the system."

Reg Stackhouse, a former Conservative member who served two different terms in the House, says that because party discipline in Canada "is tighter than in any other Parliament in the world" votes are just "an expensive waste of time." It is a system that prevents members of all parties from truly representing their constituents. "It's a goddam abuse," adds MacDonald. There are "some damn good" Conservative back-benchers who rarely get a chance to take part in Commons debates. "What they get to do is to stand up and read out a departmental speech which says all is rosy in la-la land. No wonder the system doesn't work." The role of the opposition is just as clearly defined by the party leadership – again regardless of the personal or regional interests of individual members.

Even the dumbest participants in this democratic charade realize that the system must be changed if it is ever to gain respect. In its 1991 Throne Speech, the government promised reforms. It called on all sides to become less partisan and to adopt fundamental changes in attitude that would allow members, in many cases, to speak and vote as they choose. The chief proponent of the new Utopia was Mulroney's fierce House leader, Harvie Andre, who is one of the most hot-tempered partisans in Parliament. One astute observer of the place over the last thirty years has been Douglas Fisher. In a *Sun* column after the reform proposals were announced, he wrote: "What changes in rules, what altered processes, might crib a [Sheila] Copps or a Harvie Andre into courtesy and out of black and white partisanship?" He holds out little hope that the present crop of MPs will change their behavior.

House leaders and whips in all parties have been chosen for the very quality – unquestioning loyalty to the party line – that the government suddenly sees as an impediment to Parliament. Strange! It is far more likely that those lines in the Throne Speech were prompted by public disgust and the explosive growth of the Reform Party based on its promises to clean the place up. No one believes that government leaders who have acquired all the power are suddenly prepared to hand it over to mere MPs.

Veteran columnist Charles Lynch has seen pledges of "power to the people" come to naught many times before. In a post–Throne Speech column, he wrote: " 'All eyes are on this chamber,' says the Prime Minister . . . sounding the way Prime Ministers used to sound when Parliament called itself the highest court in the land and everybody believed it." The *Ottawa Citizen*'s Paul Gessell quoted the Throne Speech line, "This session will be a turning point in Canadian history," and noted that it might well have said, "that Mulroney is hoping this session will be a turning point for Conservative fortunes."

With the motives of Commons leaders suspect and the party sheep unwilling to launch out on their own, real reforms could be a long time in coming. After all, pleas for attitudinal change, free votes, effective committees and measures to allow private members to create law are not new. Such changes were all proposed by the McGrath committee in 1985.

The government brags that it implemented 77 per cent of McGrath's 119 recommendations in whole, another 14 per cent in part. That argument simply confirms that parliamentary reform is not a matter of arithmetic. Suppose that a new country were set up on the basis of a hundred recommendations, one of which was free elections. If its leaders fulfilled all the other ninety-nine, but not that one, their percentage record would be almost perfect but in democratic terms they would have achieved nothing. The numbers mean nothing. Results can be determined only in terms of the workability of the system and its responsiveness to the people's wishes. Replacement of the current government house leader and whip who have contributed so directly to the poisonous partisan atmosphere would be a good start to a "new look" House of Commons.

The reforms proposed in the Throne Speech look good. Implementing them may be beyond the will and ability of those who created the present mess. It is easier to visualize Mulroney's ministers wearing beanies with propellers than it is to imagine them asking all-party committees to help produce legislation and budgets. A new team committed from the outset to revamp Parliament seems a more promising bet than backing those who have drawn power to themselves and have a vested interest in keeping it.

Nevertheless there is some movement. MacDonald and some Young Turks in the Liberal caucus are pressing leader Jean Chrétien for a commitment to alter the system fundamentally if their party forms the next government. A few frustrated Tory MPs occasionally test their party's commitment to reform – and several have been kicked out for doing just what the government now advocates. Jim Fulton, Svend Robinson, Ian Waddell and Bill Blaikie in the NDP caucus have long proposed looser discipline in their party – with mixed results. Pat Nowlan, no longer a member of the Conservative caucus because of his habit of expressing non-conformist views, intends to run in the next election on the issue of parliamentary reform. "Everywhere people are expressing frustration, helplessness and, more seriously, total cynicism with the political process," says the twenty-six-year veteran. "MPs are 'nobodies' – we pay them well and give them perks and privileges – yet they act like trained seals. . . . This creeping political malaise must be arrested."

The decline of Parliament due to its domination by an all-powerful cabinet and a burgeoning, unchecked bureaucracy has been talked about for decades. Numerous studies, from the Lampert report on financial accountability in 1979 to the Macdonald royal commission on Canada's economic prospects and the McGrath report in 1985, have all pointed to the same problem. They say that it is essential to shift power to committees if the Commons is to act as a counter-weight to government. They say that greater use of committees is the only way to give MPs "teeth, muscle and claws." The government pays lip-service to that idea, but in practice has kept committees tightly controlled. It usually ignores recommendations achieved by all-party consensus.

Strong, working legislatures such as Germany's Bundestag and the U.S. Congress conduct their work in vigorous, independent committees. That is where politicians specialize, initiate policy and become effective watch-dogs over the government. Germany's committee system is not as powerful as the American one but is much more effective than ours, where independence is almost unheard of. The Germans appear to have found a system that features both disciplined parties and legislators free to debate and influence policy. In the United States, congressional committees are totally independent of the executive and have real power to control the legislative process. Even the parliamentary systems in Britain and Australia give their MPs more independence than ours.

The Germans may have shown the way by selecting some of the best features of the American system, while avoiding some of its most serious handicaps. Certainly the congressional committee system works. But two-year terms for members of the House of Representatives, the corrosive power of special interests in funding elections, free-wheeling primaries and the seniority system for committee chairmen are less desirable features.

Canada has already borrowed heavily from the American system. Our first constitutional draftsmen were attracted to the American form of federalism in the nineteenth century and dazzled by the Bill of Rights in this one. Sir John A. Macdonald recognized that federalism was required to meet the regional needs of a country as large and diverse as Canada. But at the same time the Fathers of Confederation opted for the British system of simple majority rule dominated by a powerful cabinet. They did not see the need for an independent system of checks and balances. Today, cabinet and Parliament are controlled by a single small group. If that group shares power at all, it is with top bureaucrats and provincial leaders through "first ministers" and "federal-provincial" conferences from which ordinary parliamentarians are excluded. Special-interest groups gain influence through political insiders, often high-powered and high-priced lobbyists who are well connected to the Ottawa elite. Ordinary MPs are outside that process too.

The adoption of the 1982 Charter of Rights and Freedoms has fundamentally changed the nature of government. It helped to bring Canada much closer to the U.S.-style of government by giving the judiciary enormous new powers to limit both Parliament and government. "The Charter has turned the Supreme Court into a more effective centre of power that can check the executive and the legislative branch of the government," says University of Toronto professor Albert Breton. "There is no doubt we have been moving in the American direction."

Attractive features of the U.S. system include the ability of congressional legislators to act independently of their party in the best interests of their constituents. On the other hand, the beauty of a parliamentary system is the ability of the executive to deliver on its promises. In Congress, the U.S. president can see his policies adopted only after a tough review process designed to ensure that every interest gets a say. In Canada, the only voice that counts is that of the government whip carrying out the prime minister's orders. A made-in-Canada variation of the congressional system would weaken cabinet and give more authority to MPs. A better calibre of member and renewed public respect of the institution should follow.

Academics, parliamentary observers and MPs offer four means for reviving Parliament: autonomous committees, free votes, less stringent party discipline and an elected Senate to represent the regions. The basic outline has been detailed in the government's background paper to the Throne Speech, but with a degree of commitment no less vague than the commitment to prosperity and education for all. When it comes to Throne Speeches, performance invariably falls short of promises.

The fundamental changes this government has been forced by political threats to examine will not come easily. As professor and respected journalist Anthony Westell said in an *Ottawa Citizen* article early in 1991: "Parliament knows nothing of compromise . . . it is a theatrical forum for political warfare." Nevertheless, such proposed changes bear study by us all simply because the existing parliamentary system no longer works and urgently needs reform.

A well-designed committee system, allowed to work, can strengthen our parliamentary form of government in a number of important ways. It can bring the people back into the process through individual MPs, reduce partisanship, promote serious examination of legislation and spending and co-ordinate the work of MPs and bureaucrats. By not using committees effectively our system has allowed a "vast array of government activity to go unexamined," concludes political scientist Christopher Dunn. Stronger committee review would not usurp cabinet's right to initiate spending, but should make government more responsive to taxpayers' wishes as expressed through their local representatives.

Ten or twelve committees created by statute to oversee major government departments under the very public eye of television would be a good start. Each needs subcommittees to launch special investigations or study specific legislation. They must be autonomous, with broad terms of reference and enough money for professional staff. Perhaps they could use the $3 million or so now blown on overseas junkets, or some of the money MPs and their spouses now spend on up to sixty-four return flights anywhere in Canada. Members should remain on committees for the duration of Parliament in order to develop expertise in the subject area, free of the whip's authority to shuffle them at will.

A key would be a powerful Standing Committee on Government Finance and the Economy. It would examine the government's five-year fiscal plan and would play a public role in drawing up federal budgets. Instead of examining these only after they have been prepared by some mystical secret process and then dropped on a helpless nation, the committee should hold hearings on tax measures and spending during the summer and fall. Its report could be tabled before Christmas to allow for Commons debate. The minister of finance would then have a sense of the public's views before preparing a budget for presentation in February. He or she could choose to ignore the committee's recommendations, but would have to answer to Parliament and the country for the budget in a more direct way than now.

Committees must have the right to oversee spending, which is, after all, the first purpose of Parliament. Today MPs have no influence over how the government spends taxpayers' money. In the late 1960s when the spending estimates were turned over to committees for review, the ancient parliamentary right to delay was removed. Even if committees have not completed their scrutiny of departmental estimates, these are "deemed to be reported" by May 31 and are passed by June 30. The long recess in April and May 1991 meant that committees did not even begin to study the estimates until after the reporting deadline. Under a special order they got two weeks to do so.

The rigid time limit should be removed, although the government obviously must retain the right eventually to get its estimates adopted. The Canadian Bar Association has suggested that at least one department per year should be examined by the House of Commons itself. "The rationale for an experimental return to this procedure is based on the need for periodic scrutiny of a department's expenditures in a highly public forum as well as on a principle of parliamentary democracy dating back to the Magna Carta." TV coverage of a committee doing that job would achieve the same "high public" end.

The association also believes that the estimates of a limited number of departments should be selected annually, some by the opposition and some by government back-benchers, for in-depth study. Political scientist Robert Jackson has proposed a General Estimates Committee to examine all government spending and a separate committee to review Crown corporations. A General Estimates Committee, with links to the comptroller general and with its own expertise, would make the government more accountable to Parliament. It would be able to review total proposed spending in relation to available funds and determine if the government can meet its objectives.

The Public Accounts Committee, which is supposed to be the most important one on Parliament Hill, is a watch-dog without teeth. It should be able to examine all government accounts, put its findings before Parliament and demand public debate on them. Motions to concur in committee reports today are used as little more than a tactic to delay government business for an hour or so, not as true tests of accountability.

Another critically important way to make individual parliamentarians effective and reduce unproductive political warfare is to have them conduct many of the major studies that governments so often hand to commissions and task forces. When given these tasks, MPs and senators can produce first-rate reports, as they did during the 1970s on unemployment insurance and the penitentiary system and in the 1980s on acid rain and deregulation. Two years ago the Transport Committee did a major study of VIA Rail, but its recommendations to improve service were ignored by the government, which was determined to cut instead. Such reports should be regarded as valuable public contributions to policy rather than nuisances to be cast aside.

The government treats proposed legislation with the same disdain. A bill today is the product of brokerage politics among cabinet, civil servants, special-interest groups, corporations and lobbyists. This process should be moved into committees where cards are played publicly. Using ministerial guidelines, committees could even draft bills. Involving MPs early in the legislative and policy process can get them working in a less partisan way towards a goal – and possibly prevent later deadlocks, such as the one that stalled the gun-control legislation. Ministers could choose to ignore the committee product, but chances are that many of the ideas generated there would be acceptable.

Legislation brought before the House today is already in almost final form (except where faulty drafting forces "technical changes"). Ministers treat proposed amendments to their bills almost as a personal attack. To respond to suggestions for changes is to admit weakness and to risk condemnation by colleagues for holding up other business. If the process is opened up, the greater public input lessens "ownership" of a bill by a minister or the government. Cabinet members and their top officials would have to work more closely with ordinary MPs to achieve policy ends. Participation by western or Atlantic members could do much to relieve tension and reduce complaints that the regions are ignored in the legislative process.

It is the right and duty of cabinet to manage, to initiate policy and to determine budgets. But Parliament also has a duty to oversee the managers and to propose ideas and solutions. Reports of parliamentary committees must offer detailed judgements on the way the country is being run. The government should respond to them. Such "creative tension" should produce better government, even if it does make life less comfortable for ministers and their top advisers.

One key change the McGrath committee called for in 1985 dealt with "confidence" votes. They are the traditional way for the people's representatives in the Commons to show whether or not they have confidence in the government. A vote against the government on budget or major money bills means its defeat and probably an election. That is what happened in December 1979, when the combined opposition upset Joe Clark's minority Conservative government on a budget vote. Divisions on budget questions are historically votes of confidence. But McGrath pointed out that most of the hundreds of votes taken each session are no such thing. They simply decide whether the House supports a particular bill, amendment, motion or whatever item is before it. Nevertheless, all these votes are treated as confidence tests, the government voting as a block on one side, the opposition solidly on the other. Discipline enforced by the party whips ensures that members do not break ranks, but also that they are not free to vote as they believe or as their constituents may wish. McGrath said that that convention was nonsense. The few votes that are true tests of confidence in the government can be specified as such. On the rest, members can "vote their conscience."

Free votes that allow members to represent honestly the electors who sent them to Ottawa are a key part of the Reform Party platform. Amazingly, with Reform ranks burgeoning, the government has decided that it too likes the idea McGrath recommended six years ago. It promised in the Throne Speech to work for the "attitudinal" change needed, so that members who deviate from the party line are not seen as dangerous rebels signalling a split in the ranks.

Regardless of what prompted the government's change of heart, there is no doubt that free votes are a necessity in a reformed Parliament. Not only would MPs be able to represent their constituents more honestly, ministers would be forced to use persuasion, not the whip, to get colleagues to support legislation. Defeats might cost a particular item, but they would allow the government to demonstrate that Parliament has a real role and that the government is acting according to the people's wishes. A loss of party discipline would mean a gain in honest representation. The regions would have a voice in policy, and MPs would be seen on the record as personally supporting or opposing particular items, rather than behaving like a flock of sheep.

It would be more honest in many ways – once the practice is accepted by all parties, and the media learn not to gallop off whooping about the latest party mutiny. It might even remove the temptation for NDP House leader Nelson Riis to send a memo like the one he delivered to all Conservatives last spring. He asked them to vote against a government measure, but if they could not, to miss the vote and say they were sick. In the real world, such an explanation is called lying. In the Commons it is – well – an NDP tactic.

Recent free votes on abortion and capital punishment are examples of how Parliament can work if given the chance. Even then, the uniform stand of cabinet members and parliamentary secretaries left some of the more cautious Conservatives feeling a little less than free. But the two issues were magnificently argued in long debates, with MPs speaking from the heart and listening intently before rendering their individual judgements. "If we could do it on abortion why can't we do it on other pieces of legislation?" asks Ron Mac-Donald. "That was one of the most civilized, rational, reasoned, well-researched debates that the House of Commons has seen in a long time."

MPs must also be given a better chance to push their own bills into law. Private members' bills are usually "talked out" (no vote is taken before the allotted time expires) or defeated. When MPs lack the power to follow through, motions urging some course of action are forgotten after an hour of pro-forma blather in the House. Worse, most MPs assume government and opposition roles, even though such individual initiatives are supposed to be free of party influence.

"The charade has got to end if we, as members of Parliament, want to be a somebody," says Liberal MP Don Boudria. He suggests that the "talking-out provisions" be abolished and every issue be put to a vote. A day or two every few weeks should be allocated for private members' business rather than the present one hour per day. This would allow more prolonged discussion. Coupled with freer votes, private members' bills could be an important tool in redistributing power from the cabinet to the back-benchers. They could lead to greater consultation among ministers, the bureaucracy and MPs. The government would become more sensitive to grass-roots issues proposed as private members' legislation that might become law.

The enemies of parliamentary reform are the party leaders. Those with control seldom relinquish it willingly. Leaders rarely welcome questions or independent initiatives from those they lead – or, in fact, any action that makes their goals more difficult to achieve. But that is what reform means. In the words of *Financial Post* columnist and political analyst Gordon Gibson, "The solution is to address the needs of the country, rather than the needs of the politicos." Even the leaders might learn to like some things about it. MPs who were usefully employed would be happier. Public contempt for politicians and their work should decrease. Reform Party leader Preston Manning has even proposed that votes in caucus be free and the results released to the public. That would lighten the load of the whips, whose job now is to keep the entire caucus in line like counsellors at a day camp and to spread the implausible story that they all think alike. Reduction in the baby-sitting duties would logically result in a reduction in the whips' pay, staff and office overhead, and a substantial saving to the taxpayer.

Parties, of course, remain necessary. They should simply relax their iron grip on MPs, a posture that serves only to destroy their ability to act for the people who elected them. Parties should campaign on a platform detailing the major issues that their candidates subscribe to and will support if elected, such as free trade in 1988. Nowlan points out that MPs themselves don't know most of what their party plans to do if it forms a government, so obviously the voters cannot know either. He describes how members of the Conservative caucus learn about their government's plans: "It's a dog-and-pony show, with slide presentations from the minister a few hours before its [policy] is announced in the House. You find out about it just about the time it appears in the paper."

Some will argue that the reforms proposed will erode the role of political parties and make MPs a target of special-interest groups. On the contrary, they would require parties to be more honest and more specific about their plans and achieve consensus by persuasion rather than discipline. Parties no longer perform the role of public consensus builders. Studies show that Canadians subscribe to interest groups, such as Operation Dismantle or the National Citizens' Coalition, rather than to political parties. Interest groups, in turn, concentrate their attention directly on the bureaucracy and cabinet ministers not, as they did twenty years ago, on the political parties. Returning some power to MPs would force these groups to appeal to Parliament and enhance its consensus-building role. Political brokerage among regional representatives would dispel the notion that only provincial premiers speak for the regions.

There can be no meaningful reform of Parliament unless the Senate is changed from the final resting place of party hacks to an elected body representing Canada's diverse regional interests. Abolition of the upper chamber is not the answer. The regions need a way to check the power of the Commons, where heavily populated Ontario and Quebec hold sway. With Conservatives now in control of the upper chamber, it will be interesting to see if the government's eagerness to revamp it remains as fervent as when the Liberals wielded majority power there.

Senate reform can be a major step in redefining federal-provincial relations. It may be the most important way to overcome regional separatism and develop "consensual federalism." The U.S. Senate has power at least equal to that of the House of Representatives. This is not a problem in a system where the president and his cabinet are not responsible to either House. It doesn't work the same way here. The prime minister and cabinet come from, and are supposed to answer to, the Commons. They stand or fall in the lower House.

The West has been pushing for an elected Senate with equal representation from each province. But it is unlikely that Quebec, should it choose to remain in Canada, would ever stand for one-in-ten status. One change to consider is election of senators for regional blocks: British Columbia and the two territories; Alberta, Saskatchewan and Manitoba; Ontario; Quebec; and the Atlantic provinces. All senators should be elected through proportional representation to guarantee that they reflect the views of the provinces or regions.

Tom Kent, a policy guru to Lester Pearson, suggested that each of the five regions should have twenty-five constituencies, for a total of 125 senators, who would be elected in proportion to the votes cast for each party. Kent contends that regional interests would be better represented, leading to more compromises and the formation of coalitions to support regional programs and policies. Whatever the details, most authorities now endorse an elected Senate with acknowledged regional responsibilities.

Senators should have fixed terms – of, say, six years. They should not be allowed to join cabinet, because its need for solidarity would compromise their ability to speak openly for their regions. The Senate should not be able to defeat a government through a non-confidence vote and probably should have specific veto powers concerning the Constitution, linguistic rights, and key appointments, such as those to the Supreme Court of Canada. There should also be a joint Commons-Senate Committee set up to settle disputes between the two houses. Compromise, after all, is the essence of politics. The more avenues built in for consensus, the less likely the system is to fracture.

Canada should definitely not adopt the Australian system, which allows the Senate to strangle the government by refusing to pass money bills. A reformed Senate should have limited power over tax and money legislation, possibly through a six-month delay. It should not have the power to force an election by denying money, as Australia's Senate did in 1975. It should also avoid the German example, where members of the Bundesrat (or House of the Provinces) are chosen by provincial governments. Because disputes over regional funds are at the heart of Canadian federalism, the Senate should be able to initiate certain money bills affecting regional development. It would have the basic authority that Sir John A. envisaged, for "controlling and regulating, but not initiating."

The fat cabinet in the Canadian parliamentary system shows no inclination to diet. With thirty-nine ministers it is unnecessarily large and far too expensive. The political priorities of prime ministers, not the country's administrative needs, have determined its size. Mulroney could shed fifteen no-name ministers without any noticeably adverse impact. Such a visible cut would send a clear signal to the public and bureaucrats that the government is serious about tightening its own belt, not just the one squeezing taxpayers.

The British system uses junior ministers to handle departmental duties. It restricts cabinet rank and policy roles to senior ministers.

Our system could cut a further level. Instead of rewarding promising MPs with parliamentary secretaries' pay cheques, it could use their talents on special, standing and legislative committees – giving them the chance to do work of far more value than reading speeches written by faceless bureaucrats to a near-empty Commons chamber.

None of this will work until the credibility of the system and of politicians themselves is restored. Parliamentarians could begin by earning their pay with productive work, instead of the ineffective political exercises that so alienate the public. If the business of committees and the House again became important to the way Canada is run, members would be more eager to take part. Those who don't show up for Senate and Commons duty should not be paid as much as those who do. There might be a base pay of, say, $80,000, with up to $20,000 or $30,000 added according to an attendance formula. With the number of sitting days now reduced to 135 a year, there is no reason why all members cannot be active in Ottawa whenever Parliament is in session. This would be a crude but practical way to encourage diligence and punish slackers. The huge amount of parliamentary "down time" should be more than ample for constituency work and travel. It should also result in immediate reductions to budgets for staff and services, including travel to and from Ottawa.

The tax-free allowances must go. They are simply disguised pay, a special benefit that sets parliamentarians apart from the people they are supposed to identify with. The idea of tax-free payments may have been sound thirty years ago when MPs dipped into their own meagre indemnity to cover the cost of long-distance phones, travel, extra staff, equipment and constituency expenses. Today the cost of everything, whether of shipping their free framed pictures home or their cars to Ottawa, is covered by the Commons budget. MPs deserve a good salary, but it should not be in the form of tax-free allowances for which they never show a receipt. Nor should each member receive an identical sum for office staff and equipment, regardless of individual requirements or the amount of time spent working. Most MPs who get into trouble for misusing office funds do so because they have too much money to dispose of in the first place. Because the rules for politicians and those for the public are so different, it is almost impossible for the people's representatives to understand how the people themselves travel, pay their bills and taxes and work within strict budget limits.

The most extreme example of that double standard is the parliamentary pension plan, the most generous in North America. Our leaders cheerfully plan it and pocket it, while lecturing us about fiscal restraint. If parliamentarians wonder about their poor public image, they need look no further for the cause than that lucrative scheme: 30 per cent pay after six years, 75 per cent after fifteen, collectible immediately and fully indexed at age sixty.

At a time when Ottawa limits welfare payments and social housing, it is a disgrace for MPs to award themselves pensions that can exceed a million dollars for those who leave in the prime of life. The age to begin collecting should be fifty-five or sixty, as it is with other Canadians, with indexing limited to the average formula of outside plans. As David Somerville of the National Citizens' Coalition has said: "A large step back onto the road to respect would be taken by MPs if they fundamentally reformed their pension plan."

Reasonable rather than excessive pay and allowances might ensure that Canadians again sought office in order to serve the public. Today we get, as B.C. New Democrat Dave Barrett said of officeholders in his home province, "the best politicians money can buy." Charles Gordon put it just a bit differently in a *Maclean's* column in April 1991. "There is nothing wrong with the system. It is the politicians who aren't working."

Another necessary change is an end to double-dipping. That proposal was made by Liberal MP David Kilgour and rejected by MPs from all parties. The practice of paying rich pensions to former MPs while they receive six-figure incomes from patronage appointments is, as the *Edmonton Journal* editorialized, "the worst type of greed, villainy and general thievery." Can Ed Broadbent, who gets a parliamentary pension of $45,000 plus a salary of over $100,000 as head of a federal human-rights agency, believe that the Oshawa auto workers who elected him seven times or the social democrats he led for a dozen years respect the example he sets today? Does eighty-one-year-old George Hees' work in surveying our aid to the Third World's starving millions warrant an income of well over $150,000 from combined sources? Is it any wonder that Canadians perceive politicians as pigs at the trough? "The gap between MPs and other Canadians is wide and getting wider," says Kilgour. "It explains in part the widespread view that MPs only look to serve their own interests."

Most defeated or retired members of the governing party board the gravy train for another long ride at public expense. Their post-election stops include the courts and government boards, commissions and agencies, where fat salaries and perks await. Without doubt many are qualified for the jobs, but so are others who don't happen to be members of the governing party or recipients of parliamentary pensions. Many of these jobs should be filled in the same way as other public service positions, through competition. Removing the stench of patronage would improve the credibility of many federal boards. It would not prevent former politicians from applying. It would simply ensure that candidates are chosen for their qualifications, not their political credits. Other Order in Council appointments such as judgeships should be scrutinized by Commons committees with veto power.

Most nations have conflict-of-interest or disclosure rules to safeguard the public from crooked politicians. Instead of rules, Canada has promises and a system where the Criminal Code, rather than a moral code, is the guide. The United States has fairly stiff disclosure rules. These are based on the belief that full knowledge of a member's assets and interests provides public protection. Senators and representatives must file detailed reports of their finances, including gifts, outside income and debts, and make those public to any citizen who asks.

Public disclosure would not only curb possible abuses but also help restore lost confidence in the political system. The Mulroney government has proposed conflict-of-interest rules, but they fall far short of full disclosure. Although MPs and senators would be required to file personal financial information (and more limited statements on the holdings of their spouses and children), all the information, except a summary of the parliamentarians' statements, would be kept secret.

Under such a system Canadians would not know if party leaders are receiving trust funds or extra spending money from wealthy supporters. The $3,000 that the Liberals paid for John Turner's apartment in Toronto would not be revealed, nor would the $300,000 doled out to the Mulroneys to fix up their Sussex Drive residence. No one would know if an MP was receiving money from his riding association or rich friends (quite a few do, claiming they need the supplement to meet the expenses of office). Conflict-of-interest legislation must be introduced to include many of the U.S. features. Some possibilities, as proposed in a *Toronto Star* article by Geoffrey Stevens, might be:

– a requirement to report any arrangement that the member may have for leave of absence while he serves in elected office or for employment in the future;

– detailed reporting of debts in excess of $10,000 (including credit card balances and under-secured loans);

– disclosure of any hospitality accepted in excess of $250.

The Reform Party has taken its own approach to preventing scoundrels from running. All those wishing to become candidates under its banner will be asked to open their books and private lives to a panel of local riding executives. A detailed questionnaire asks them about finances and personal histories, but also deals with families – to ensure that those around the candidate are prepared for the sacrifices and trials of public office.

People who enter public life must be prepared to account publicly for their behavior. Politicians often say that many good people stay outside because they don't want their private lives on display. It is probably best that they do not run for election if they cannot understand the special demands of public service and the need for guidelines. It is their decision to seek office, but they should know that the windows must be kept open. As David Kilgour told the Commons in the spring of 1991: "As far as I know none of us was forced to run for office, all of us chose to run for office. . . . No one was ever forced to run for Parliament."

The rules should also be changed to ensure that any MP who breaches the public trust is denied severance pay. It would serve as a deterrent to MPs with criminal intentions. Former Tory MP Michel Gravel qualified for $29,150 in severance pay by waiting until after the 1988 election to plead guilty to fifteen counts of bribery and influence-peddling while in office. He was sentenced to one year in jail in 1989 and ordered to pay a fine of $50,000. Yet he also qualified to claim up to $10,000 in resettlement costs, covering job retraining, stress-management programs and the rental of temporary office space. Few non-criminals get breaks like that.

MPs who are merely investigated for possible offences but not charged have their legal fees covered by taxpayers. Six Tories got thousands of dollars in taxpayer-funded legal help to fight warrants obtained by the Mounties to search their Parliament Hill offices. Payments stopped if the MP was charged. Last December the Board of Internal Economy agreed that MPs should be reimbursed "up to the beginning of the trial, if any." Three of the MPs investigated in this Parliament were eventually charged, although the charges against one were later dismissed. Few other Canadians who come under investigation for possible offences at work can expect the boss or the public to pay their legal costs. Those involved in the Doug Small budget-leak case got no relief from legal fees when wrongly charged by the government. Again, the double standard may pay the politicians' bills, but it is tremendously costly in terms of public respect.

No group waxes more eloquent about freedom and open government than Canadian parliamentarians – or practises greater secrecy in its affairs. Sessions of the Senate and Commons Boards of Internal Economy that run our most public institutions are secret. These are the sessions where allowances, perks, travel and benefits are decided on, free of questions and public interference. It is one area where all parties readily reach agreement.

To overcome the public's disgust with such a process, meetings and minutes of committees dealing with benefits for senators and MPs must be open to the public. MPs probably would not have dared to exempt their office budgets from the GST or to award themselves a $6,000 "housing/travel allowance" at the height of the recession if the press and the public had been allowed to see what they were doing. Of course, hearings that deal with individual employees' wages and discipline must be secret, but the public has every right to know what these high-powered boards are doing with its money.

Openness should be the cornerstone of parliamentary government, as Michael Wilson said in 1990 while defending the $800,000 spent on a video promoting the GST. "In a democracy it is important that citizens be fully informed about what government is doing with their money." He is right. That is why detailed accounts should be provided to the public as a matter of course.

There are Blue Books that show the spending estimates of all departments and agencies. They are released annually to the press and public except for one set – the ones that cover the House of Commons and Senate. The only people who routinely have copies of those volumes are members of the Commons' and Senate's Internal Economy committees. Few parliamentarians even know those volumes exist. The palace guard keeps them under lock and key for fear that reporters will let the public know how its money is lavished on politicians. The guardians of the Commons secrets now say the budget figures will be released to MPs who make a formal request.

The Blue Books reveal the millions parliamentarians spend flying around the world on so-called fact-finding missions that are often simply paid vacations for the well-to-do. It is even more inappropriate for the public to pick up the tab for spouses and lovers. Certainly some trips by parliamentary associations are justified, particularly exchanges between Canadian and American legislators. But most are expensive junkets that should be scrapped or significantly chopped, along with the costly associations that arrange them.

For anyone who believes that members of the Commonwealth Parliamentary Association are working for us each February on the beaches of the Caribbean we can only suggest a major investment in a Baie Comeau rock farm. The acceptance of all-expense-paid trips from foreign governments and lobbyists should cease. They leave the impression, not necessarily wrong, that Canadian lawmakers can be bought for the price of an airline ticket, hotel room and, in particularly tough cases, massage.

Another step towards integrity and restored public trust would be to allow the auditor general to comb the books regularly, without restrictions. In a 1991 audit of the Commons, the auditor general was not given access to "supporting documentation or briefing notes nor to any of the Board's [Internal Economy] minutes which have not yet been tabled in the House." He should be permitted to make value judgements on the type of services offered to MPs and senators. There would probably not be three cut-rate barber-shops, a hair-styling salon, four gyms and a furniture showroom if any reasonable value-for-dollar appraisal were used. Likewise, Parliament should lay down clear spending guidelines for MPs' operating budgets, so that the RCMP can determine if a member has broken the law. Allowing that judgement to rest with the BOIE is a clear case of the fox guarding the chickens.

Real parliamentary reform is long overdue. There is no mystery about why the public has lost faith in Parliament, just an unwillingness by parliamentarians to climb out of the vault and face the truth. Canada's huge economic and unity problems can only be dealt with by a system and politicians whom the people trust. Trust is not earned when power is concentrated in the prime minister and a handful of agents around him, when MPs vote like robots or when parliamentarians preach the virtues of restraint and openness that they are unwilling to practise themselves.

But Canadian voters must also share the blame. It is up to them to demand an accounting from their present MPs and to throw the rascals out if they do not provide it. A change of government alone is not the answer. Each party quickly adopts and expands on the self-serving practices of its predecessor in office. The parliamentary system must be fundamentally changed. So must attitudes, so that an honor code truly becomes Parliament's guide. The people have a vital part to play in making Parliament the effective counterweight to government that it was designed to be. As former Conservative MP Ged Baldwin observed: "Parliament did not create democracy, the people did." There are Canadians willing to dedicate themselves to public service, not self-service. We must find them soon.

BIBLIOGRAPHY

Annotated Standing Orders of the House of Commons.

Bercuson, David, J.L. Granatstein and W.R. Young. *Sacred Trust? Brian Mulroney and the Conservative Party in Power*. Toronto: Doubleday, 1986.

Biggar, E.B. *Anecdotal Life of Sir John A. Macdonald*. Montreal: John Lovell, 1891.

Bishop, Peter V. "Restoring Parliament to Power," *Queen's Quarterly* 77 (1970).

Bosc, Marc. ed. *The Broadview Book of Canadian Parliamentary Anecdotes*. Peterborough, Ont.: Broadview Press, 1988.

Bourinot, J.B. "The House of Commons in Session," *Canadian Monthly* 2 (1877).

Broad, Debra. "Privileged to Meet You . . . At the Bargaining Table." Unpublished paper, 1986.

Cameron, Stevie. *Ottawa Inside Out*. Toronto: Key Porter, 1989.

Camp, Dalton. *Points of Departure*. Ottawa: Deneau and Greenberg, 1979.

Chenier, John. A. "Ministers of State to Assist: Weighing the Costs and Benefits," *Canadian Public Administration* 28:3 (Fall 1985).

Cody, Howard. "Some Implications of Commons Reform for 'Out' Canada," *Canadian Parliamentary Review* (Winter 1990-91).

Courtney, J.C., ed. *The Canadian House of Commons: Essays in Honour of Norman Ward*. Calgary: University of Calgary Press, 1985.

Cross, A.F. *The People's Mouth*. Toronto: Macmillan, 1943.

D'Aquino, Thomas, G. Bruce Doern and Cassandra Blair. *Parliamentary Democracy in Canada: Issues for Reform*. Toronto: Methuen, 1983.

Diefenbaker, John. *One Canada*. (3 vols.) Toronto: Macmillan of Canada, 1977.

Donaldson, Gordon. *Fifteen Men*. Toronto: Doubleday Canada, 1975.

Downey, Terrence. *Representation versus Efficiencies: Confronting the Size of Cabinet Dilemma in Canada*. Ottawa: Library of Parliament, 1985.

Dunn, Christopher. "Executive Dominance in Provincial Legislatures," *Canadian Parliamentary Review* (Spring 1990).

Exempt Staff Budget, Accommodation, and Human Resource Management in Ministers' Offices. Ottawa: Library of Parliament, 1986.

Expenditures of Offices of Ministers and Offices of Ministers of State for the Period 1980-81 to 1985-86. Ottawa: Library of Parliament, 1986.

Fleming, Robert. *Canadian Legislatures*. Ottawa: Ampersand, 1988.

Fletcher, Frederick J. and Donald Wallace, eds. *Canadian Politics through Press Reports*. Toronto: Oxford University Press, 1984.

Ford, Arthur R. *As the World Wags On*. Toronto: Ryerson Press, 1950.

Forsey, Eugene, *A Life on the Fringe: The Memoirs of Eugene Forsey*. Toronto: Oxford University Press, 1990.

Gollner, Andrew B., and Daniel Salee, eds. *Canada under Mulroney: An End of Term Report*. Montreal: Véhicule Press, 1988.

Horner, Jack. *My Own Brand*. Edmonton: Hurtig, 1980.

House of Commons Estimates 1990-91.

Jackson, Robert. "Executive-Legislative Relations in Canada." Paper delivered to the 25th anniversary of the research branch of the Canadian Library of Parliament. October 24, 1990.

——, and Doreen Jackson. *Politics in Canada*. Scarborough, Ont.: Prentice-Hall, 1990.

————, Doreen Jackson and Nicholas Baxter-Moore, eds. *Contemporary Canadian Politics*. Scarborough, Ont.: Prentice-Hall, 1987.

Johansen, David. *Parliamentary Privilege with Special Reference to Confidentiality*. Ottawa: Library of Parliament, 1982.

Kornberg, Allan, and William Mishler. *Influence in Parliament: Canada*. Durham, N.C.: Duke University Press, 1976.

Lemco, Jonathan. "The Fusion of Powers, Party Discipline and the Canadian Parliament: A Critical Assessment," *Presidential Quarterly* (Spring 1988).

Levy, Gary. "Collective Bargaining for Parliamentary Employees," *Canadian Parliamentary Review* (Summer 1986).

Mallory, J.R. *Cabinet Government in Canada in the Seventies*. Toronto: New Civics Group, 1979.

March, Roman. *The Myth of Parliament*. Scarborough: Prentice-Hall, 1974.

McCauley, Janet Marie. "The Senate of Canada: Maintenance of a Second Chamber through Functional Adaptability." Ph.D. diss., Pennsylvania State University, 1983.

Martin, Paul. *A Very Public Life*. Ottawa: Deneau, 1983.

Matheson, W.A. *The Prime Minister and the Cabinet*. Toronto: Methuen, 1976.

McLeod, Jack. ed. *The Oxford Book of Canadian Political Anecdotes*. Toronto: Oxford University Press, 1988.

Nielsen, A.W., and J.C. MacPherson. *The Legislative Process in Canada: The Need For Reform*. Montreal: Institute for Research on Public Policy, 1978.

Nielsen, Erik. *The House Is Not a Home*. Toronto: Macmillan of Canada, 1989.

O'Leary, Grattan. *Recollections of People, Press and Politics*. Toronto: Macmillan of Canada, 1977.

Report of the Canadian Bar Association Committee on the Reform of Parliament. Ottawa: Library of Parliament, 1982.

Simeon, James. *Prime Ministers and Cabinet Decision-Making: Political Leadership in Canada in the Post-Trudeau Era.* Ottawa: Library of Parliament, 1989.

———. "Thoughts on the Canadian and American Political Systems," *Canadian Parliamentary Review* (Summer 1988).

Simpson, Jeffrey. *Spoils of Power: The Politics of Patronage.* Don Mills, Ont.: Collins, 1988.

Stewart, J.B. *The Canadian House of Commons.* Montreal: McGill-Queen's University Press, 1977.

Stoett, Peter J. "Elect Senators by Proportional Representation," *Policy Options* (March 1991).

Sulzner, George. "Collective Bargaining Comes to Parliament," *Canadian Parliamentary Review* (Spring 1990).

Thomas, Paul. *Parliamentary Reform through Political Parties.* Ottawa: Library of Parliament, 1985.

———. *Parliament and the Purse Strings.* Ottawa: Library of Parliament, 1989.

Ward, Norman. *The Public Purse.* Toronto: University of Toronto Press, 1962.

———. "The Formative Years of the House of Commons, 1867-91," *Canadian Journal of Economics.* Vol. 18. Toronto: University of Toronto Press, 1952.

Westell, Anthony. *Paradox: Trudeau as Prime Minister.* Scarborough, Ont.: Prentice-Hall, 1972.

Whelan, Eugene. *The Man in the Green Stetson.* Toronto: Irwin, 1986.

INDEX

INDEX

INDEX